AMERICAN BEAUTY

AMERICAN BEAUTY
William Carlos Williams and
the Modernist Whitman

Stephen Tapscott

COLUMBIA UNIVERSITY PRESS

New York

1984

2935256

Library of Congress Cataloging in Publication Data

Tapscott, Stephen, 1948–
American beauty.

Bibliography: p.
Includes index.
1. Williams, William Carlos, 1883–1963—Criticism
and interpretation.   2. Whitman, Walt, 1819–1892—
Influence—Williams.   I. Title.
PS3545.I544Z887   1984   811'.52   83-15216
ISBN 0-231-05774-1
ISBN 0-231-05775-X (pbk.)

33 ʹ   Columbia University Press
New York   Guildford, Surrey

Copyright © 1984 Columbia University Press
All rights reserved
Printed in the United States of America

Clothbound editions of Columbia University Press books are Smyth-
sewn and printed on permanent and durable acid-free paper.

Book design by Ken Venezio.

I would like to express my gratitude to the community of
         scholars in the Literature Faculty at M.I.T.:
to my students, who are patiently teaching me how to read,
to my junior colleagues, who are teaching me how to think,
to my senior colleagues, who are teaching me how to draw conclusions;
and to Monica Kearney, Administrator,
who keeps all of us organized, and who teaches us gusto.
                 This book is for them.

Contents

Acknowledgments

I am grateful to the following publishers and authors for permission to quote or to translate for this volume extracts from the following works:

Hart Crane, *The Bridge,* reprinted by permission of Liveright Publishing Corporation. Copyright 1933, © 1958, 1970 Liveright Publishing Corporation.

Hart Crane, *The Letters of Hart Crane,* ed. Brom Weber. Copyright © 1965 The University of California Press.

Rubén Darío, "Walt Whitman," and "Oda a Roosevelt," *Poesías Completas, Azul.* Copyright © 1969 Editorial Losada, S.A.

D. H. Lawrence, from *The Complete Poems of D. H. Lawrence,* Collected and Edited by Vivian de Sola Pinto and F. Warren Roberts. Copyright © 1964, 1971 Angelo Ravagli and C. M. Weekly, Executors of The Estate of Frieda Lawrence Ravagli. Reprinted by permission of Viking Penguin Inc.

Federico García Lorca, *Poeta en Nueva York* (7th ed.) Copyright © 1962 Editorial Losada, S.A.

Hugh MacDiarmid, *Lucky Poet,* copyright 1943 Methuen and Co., reissued by Jonathan Cape, copyright © 1972 Michael Grieve and Valda Grieve, Executors, Hugh MacDiarmid Estate.

Marianne Moore, "Marriage," reprinted with permission of Macmillan Publishing Company from *Collected Poems* of Marianne Moore. Copyright 1935 by Marianne Moore, renewed 1963 by Marianne Moore and T. S. Eliot.

Vladimir Mayakovsky, "The Brooklyn Bridge," © 1958, Progress Publishers, Moscow.

Pablo Neruda, "El Hombre Invisible," and "Oda a Walt Whitman," copyright © 1954, 1963, 1980. Published by Editorial Losada, S.A.

Charles Olson, *The Maximus Poems,* copyright © 1960, published by The Jargon Society / Corinth Books.

Ezra Pound:

——*The Cantos of Ezra Pound.* Copyright 1934 Ezra Pound.

——*Literary Essays.* Copyright 1918, 1920, 1935 Ezra Pound.

——*Personae.* Copyright 1926 Ezra Pound.

——*Selected Prose 1909–1965.* Copyright © 1973 The Estate of Ezra Pound.

——*Spirit of Romance.* Copyright © 1968 Ezra Pound. All Rights Reserved.

Gertrude Stein, "The Gradual Making of 'The Making of Americans,' " copyright 1925, © 1969. Published by Peter Owen Ltd., London.

Wallace Stevens, "Gigantomania," "Esthétique du Mal," and "Metaphors of a Magnifico," from *The Collected Poems of Wallace Stevens,* copyright © 1967. Published by Alfred A. Knopf, Inc.

Walt Whitman, *Leaves of Grass: Comprehensive Reader's Edition,* edited by Harold W. Blodgett and Sculley Bradley. Copyright © 1965 New York University. Reprinted by Permission of New York University Press.

William Carlos Williams:

——*The Autobiography of William Carlos Williams.* Copyright © 1951 William Carlos Williams. Published by Random House.

——*Collected Earlier Poems.* Copyright 1917, 1921 The Four Seas Company. Copyright 1934 The Objectivist Press. Copyright 1935 The Alcestis Press. Copyright 1936 Ronald Lane Latimer. Copyright 1938 New Directions Publishing Corp. Copyright 1938, 1941, 1951 William Carlos Williams. Published by New Directions Publishing Corp.

——*The Collected Later Poems.* Copyright 1944, 1948, 1949, 1950 William Carlos Williams. Copyright © 1963 the Estate of William Carlos Williams. Published by New Directions Publishing Corp.

——*The Embodiment of Knowledge.* Copyright © 1974 Florence H. Williams. Published by New Directions Publishing Corp.

——*Imaginations.* Copyright © 1970 Florence H. Williams.

——*In the American Grain.* Copyright 1925 James Laughlin.

——*New Directions in Prose and Poetry, 1931.* Copyright 1931 James Laughlin for the New Directions Publishing Corp.

——*New Directions 17.* Copyright © 1961 New Directions Publishing Corp.

——"New From New Directions," news release May 31, 1951. Copyright 1951 James Laughlin for New Directions Publishing Corp.

——*Pictures from Brueghel.* Copyright © 1959, 1962 William Carlos Williams. Published by New Directions Publishing Corp.

——*Selected Essays.* Copyright 1954 William Carlos Williams. Published by the New Directions Publishing Corp.

——*Selected Letters of William Carlos Williams.* Copyright © 1957 William Carlos Williams. Published by Oblonsky Publishers.

Unpublished material by William Carlos Williams, copyright ©
1983 William Eric Williams and Paul H. Williams. My special thanks
also to the curators and staff of the Collection of American Literature, Beinecke Rare Book and Manuscript Library, Yale University, and of the Poetry / Rare Books Collection of the University
Libraries, State University of New York at Buffalo, for making
those materials available and for permission to print them here.

The first section of chapter 7 first appeared in *American Literature*
53, no. 2, under the title "Whitman in Paterson," and the second
section of chapter 7 first appeared in *The Yearbook of English Studies,* no. 8 (1978), under the title "Williams' Paterson: Doctor and
Democrat." (Reprinted here by permission of the Editor and of
the Modern Humanities Research Association, publishers.) Several paragraphs of the last two chapters were incorporated into an
essay for *The Arizona Quarterly* 33, no. 4, "Paterson A'Bloom:
Joyce, Williams, and the Virtue of 'Abcedmindedness.' " My thanks
to the editors of those periodicals for their gracious editorial help
with those essays and for permission to reprint those materials
here.

Introduction

To Elsie

The pure products of America
go crazy—
mountain folk from Kentucky

or the ribbed north end of
Jersey
with its isolate lakes and

valleys, its deaf-mutes, thieves
old names
and promiscuity between

devil-may-care men who have taken
to railroading
out of sheer lust of adventure—

and young slatterns, bathed
in filth
from Monday to Saturday

to be tricked out that night
with gauds
from imaginations which have no

peasant traditions to give them
character
but flutter and flaunt

sheer rags—succumbing without
emotion
save numbed terror

under some hedge of choke-cherry
or viburnum—
which they cannot express—

Unless it be that marriage
perhaps
with a dash of Indian blood

will throw up a girl so desolate
so hemmed round
with disease or murder

that she'll be rescued by an
agent—
reared by the state and

sent out at fifteen to work in
some hard-pressed
house in the suburbs—

some doctor's family, some Elsie—
voluptuous water
expressing with broken

brain the truth about us—
her great
ungainly hips and flopping breasts

addressed to cheap
jewelry
and rich young men with fine eyes

as if the earth under our feet
were
an excrement of some sky

and we degraded prisoners
destined
to hunger until we eat filth

while the imagination strains
after deer
going by fields of goldenrod in

the stifling heat of September
Somehow
it seems to destroy us

It is only in isolate flecks that
something
is given off

No one
to witness
and adjust, no one to drive the car

This book began with a good question from a student. We were
reading William Carlos Williams' poem "To Elsie" (1923) and
thinking about its long detailed approach to its central subject:

The pure products of America
go crazy—
mountain folk from Kentucky

or the ribbed north end of
Jersey
with its isolate lakes and

valleys, its deaf-mutes, thieves
old names
and promiscuity between

devil-may-care men. . .

and young slatterns, bathed
in filth
from Monday to Saturday

One of the students in the class, a sophomore with a genius for
asking the obvious and difficult question, wondered aloud why
Williams calls the poem "To Elsie": in what sense, he asked, does
this panoramic description of the harsh local circumstances make
a dedication "to" Williams' housemaid appropriate? The poem
never does address Elsie directly but represents her as one of those
"pure products" of the local scene. She is not a subject but a suffering representative object in a world that may from time to time
generate "some Elsie":

sent out at fifteen to work in
some hard-pressed
house in the suburbs—

> some doctor's family, some Elsie—
> voluptuous water
> expressing with broken
>
> brain the truth about us—

The other students in the class picked up the question, turned it over, and argued, in effect, that the poem is not so much an address "to" Elsie the young woman as an approach "toward" Elsie as a metonymic personalization of the forces that produced her: she results from those forces, summarizes and embodies them, and yet transcends them. Elsie represents—or rather *is*—the intersection of the public circumstances of north Jersey and the private life of the "doctor's family." As the students continued we began to see the poem as an hourglass, beginning with a wide field of conditions (the geography, the mountain families, their behavior), narrowing through a desolate "marriage" and through the intervention of state agents, toward Elsie herself. Then, after her depiction, the poem expands again, into a different kind of generalization: no longer sociological and objective ("they") but passionate and compassionate ("we").

> as if the earth under our feet
> were
> an excrement of some sky
>
> and we degraded prisoners
> destined
> to hunger until we eat filth

At that intersection of the sociological and the private, Elsie lives in the hard-pressed doctor's family. She is both a particular self *and* the representative product of a larger ("general") social condition which she personifies.

> It is only in isolate flecks that
> something
> is given off

But still my sophomore persisted: does this use of Elsie as a symbol make her more or less a person in the poem? Isn't Williams depersonalizing Elsie, even if he is using her presence (paradoxically) as an occasion for sympathy? The poem does seem a marvel of tact, as Williams negotiates between a purely external, objective interpretation of Elsie's presence and a purely subjective, private sympathy with her experience. Elsie is that nexus between public and private worlds: her presence is an intrusion of the outside into the inside world, and yet the family had been "hard-pressed," like the rest of this world, before she had appeared. Her subjective absence at the center of the poem is, then, both a tribute to her opaque physicality ("her great/ungainly hips and flopping breasts") and a rebuke to the circumstances that shaped her and that keep her imaginatively mute:

> No one
> to witness
> and adjust, no one to drive the car

The world she embodies lacks external witness and guidance. Such functions should be the work of the local inhabitants, and yet Elsie herself is "no one" capable of those meliorative functions.

The class concluded that Williams had done something remarkable in "To Elsie": without sentimentality or propagandistic rhetoric, he had managed both to work that objective sociological information toward an informing sympathy with Elsie, and to work her private experience toward a public social conclusion. Further, they suggested, this achievement reminded them of "Song of Myself," in which Walt Whitman offers himself as an ideally inclusive metaphor, an intersection of public and private experiences:

> I celebrate myself, and sing myself,
> And what I assume you shall assume

Where Whitman offers himself—an idealized image of himself—as that intersecting personality, Williams puts the mysterious physical presence of Elsie at the intersection of those outer and inner forces. And just as Williams locates Elsie at the center of his poem, in that hourglass effect that balances the public information and the private response, Whitman saves his own name until "Song of Myself" is nearly half over. Then (in section 24) the announcement of his own name seems an important occasion—as if the name itself, objectified and pronounced, has the power forcibly to send us onto the Open Road:

> Unscrew the locks from the doors!
> Unscrew the doors themselves from their jambs!

Williams saves Elsie's name but makes it both public ("some") and private ("Elsie").

My students first made this connection between the expansive and representative egotism of Whitman and the expansive generosity of the Williams voice; they saw also that the connection is both tonal and formal. This study continues their first insights by locating Williams more specifically in two contexts: in the history of American poetry (essentially Whitmanian, as Williams construes the tradition) and in the American modernist movement. Of course the two contexts are inseparable: Williams works retrospectively to invent a Whitmanian "American" tradition, because he suspects that his own American version of modernism lacks the stability of a tradition, like the stability he envies in the international modernists Pound and Eliot.

To trace this pattern of Whitmanian "influence" through to its effects in Williams' later work, especially in *Paterson,* I realized I would have to address three points; they became the three parts of this book. In Part 1 we begin with Williams' version of Whitman and read shorter Williams poems, focusing on the modernists' two related images of Whitman: as a giant and as a "simple separate person." Part 2 concentrates more exclusively on Williams' reworking of Whitman's theories of language, bringing Whitman's tonal attitudes into the context of Williams' modernist poetics. In Part 3 we consider Williams' overt use of Whitman in *Paterson* and finally the doubled perspective of intimacy-and-distance that is Williams' largest single response to Whitman's example.

Before we get to the immediate evidence of Whitman's "influence" on Williams' poems, however, we need to put Williams into the historical context that provoked his response to the Whitmanian "tradition." Though its threads are occasionally tangled, that contextual network should help us to see Williams' use of Whitman not only as formative in his own work but as representative of a pattern of modernist uses of Whitman. Williams' reworking of the Whitmanian model is representative in two ways: first, in his appropriation of Whitman's themes and tones (in works by Pound, Lawrence, Stevens, and others, pp. 44–60 below) and second, in his application of Whitmanian principles of style to a modern cultural situation (as in the Hispanic and Russian adaptations of Whitman, pp. 66–88 below). As he invents a Whitman to satisfy his own need for an American tradition, Williams' career encapsulates many of these modernist and postmodernist responses to the Whitman-problem. For the moment, then, we postpone a full discussion of William's own work (in Part 2), in order to consider briefly those historical backgrounds and analogies. Along the way we'll be looking at shorter Williams poems, in the order he wrote them, from his earliest work to *Paterson* V. I suspect that the way to approach this delicate question of comparative influence is through a somewhat detailed route through a few poems— by Williams and by others—that illustrate different attitudes toward Whitman's example. Our goal ultimately is to look at the structuring principles of Williams' own poems—"no ideas but in the facts"—but Williams' contextual sense, his alertness to directions and discoveries among his contemporaries' works, is stronger than we usually suppose. Williams' creation of a protomodernist Whitman is, in fact, largely a response to those contextual considerations; he invents the Whitman he thinks he and his contemporaries need.

Part 1 thus circles around the central subject (Williams), as if to map a field before Parts 2 and 3 penetrate it. Eventually I want not only to suggest a way to apprehend and to appreciate Williams' poems, but also to see his poetic in several ways: as an example of the "line of Whitman," as an enactment of an objectivist ethos, and (especially with focus on the modernist epic *Paterson*) as a peculiarly American effort to marry local specificity of detail and diction with the visionary idea of a new language, a new cultural dispensation, a new heaven and earth. I approach Williams and his poems, therefore, from several angles of vision; in order to place the work in the contexts of its inheritance from Whitman, its metrical pioneering, and its adaptation of essential energies from

such movements as Imagism, Vorticism, and Objectivism, I incidentally consider a variety of subthemes (the range of Whitman's
influence, for instance, or the fate of the long poem in English
since Milton). I trust that the relation of these peripheral parts
(especially the topic of the modernist uses of Whitman) to the
whole will become clear. I take as my essential topic a reading of
Williams as a crucially inventive—and representative—artistic figure of his time: a subtle and intelligent writer whose work is
sometimes underestimated, ironically, because of the obvious joys
of its surface. In Williams' best work the idea is inseparable from
the thing. I hope to take Williams' joyous dictum as an ideal for
criticism, as Williams did for his poetry: no ideas but in the thing
itself.

PART I

A Whitman for Moderns

ONE

The Problem of an American Self

The history of one branch of American literary aesthetics begins with the temptations of Milton's Satan: even Walt Whitman, who says he wants to sound like "Adam early in the morning," soon discovers Satanic energies implicit in his self-assertion. The influence is primarily formal; I do not mean to stress the overtly historical argument, by which rationalist Puritanism influences American thought, from Bradford through Emerson and beyond. Nor do I mean the exclusively literary-historical influence of Milton on the English Romantic poets and thus indirectly on the later American Romantic writers. Rather, the formal influence of Milton's Satan on American poetic theory is that problem of the Egotistical Sublime to which Blake alluded in "The Marriage of Heaven and Hell": "The reason Milton wrote in fetters when he wrote of Angels & God, and at liberty when of Devils & Hell, is because he was a true Poet and of the Devils party without knowing it." Milton's unacknowledged desire for liberty takes form as the unfettered vividness of Satan and Pandemonium, in *Paradise Lost*.

Blake deliberately conflates the two related lines of argument, but we should, I think, notice the distinction between the ethical and the aesthetic issues. In moral terms, the poet of the "Devils party" inadvertently asserts, through his individuation, a pride that amounts to an assault on order, propriety, and reason. (Thus Shelley sees in Satan an example of human regeneration through suffering, Byron identifies in Satan an archetypal political rebel, and Hazlitt thinks Satan represents the abstract revolt of energy against form.) But the imaginative creation of a vivid Self invites a structural problem within the poem that Self inhabits: Milton reveals himself of the Devils party as much by stylistic asymmetry as by tacit argument. The opening books of *Paradise Lost* portray a Satan so sympathetic and sovereign unto himself that the subsequent books of the poem never quite dispel the largesse we first sense in him. Milton's Satan creates himself through heroic resistance, and through that self-creation he generates his own place in the universe:

> The mind is its own place, and in itself
> Can make a Heav'n of Hell, a Hell of Heav'n. (I, 254–55)

The moral problem Satan has in subordinating himself to the cosmic form of God's universe repeats Milton's structural problem of subordinating a grand Self within the poem's formal proportions: thus Blake could associate the moral problems of energy with the structural problem of poetic form. A celebrated Self is hard to control, because of its tendency to dominate its "place."

In North America for the last 150 years, however, the aesthetic problem has presented itself in political, not in theological, vocabularies. In the literature of the United States since Joel Barlow's *Columbiad,* writers have worked to develop a formal tradition of quintessentially American writing—especially of poetry—that could declare itself rebelliously indigenous to the North American landscape and culture.[1] Often these attempts have taken the form of long poems that relate the conditions of a large poetic project to the conditions of a broad prosaic country. These poems, that is, claim to represent the nation as it "speaks" itself. Often the method has been to assert an enlarged personal Self (in Whitman, for instance), or a representative figure (in Ezra Pound's surrogate heroes, in Wallace Stevens' Crispin, in Charles Olson's Maximus), or a central idiosyncratic and loquacious narrator (as in the meditative experiments of Hart Crane, John Berryman, A. R. Ammons, and John Ashbery).

Difficulties arise, however, when the need for unity within the poem begins to assert itself. However inclusive and democratic its contents, an extended piece of writing demands an organizational structure to relate the parts to the whole. As Poe argued in 1850, a single lyric cannot be both unified and long; appropriately, the new lyrical-epic poem tends almost immediately to break into mentally and visually comprehensible separate units.[2] But the systems of order that result are often discriminating, arbitrary, or subordinating, and for a poem claiming to represent an "American" or "democratic" open condition, such order can be problematic. Since 1855, the diverse parts of the American epic have experienced the same tensions between sovereignty and union that the diverse citizens and states of the nation have encountered: the dilemma of Milton with his creation Satan.

For political institutions, the alternatives in this dilemma tend either toward an ideal synchronicity and coexistence or toward the establishment of new organizing principles, either through legislation or through force. (The problem that had been for Milton a theological conflict of ethical versus aesthetic forces becomes in the new political vocabulary a conflict of "historical" (horizontal) versus "structural" (vertical) forces in the field of the poem. Within a decade of the first *Leaves of Grass,* for instance, the American states broke into civil war over those questions of unity and diversity that Whitman had tried verbally to resolve in "Song of Myself.") The poem, however, has to reconcile its conflicts within itself. To be responsibly comprehensive, the long American poem must find some adhesive power like that of Whitman's theoretical democracy, in order to reconcile the actual demands of unity and diversity with which the nation has had to struggle. The problem for the long American poem—as for the American political system—is one of comprehensive form. Whatever cohesive power the poem assumes must prove compatible, in language and in organization, with the facts of cultural experience—not only compatible, that is, but proleptic. In the name of the culture, the poem makes both a self and a proportionate place for that self: both must be large enough to encompass diversity but specific enough to be comprehensible and orderly.

For practical reasons of focus, I have limited this essay to the problems of an "American" form in the work of William Carlos Williams, especially in his long poem *Paterson,* as he aligns himself with a paradoxical American tradition of rebelliousness against tradition—that is, especially as Williams summons Walt Whitman to ratify his modernist attempts to reconcile the Many and the One. I confess that my choice of Williams and of Williams' Whitman is largely a matter of personal enthusiasm. Nevertheless, the relation between the two poets does, I think, suggest a pattern. The deceptively simple dance of avoidance and appropriation by which Williams encounters Whitman is significant for its own sake in literary history, and it also summarizes the Whitman problem for many other modern writers.

What interests me about the American modernist image of Whitman is that it links two of the major premises of international modernism. The historical issue (the tension between a writer's meliorist hopes for the culture and the problematic factual reality) intersects with the formal issue (the self-consciousness of the modernist artist, who works in a self-referential form), in an intersection that is like the crux of the most representative modernist poems ("Hugh Selwyn Mauberly," *The Waste Land,* "Meditations in Time of Civil War," *The Bridge, In Parenthesis,* and others). For Williams and Pound and other poets, Whitman provides an available image of a formal predecessor; he is a poet who worked within the poetic line to redefine the relation of the observing self to a problematic cultural context. Though Whitman's experiments in a "democratic" mode are now inappropriate as formal models, the figure of Whitman is useful as an image of a protomodernist who demonstrated that the ratio of the historical and the structural could be negotiated within the self-reflexive form of the new poem. Ironically, to write a long poem means coming to terms not only with theoretical questions of form and of diction, but also with this image of Whitman. The rebel makes a problematic and even conservative father. Thus theoretical problems of form become practical questions of the newer poet's artistic identity within a paradoxical American tradition of rebellion against tradition.

Eventually, the argument could be extended to the problems of form and of poetic identity for writers in other cultures and in

other languages—though I would argue that the North American
model is still essential, because of two courses of influence. In the
first case, Whitman is the model for many writers in developing
countries, where his work represents forms of possibility for emergent literary identity in newly self-conscious nationalist movements. (We'll return to this point later in this chapter.) In the
second case, the long poem in twentieth-century writing—although not an exclusively North American form—has been so
largely shaped by the experiments of early North American modernists that that American model is still centrally pertinent. We
tend to forget how American the *Cantos* are, in theme and in execution, or how closely Pound's excursions into Confucianism, into
Greek mythology, and into Renaissance history parallel that search
for an ideal society Pound finds in the writings of Adams and
Jefferson. For all his cosmopolitanism, Pound remains centrally
within the American tradition. Similarly, T. S. Eliot returns, even
literally, to a concern with local time and American place, in the
Four Quartets. From Pound and Williams, and from Eliot separately, the major directions of the modern "lyric epic" poem begin:
we can recognize for instance a "Pound-and-Williams" tradition
(in the work of writers like Basil Bunting in England, Charles Olson in America, David Jones in Wales) and an "Eliot" tradition
(in the early Auden, for instance, or in Patrick Kavanagh and
Thomas Kinsella in Ireland). To follow these newer traditions back
toward their shared, fundamentally North American, concern with
a cultural-and-literary form is not, I think, to be too reductive; in
any case, many of these postmodernist writers are candid about
tracing their assumptions back through the modern poets, to their
Whitmanian origins. Just as the Romantic poets' encounters with
Milton shaped much of the high Romantic concern with tradition
and rebellion for several generations, so the example of Whitman
remains pertinent for writers of the contemporary long poem in
cultures that experienced modernism strongly. Increasingly, too,
Williams himself—distinct from Pound—is becoming influential
in the aesthetics of the international long poem; thus Williams'
dialogues with Whitman come to seem doubly germane.

In the 1960s James Breslin wrote the seminal articles tracing the
influence of Whitman on Williams' early development as a nativist

writer.[3] In those exciting essays Breslin followed the influence of Whitman specifically on Williams' early career, tacitly concluding that by the time of the publication of his early work, Williams had learned what he was to learn from Whitman. That influence, according to Breslin, affected primarily Williams' tone. I wish that Breslin had continued to trace those Whitmanian tendencies throughout Williams' career. This essay is, in part, an attempt to complement Breslin's important essays by watching the later Williams continue to invent the Whitman he needs. The influence— or projection—becomes more complex when Williams starts to work on a longer poem, in a form more obviously identified with Whitman. At that point, in the long approach to *Paterson,* the "influence" becomes formal as well as tonal: Williams summons Whitman both as a predecessor and as a failed model, whose "failure" to complete his experiments requires Williams' modern completions.

As Williams pictures him, Whitman first faces the question of form squarely, trying to appropriate the energies of abstract democracy as poetic energies. Postulating an ideal spiritual democracy toward which the American landscape and people could aspire, Whitman writes to influence his fellow citizens to follow him toward that ideal by following the implications of his form.[4] Only America, in Whitman's estimation, has the resources, the linguistic potential, and the freedom from historical contingencies to approach that ideally synthetic unity-within-diversity that is his cultural goal. Though he insists on "reality" and on accurate representation in language and in detail, Whitman's rhetoric is one of ambitiously self-fulfilling idealist prophecy: he incorporates into his form enough of the palpable reality around him to make his ideally democratic vision seem organic and credible.[5]

> Thy body permanent,
> The body lurking there within thy body,
> The only purport of the form thou art, the real I myself,
>   An image, an eidólon.
>
>   Thy very songs not in thy songs,
> No special strains to sing, none for itself,

> But from the whole resulting, rising at last and floating,
>   A round full-orb'd eidólon.
>
> 　　　　　　　　　　　　　(*LOG,* p. 8)

Whitman, that is, writes to bind. His vehicle is an eidolon of that giant Adamic Self who can incorporate into his "body" the geography, the population, and the energies of his present reality, in order to transmute them into an ideally spiritual democratic monad.[6] Through this magnanimous Self, Whitman hopes to influence his fellow citizens by supercharging them with the same "democratic" energies that vivify him.

William Carlos Williams, by contrast, writes to define or to reveal, more locally. In his short poems Williams attends to the structure of short units of perception. In *Paterson* Williams seeks "an image large enough to embody the whole knowable world" around him, and that inclusive attitude toward the matter of his poem extends also toward his diction and his tone. Whitman wants to be his world; Williams wants to know his. Williams' vehicle, like Whitman's, is a corporate personality—but not a uniformly ideal one. Even more than Whitman does, Williams makes his central voice that of a "simple" and "separate" citizen. Williams does follow Whitman's lead into American themes and details and patterned organizations. But Williams diverges from Whitman, separating the modernist from the American Romantic work, when the form of the modern poem seems to demand a choice between the Whitmanian projection of an ideal condition and a more objective representation of the thing-as-itself, registered in a self-reflexive language. Williams is concerned about the injustices and inadequacies of modern America, but his purpose is political only in a large sense. In *Paterson,* his "reply to Greek and Latin with the bare hands," Williams details the specific place and circumstances of his city in order to teach others how, not what, to see.

This broad sense of ordinary perception as a mode of political vision relates to Williams' historical sense, which is less prophetic than Whitman's. Whitman writes to link with others beyond time, while Williams writes to link not by merger but by analogy, through time: what is true now for a small New Jersey city is true for that place and time only, but by probing that "local" truth

Williams hopes to find an "essence" or "gist" analogous to the gist of experience in other places and times. Whitman inscribes *Leaves of Grass* with this theme:

> One's-Self I sing, a simple separate person,
> Yet utter the word Democratic, the word En–Masse.
>
> .   .   .
>
> Of Life immense in passion, pulse, and power,
> Cheerful, for freest action form'd under the laws divine,
> The Modern Man I sing.
>
> (*LOG*, p. 1)

Whitman is writing for Americans—or for democratic spirits—in order to demonstrate what we obviously share, and to celebrate that ideal (though vague) mutuality in an inclusive single Personality. Williams, by contrast, insists on formal specificity; he is interested in experience, not in "Life." The projective and social directions of his quest, like the future-orientation of Whitman, make his effort similarly generative, however. From Whitman, Williams seems to learn that American ambition, to write a long poem that would be "experimental and endlessly incomplete."[7] What Williams and Whitman share is the recognition of a formal link between an expanded place and an expansive style of the Self: "the mind is its own place."

The largest problem for the long poem in the American idiom is thus the old Miltonic problem of shape or proportion within a poem that centers on a dominant Self. In the North American tradition the problem is a question of the evolving "shape" of a "new language" for that self: the language of the poem makes both a self and a place for that self to inhabit. Late in *Paterson* [8] Williams sets the question:

> How to begin to find a shape—to begin to begin again,
> turning the inside out : to find one phrase that will
> lie married beside another for delight   .   ?
> —seems beyond attainment   .
>
> (*P*, p. 140)

Williams claims that this tradition of prophetic, progressive verbalism begins, for North America, with Whitman. (Williams selectively ignores the eighteenth- and nineteenth-century American traditions of anticipatory criticism, though for decades before Emerson writers had been calling for an indigenous American literature.) By identifying Whitman as the origin of the tradition, Williams stresses the realization of the prophecy, not the prophecy itself—though Williams' own use of Whitman is frankly speculative and admonitory, as if Williams were prophesying a new Whitmanian movement for American poetry. Whitman's "influence" on Williams operates not through specific lines or poems, but through an internalized image of Whitman—or, more specifically, through several images that define related attitudes and tones; Whitman's example seems to demand that his discoveries be retranslated to make them appropriate vehicles for the modernist work. That process of translation, or integration, constitutes Whitman's "influence" on Williams' career. Williams' reading of Whitman is interesting because it is both formative for Williams' work and representative of the Whitman problem for other modernist writers. As a theory about Whitman, it is not particularly novel, or scholarly, or profoundly insightful about specific Whitman poems. It is, rather, a series of personal encounters with a literary "figure," as if Williams were responding directly to Whitman's own self-representations, especially to the iconoclastic dissolution of the Father at the end of "Song of Myself":

> I depart as air, I shake my white locks at the runaway sun,
> I effuse my flesh in eddies, and drift it in lacy jags.
>
> I bequeath myself to the dirt to grow from the grass I love,
> If you want me again look for me under your boot-soles.
>
> (*LOG*, p. 89)

This argument about father-figures and internalizations may recall Harold Bloom's theories of misprision and of anxious influence—though with several qualifications. First, Whitman's influence does not operate on Williams (or on his compatriots) through specific texts, but through an internalized attitude toward experience, an attitude that eventually demands adjustments in the language and form by which the newer poet shapes the world. This literary history, that is, is the story not of an argument between competing texts, but of a struggle among formative pre-verbal assumptions about language, form, and personal identity. For all his reference to Whitman's importance, Williams does not often refer to specific Whitman poems; at best he quotes the beginning of *Song of Myself* or alludes to other poems. Second, I'd argue that the influence of Whitman on twentieth-century writers seems often to fit this pattern. Bloom's theory of oedipal struggle with the parent-poet may still obtain, but the case of Whitman demands a wider, more socialized literary history; to keep within Bloom's Freudian schema, we might postulate a fraternal or sibling approach to a common father. In Williams' case, the early influence of Whitman is tangled with the influence of Williams' friend Ezra Pound, for instance, as both younger poets discover Whitman's gestures and generosity.

TWO

The Road to Whitman

Whitman and Pound and Williams: A Sibling Rivalry

Williams met Whitman's work as early as his student days at the University of Pennsylvania. Fascinated simultaneously by the formal melancholy of Keats and by the "raw vigor" of Whitman, Williams recalls in his *Autobiography,* he imitated both.[9] After Keats, Williams wrote yeasty formal sonnets; after Whitman he kept notebooks of "Whitmanesque 'thoughts,' a sort of purgation and confessional, to clear my head and my thoughts of turgid obsessions."[10] As he tried to sustain this curious mixture, then, Williams met the young Ezra Pound, also a student at Penn. Williams recalls later that the difference in his poems Before Pound and After Pound was "like B.C. and A.D."

Oddly, Williams' poems Before Pound are more overtly Whitmanian: quick, spontaneous, lurchingly emotional. He had read *Leaves of Grass* and hadn't liked most of it, but he had been impressed with the opening lines of "Song of Myself"; the prolonged adolescence of Whitman apparently appealed to the adolescent Williams. Pound's poems were already more literary, almost derivative, and he and Williams wryly discovered they had something in common. Williams recalls: "He was impressed with his own poetry; but then, I was impressed with my own poetry, so we got along all right."[11] Eventually, however, Pound's persuasive carefulness began to filter into Williams' work, displacing the early yawping.

From the beginning of their friendship, Pound asserted his own style of cosmopolitan erudition as a requirement for verse, and he quickly defined two of his most insistent complaints about Williams. On the one hand, Pound assaulted Williams for his lack of education, proposing, as he did for others, a corrective program of wide cross-cultural reading. Yet Pound also taunted Williams for not being "American" enough; Pound pointed to Williams' mixed genealogy as proof that Williams' "local" ties with the American landscape and language were at best one-generational and two-dimensional. For Pound, Williams remains a "dago-immigrant" in America.[12] In fact, to Williams' dismay, Pound continued for years to press this theory of Williams' "immigrant" status in America, suggesting that as a result of this perspective Williams consistently perceives America as somehow exotic or paradoxically foreign. Rather than respecting the local truth, as Williams claims to do, in Pound's view Williams seems fascinated by the local elements he finds in America, as an authentic American might be captivated by the exotic circumstances of another country. Other writers of the 1920s may seek exile because they already know their homeland and its limitations, but Williams, by staying at home in New Jersey, remains in Pound's view within a tradition of exiled or immigrant writers. Though Pound assails Williams with his "immigrant" family history, often Pound's taunts seem intended to recall Pound's own American birth and family history and to justify, at the same time, his own increasingly cosmopolitan orientation.

From the first, however, Pound seems to have worked as an astringent against Williams' early fascination with the raw vigor of Whitman. "The copybook poems, my secret life, the poems I was writing before I met Pound, were what I can only describe as free verse, formless, after Whitman," Williams recalls.[13] But though this initial influence of Pound tightened and polished Williams' early style, it also colors many of Williams' early efforts with a melancholy preciousness that works against his purpose in the poems. That occasional note of erudite glibness one hears in Pound's *A Lume Spento* rings equally false in Williams' earliest work, and soon Williams finds himself pulling gently away from Pound's direct influence. Perhaps coincidentally, he returns at the same time to Whitman, with a more sympathetic and less imitative response. Thus, in the opening decade of the twentieth century both Williams and Pound begin to come to terms with Whitman's identity as an indigenous American writer and, through Whitman, with the America he claims to represent both thematically and formally. At first Pound helps to subvert Williams' trust in the "raw vigor" of Whitman.[14] As they mature, however, Williams' recognition of his primary poetic identity—of the self as local inhabitant, writing in a culture with its own distinct flavor, language, and thematic needs—requires a break with Pound's increasing internationalism *and* with Whitman's idealizing and cosmic Americanness (an image of Whitman that comes through Pound). Williams goes to work in a hospital, meeting Whitman's Americans in the flesh, while Pound moves into more abstract historical themes. Pound begins to envision for himself a heroic Whitman-figure of resounding personality, whose yawping largesse seems to anticipate Pound's own ambitions for his poems and for the culture.

As early as 1909, several years out of college and several thousand miles from the United States, Pound evaluates the influence and utility of this Whitmanian message. Somewhat grandly, Pound concludes that Whitman's

crudity is an exceding great stench, but it *is* America. He is the hollow place in the rock that echoes with his time. He *does* "chant the crucial stage" and he is the "voice triumphant." He is disgusting. He is an excedingly nauseating pill, but he accomplishes his mission.[15]

Though publicly skeptical of Whitman (as in the marvelous parody in *The Spirit of Romance:* "Lo, behold, I eat water-melons. When I eat water-melons the world eats water-melons through me"),[16] privately Pound is working toward an image of Whitman that can fit his own modernist ambitions. Instead of appearing more "American" because of his specificity, Whitman becomes for Pound the representative of a "cosmic consciousness," whose "message" Pound will "drive. . . . into the new world."[17] Within several years Pound has consolidated this attitude toward Whitman until, in a 1913 sequence of poems remarkable for their Whit-

manian rhythms, tone, and techniques, Pound makes public his
most memorable "pact" with the older poet. Significantly, he describes that acceptance as a filial reconciliation, in images of graft-
ing a new fruitful branch to an established rootstock.

> I make a pact with you, Walt Whitman—
> I have detested you long enough.
> I come to you as a grown child
> Who has had a pig-headed father;
> I am old enough now to make friends.
> It was you that broke the new wood,
> Now is a time for carving.
> We have one sap and one root—
> Let there be commerce between us.[18]

The continuity of "one sap and one root" promotes a "commerce"
between the two poets: by changing the horticultural image (reminiscent of Romantic theories of "organic" form) to the commer-
cial image, Pound illustrates how his own work should "graft"
onto Whitman's example Pound's modern social concerns. In all
these poems in his 1913 sequence, Pound wryly considers the relations among the poet, the poem, and the social world:

> Go, my songs, to the lonely and the unsatisfied,
> Go also to the nerve-wracked, go to the enslaved-by-convention,
> Bear to them my contempt for their oppressors.
> Go as a great wave of cool water,
> Bear my contempt of oppressors.

These poems appear in a book entitled *Lustra;* Pound gives the
definition of the noun "lustrum" as "an offering for the sins of the
whole people," made at regular intervals by ancient Roman rulers.
In his urge to claim a similar culturally reformative power for the
poem, Pound adopts not only Whitman's tone, but also his characteristic trope of paralleled enumeration—listing—as if Pound
acknowledges the utility of Whitman's style in that association of
tone, form, and social impulse. Enumeration as a trope suggests
both a centrifugal freedom (in the observations of concrete particulars) and also a centripetal ordering (through the implied observer who sets those particulars in parallel and in sequence). Par-

allelism is often a trope of praise and of unity-within-diversity: Whitman himself learned it from the Psalms, in which David uses it to illustrate both Yahweh's dominion and the wonders of His creation. Paradoxically, it is both an empirical and rhetorical form, like a scientific experiment that generalizes data,[19] and also a form that suggests an argument based on the character of the speaker.

Pound makes his pact with Whitman, his acknowledgment of the utility not only of Whitman's tone but of his rhythms and structures as well, at the same time that he is developing the terms of Imagism, with its insistence on the spare image and on the "direct treatment of the 'thing.' " Pound is also increasingly interested in principles of juxtaposed composition that assert an order based on individual character and on proper perception, Emersonian and Confucian principles Pound later formalizes in his notion of the ideogram.[20] At the same time he is reevaluating Whitman, in his prose Pound is also beginning to propose for the poem a "new" formal concept, one that asserts an order based on sharp verbal contrasts and abutments.

From this early period of Pound's career, through the *Cantos,* the voice of Whitman is submerged in the increasingly assertive voice of Pound himself, in his various personae. The line-unit of the *Cantos* is often the noun clause; the characteristic trope remains Whitmanian parallel enumeration. Pound finds little more to learn from Whitman's style after this early period of ambivalence (also the period of Pound's strongest influence on Williams), but Pound does seem increasingly to adopt a Whitmanian persona as one of the shifting centers around which the *Cantos* revolve. The essential Americanness of the Whitmanian "father" passes to Pound the "son" both through an interest in the American configuration of politics and language and also through the Whitmanian ideal of a representative cultural hero. Whitman's representativeness becomes Pound's ideal in an international (not nationalistic) field, as Pound works to portray that hero with various historical masks (Odysseus, Confucius, Malatesta, Jefferson, and others). If Whitman's crudity "is" America, in a literary sense Pound's ambivalence toward Whitman is an ambivalence toward the America that produces him, the twentieth-century son of that father, and then expels him. Only in exile does Pound encounter Whitman seri-

ously. Whitman's ideal of progress, as he postulates on the basis
of a model Self a future state of justice and of democratic equality,
appeals to Pound's own propadeutic sense, and throughout his
career Pound continues to allude to this overriding "message" of
Whitman. In the *Pisan Cantos,* Pound makes his final truce with
this American forefather who represents his nation with chthonic
humility:

> 'Fvy! in Tdaenmarck efen dh'beasantz gnow him,'
>   meaning Whitman, exotic, still suspect
>   four miles from Camden
>   'O troubled reflection
>   'O Throat, O throbbing heart'
>   How drawn, O GEA TERRA,
>   what draws as thou drawest
>   till one sink into thee by an arm's width
>   embracing thee. Drawest,
>   truly thou drawest.
>   Wisdom lies next thee,
>   simply, past mctaphor.[21]

Thus Pound gradually identifies his own ambition as the reworking of Whitman's nationalistic "message" toward an international
cultural synthesis. As this section of Canto 82 suggests, too, the
generosity and crude vigor Pound had earlier found dominant in
Whitman seem less important, in Pound's later career, than the
image of a Whitman neglected by the country that generates him
and that needs him without knowing its need. Pound uses Whitman's metaphors of submission and of oceanic merger (quoted
from "Out of the Cradle Endlessly Rocking"), and he reinforces
the spirituality of those metaphors, paradoxically, by insisting on
Whitman's longing for the "GEA TERRA." By 1949 the Whitman
who had been a model of a confident antagonism toward the
dominant American culture has come to seem a representative vic-
tim of America's refusal to listen to its own antinomian impulses.
Thus Pound associates Whitman not with the society that refuses
him, but with the precultural earth: his earthiness *is* America in a
revised sense. Similarly, Canto 80 ("Nancy where art thou?") associates the neglect of Whitman as a poet, and therefore as a po-

tential cultural leader, both with the decay of information in a poetic tradition ("the texts of his early stuff are probably lost") and with Whitman's childlessness. Pound alludes to Whitman's "affair of the Southern Nancy," recalling a spurious anecdote— also one of Williams' favorites—according to which the racial prejudices of his friends and family forced Whitman to leave his first love, a Creole woman in New Orleans. Such a union, Pound suggests, could have produced children as important to the physical polis as Whitman's poems should be to the culture. Instead, both children and poems are thwarted: unconceived, lost, or neglected.

> a few more of him,
> were that conceivable, would have enriched
> the life of Manhattan
> or any other town or metropolis
> the texts of his early stuff are probably lost

Both the decay of verbal information and the loss of physical continuities (what Williams calls "divorce") then combine to summon the images of other poets America has ruined through its benign neglect: Richard Hovey, Frederick Wadsworth Loring, and Trumbull Stickney ("the lost legion . . ./ They just died/ They died because they/ just couldn't stand it.") And this list leads to an American-Chinese-Elizabethan question: "Nenni, Nenni, who shall have the succession?" By this point in Canto 80 and in Pound's career, however, the honor of carrying the American tradition in "succession" seems personally problematic—though culturally urgent:

> Nenni, Nenni, who shall have the succession?
> To this whiteness, Tseng said
> 'What shall add to this whiteness?' [22]

The continuity between Pound's earlier and later versions of Whitman ought to be clear. Pound learns his formal lessons from Whitman early, then works to continue the Whitmanian "message." He makes Whitman a metaphor first of America itself, then of America's neglect of its poets and of its own best possibilities:

in short, Pound uses Whitman as a metaphor of Pound's own troubled modern relations with his homeland. Williams similarly makes Whitman a figure of America's dormant potential (that is, Williams more nearly accepts Whitman's use of himself as a metaphor of American potential), but Williams works the question in another direction, asking what the formal implications of that metaphor might be. The difference between these two adult versions of Whitman reflects the difference in the two younger writers' relations to North America and to the challenge of a socially formative American poetic. As their careers diverge, Pound and Williams refine their separate concepts of Whitman, as if to use that "Father" to ratify their individuation. Pound stresses Whitman's self-aggrandizement, obstinacy, and melancholy, while Williams (annoyed by just those qualities in Pound) points to Whitman's idiomatic talk, his experiments with form, and his doubled tone of intimacy-and-distance, to defend his own modernist assumptions, which differ slightly from Pound's. Pound's Whitman and Williams' do develop from the image of Whitman they share just before World War I: while Pound is working past his early preciousness toward his "pact" with a "pig-headed father," Williams is returning to an earlier enthusiasm, having almost accidentally discovered its appropriateness.

Williams Alone in America: A Father for Theme, A Quest for Form

Florence Williams gave her husband a new copy of *Leaves of Grass* shortly after their wedding in 1913, and during the years just before World War I Williams' interest in Whitman revives. Besides suggesting the influence of Browning's narratives and of fin de siècle lyrics, Williams' poems of this period often show traces of a robust and mystic materialism that recalls Whitman's tones and methods. Williams' early poem "The Wanderer" is a good example of this similarity, as Williams deliberately echoes "Crossing Brooklyn Ferry." But where Whitman had been crossing to his home in Brooklyn, outward from the mainland, at evening, Williams' speaker is returning toward the city, inland, in full daylight:

> But one day, crossing the ferry
> With the great towers of Manhattan before me,
> Out at the prow with the sea wind blowing,
> I had been wearying many questions
> Which she had put on to try me:
> How shall I be a mirror to this modernity?
> When lo! in a rush, dragging
> A blunt boat on the yielding river—
> Suddenly I saw her![23]

Throughout "The Wanderer" Williams' speaker pursues an abstract "female" truth that eludes him until at last he jumps into the Passaic River. In that filthy local wash he finds a credible truth and a union with his grimy Muse. The gesture of the final section recalls Whitman's mystical mergings with the sea in poems like "Out of the Cradle Endlessly Rocking," "As Ebb'd with the Ocean of Life," or even "The Sleepers." Unlike Whitman's mergings, however, in Williams' poem an abandonment to the water precedes a specific rebirth:

> Then the river began to enter my heart,
> Eddying back cool and limpid
> Into the crystal beginning of its days.

This etiological refluence requires that the local "thing"—in this case the muddy river—be encountered on its own terms. In "The Wanderer" the river finally reasserts itself as a Heraclitean river of time and change and detail:

> Muddy, then black and shrunken
> Till I felt the utter depth of its rottenness
> The vile breadth of its degradation
> And dropped down knowing this was me now.
> But she lifted me and the water took a new tide
> Again into the older experiences,
> And so, backward and forward,
> It tortured itself within me
> Until time had been washed finally under. . . .

This early Williams poem ends with the image of a marriage of the woman-figure with the river-sodden poet. Just as in *Paterson* Williams pictures a Whitmanian giant whose marriage with the natural world promises the birth of a new language, so in "The Wanderer" the marriage of the poem with the fecund local scene produces a son. That child will live in a "bird's paradise" like that of the "solitary singer," Whitman's ariatic bird that sings in a swamp its cradle song of death and of oceanic merger (in "When Lilacs Last in the Dooryard Bloom'd"). Williams' poem ends with this marriage of speaker and circumstance, and with a prophecy that the poet's wandering has not yet ended, because his "son" will continue the quest:

> "Here shall be a bird's paradise,
> They sing to you remembering my voice:
> Here the most secluded spaces
> For miles around, hallowed by a stench
> To be our joint solitude and temple;
> In memory of this clear marriage
> And the child I have brought you in the late years.
> Live, river, live in luxuriance
> Remembering this our son,
> In remembrance of me and my sorrow
> And of the new wandering!"
>
> (*CEP*, pp. 11–12)

"The Wanderer" is interesting as a pivotal point for Williams, though the poem is an unlikely crossing of Keats ("To Psyche," "Lamia") and Whitman. In lines like those of the ending, Williams seems determined to learn from Whitman, without quite identifying what the formally useful lessons from Whitman might be. While Pound at this time is working toward an image of Whitman as a robust father, the necessary stylistic antidote to American oppressiveness, Williams is using Whitman as a model of thematic possibilities; Williams has not yet made his eventual connection between ideology and style. Eventually the success of Eliot in England will force him to make that association; at that point Williams' image of Whitman will change from the early model (as explained by James Breslin) to a more constant referent, one with structural and cultural implications. When in the "Broadway" section of "The Wanderer" Williams rewrites lines from "Crossing Brooklyn Ferry," for instance, he is still incompletely internalizing Whitman's style.

He repeats the expansive Whitmanian gesture—even turning it to socially critical purposes, in a Baudelairean nightmare—without yet hearing the verbal vigor and syntactical excitement of Whitman's example:

> It was then she struck—from behind,
> In mid air, as with the edge of a great wing!
> And instantly down the mists of my eyes
> There came crowds walking—men as visions
> With expressionless, animate faces. . . .
>
> (*CEP,* p. 5)

Flow on, river! flow with the flood-tide, and ebb with the ebb-tide!
Frolic on, crested and scallop-edg'd waves!
Gorgeous clouds of the sunset! drench with your splendor me, or the
    men and women generations after me!
Cross from shore to shore, countless crowds of passengers!

> (*LOG,* p. 164)

If Williams had early rejected the "raw vigor" of Whitman in his own practice, at this time—early in World War I—he nevertheless seems taken with Whitman's tones and emotions. James Breslin succinctly characterizes this influence of Whitman on Williams' early development:

in "Leaves of Grass" Williams discovered a poet who had defiantly shattered conventional forms in order to release *his* feelings. Williams was thus stirred to affirm the ardent, extravagant side of his own nature—to achieve, in his broken, oppressive world, a version of Whitman's process of continual renewal.[24]

As Breslin explains, however, the sense of an exultant omniscient self that had characterized Whitman's Jacksonian optimism was no longer tenable for Williams. After 1913, the "central theme" of much of Williams' poetry is not exclusively the ardent, expansive side of himself, but is rather the effort of that self to "break through restrictions," to "generate new growth." By 1917—the same year as the publication of *Prufrock and Other Observations* to critical acclaim, first in England—Williams is asserting the continuity of his quest with Whitman's. The frontispiece of Williams' *Al Que Quiere!* (1917) carries this breezy Whitmanian blurb:

To Whom It May Concern!

This book is a collection of poems by William Carlos Williams. You gentle reader, will probably not like it, because it is brutally powerful and scornfully crude. Fortunately, neither the author nor the publisher care[s] much whether you like it or not. The author has done his work, and if you *do* read the book you will agree that he doesn't give a damn for your opinion. We have the profound satisfaction of publishing a book in which, we venture, the poets of the future will dig for materials as the poets of today dig in Whitman's "Leaves of Grass."[25]

The book *Al Que Quiere!* oddly combines poems of lurching exuberance with poems of rhetorical ponderousness; even allowing for the retrospective pressure a reader exerts on a writer's early work to make it seem to anticipate later developments, the effect of the volume is one of discontinuous transition. Williams seems still to be learning the power of the word to transmute the experience it records. Earlier poems like "The Wanderer" had described experiences; as in early studio photography, the image had been artificial but not yet fully artificed, not yet simulating spontaneity. In the best early work of Williams, however, the language does not record but transmogrifies experience, making the verbal experience of the poem analogous to—but not identical with—the experience the poem re-presents. But watch in the poem "Pastoral," for instance, how Williams wants to impose two modes of language onto the same scene, one to present the experience and another to interpret it. Here is the whole poem:

PASTORAL

If I say I have heard voices
who will believe me?

"None has dipped his hand
in the black waters of the sky
nor picked the yellow lilies
that sway on their clear stems
and no tree has waited
long enough nor still enough
to touch fingers with the moon."

I looked and there were little frogs
with puffed-out throats,
singing in the slime.

(*CEP,* p. 161)

By now Williams has at least abandoned the great Keatsian self-dramatizing symbolic gesture. Overtly the argument of the poem is that the "voices" of the little frogs suggest the (presumably) more profound ariatic outburst of the middle section. The "emotional" middle of the poem is obviously the "poetry"—but somewhat too obviously. The problem is that we cannot read the poem as ironic in its relation to that central section: Williams apparently wants us to accept that warbling stanza as representing the emotional truth of the situation—so that we would be surprised to find such sublimity ascribed to the frogs (or to his response to their song). Their singing "in the slime" is the "surprise" ending, working awkwardly to credit mundane experience with the emotion of the middle section. But that emotion, expressed with the residual vocabulary of fin de siècle ornament, is only asserted. That is, Williams doesn't yet trust his own argument; he does not yet credit the frogs' song with an adequate, uninterpreted, innate sublimity. Several of the poems in *Al Que Quiere!* work in this way, insisting through comparison on the emotional profundity of mundane experience. What bothers me about this "Pastoral," however, is that it relies on an inherited rhetoric to suggest situational emotion; it doesn't find its own figure verbally or dramatically self-complete. Despite its overt argument, Williams' "Pastoral" is stylistically derivative. Nevertheless, the poem marks an advance on the primary derivativeness of poems like "The Wanderer" (which Williams gives as the first poem in *Al Que Quiere!*)

Clearly, Williams is working past the rhetorical stiffness of his early poems, and in the transitional process he seems to find the influence of Whitman salutary. Whitman's tone informs much of this early work; early in World War I, Williams undergoes a liberating conversion, which in hindsight seems to lead with certainty toward the style we now associate with his most accomplished shorter lyrics. Two events bracket this period in the standard biographical accounts of Williams' development: the Armory Show in 1913 and the publication of Eliot's *The Waste Land* in book form in 1922. Williams himself is in part responsible for the literalness of this historical account. In his prose he repeatedly alludes to the Armory Show as the occasion for his liberating discovery of a "local assertion," just as he repeatedly objects to the conservatism and dominance of Eliot's poetic. Both the Armory Show and Eliot's success were clearly formative, but they are important primarily as occasions that mark stages in a decade of development for Williams. The two occasions are important for complementary reasons: in a positive and in a negative way, Williams uses them to date—and thus to formalize—tendencies that had been steadily developing in his own aesthetic.

Williams' sense of a "local virtue" intensified, he recalls, about the time of the Armory Show of modern painting in New York (and Chicago and Boston) in 1913—the same year as Pound's "pact" with Walt Whitman. In his *Autobiography* Williams characterizes the importance of the show's paintings by Kandinsky, Duchamp, Matisse, and others:

Whether the Armory Show in painting did it or whether that also was no more than a facet—the poetic line, the way the image was to lie on the page was our immediate concern. For myself all that implied, in the materials, respecting the place I knew best, was finding a local assertion—to my everlasting relief. I had never in my life felt that way. I was tremendously stirred.[26]

For Williams and other writers and visual artists, the exhibit by the American Association of Painters and Sculptors (in the Sixty-Ninth Regiment Armory in New York) was more potent as a metaphor than as an historical reality. The show popularly seemed to herald the emergence of a native American modernism (even though eventually the work by European painters proved to be of larger importance and critical interest); the show seemed to offer evidence of a liberating American break with tradition (even though the show began with a room of paintings by Ingres, Delacroix, and the Impressionists, acknowledged predecessors of the modernists); the show was repeatedly credited with having defined a "new aesthetic" (even though, as art historians like Meyer Schapiro have observed, the show was definitive largely because it publicized the pioneering work of several earlier generations of modern artists). The popular accounts of the Armory Show's importance, however, became historically more important than the facts. When he credits his own discovery of a "local assertion" to the effects of the Armory Show in 1913, Williams makes a metaphor of the occasion in order to associate his own experiments with this popular notion of the aesthetic the Show represented. Schapiro characterizes that aesthetic in ways that associate it with Williams' developing image of his own ambitions—and with his image of Walt Whitman:

The individual, his freedom, his inner world, his dedication, had become primary; and the self-affirming nature of the new art, with its outspoken colors and forms and more overt operations, was a means of realizing the new values, which were collective values, for individuality is a social fact, a matter of common striving, inconceivable without the modern conditions and means.[27]

Marcel Duchamp's "Nude Descending a Staircase" illustrates the case. By breaking the motion of the body into a series of interrelating planes ("the way the image was to lie on the page,"), Duchamp shapes a motion in a series of arrested perceptual moments: the painting is not so much about the body as about a perception of a body-in-motion. Our sense of the continuity of the narrative (the "descent") comes from our subjective fusion of different movements represented synchronically on the single flattened plane. What seems at first eccentric or subjective in the painting proves to require the participation of the viewer in the recombination of the represented event. In this sense its geometrical forms and angular stripes of color make the painting a collective or collaborative event. The painting has elegance, but it is the purified elegance of a scientific axiom; we see the "objective" truth of the represented objective fact (one body), but only because the painting articulates the specific empirical stages by which we subjectively perceive it.

When Williams claims the Armory Show as a formative occasion in his own development, therefore, he is working to associate his own ambitions at this point with the popularly accepted implications of the Show: both the modernist paintings presented there and Williams' own aesthetic ambitions committed the artist to a "local virtue." The "location" of this new ambition is both the American artwork and the American scene from which it comes, "singing in the slime." That is, the terms in which Williams positively describes the Armory Show are the same terms he uses, pejoratively, to describe the influence of T.S. Eliot on American letters. Before the publication of *The Waste Land,* Williams and other American artists had been working, he recalls, for a new formal freedom and for an American spirit of rebellious enterprise in the arts. Then came the "great catastrophe" of Eliot's international success, the triumph of a "Puritan," Anglo-American, conservative poetic, which seemed to Williams to preclude the continued development of the neo-Whitmanic populist American aesthetic. "I had not known how much the spirit of Whitman animated us," he remembers, "until it was withdrawn from us. Free verse became overnight a thing of the past." The first book Williams published after the Eliot-catastrophe is, in fact, entitled *Sour Grapes.*[28]

In these allusions to Eliot, the elements of Williams' professional indignation are difficult to distinguish from the elements of his personal hostility; at the most unexpected moments in his essays Williams seems to veer unnecessarily out of his way to savage Eliot. Williams' disappointment over the disruption of his own native modernism is clearly allied with a virulent personal dislike for Eliot and with a disappointment in his old friend Pound. Louis Simpson interestingly graphs Williams' aesthetic development against his private antagonisms, observing that Williams' mistrust of Eliot's anglophilia, though strong, does not account for all of Williams' personal animosity. Simpson concludes that Williams' hostilities sprang in part from feelings of betrayal when Pound, who had been an important influence and a contact with an international realm of letters, began to sponsor Eliot, promoting him as the most important new voice in English-language-based poetry. (By 1914 Pound was sending Eliot's poems to *Poetry* magazine, describing them as "the most interesting contributions" by a contemporary.) Williams reacted with hostility toward his "rival" Eliot, with contempt for Eliot's "dangerous" and "conformist" anglicized poetry, and with temporary harshness toward Pound him-self.[29] By the time of *Kora in Hell* (in 1920—even before *The Waste Land* volume), Williams ambiguously calls Pound "the best enemy United States verse has." Without compromising his en-thusiasm for Eliot's work, Pound defended himself to Williams and tried to conciliate, maintaining that "we need . . . both." In 1920 he wrote in a letter to Williams that it was "possibly lament-able that the two halves of what might have made a fairly decent poet should be sequestered and divided by the —— buttocks of the arse-wide Atlantic Ocean."[30]

But Williams' personal antagonisms toward Eliot modulate, within a few years, into a more precise formal objection. Williams remains defensively committed to "local" experience, but he de-fines this "local" fidelity in such a way as to criticize the cosmo-politanism of Pound and Eliot in terms of the poetic line. "Local-ity" is "the sense of being attached with integrity to actual experience," he insists[31]—and he concludes that the danger of Eliot's success is the danger of the domination of the "English" iambic line, a cultural form unrelated to "actual experience" in America. Coincidentally, Whitman, too, had had to face that chal-lenge of the iambic line:

He always said that his poems, which had broken the dominance of the iambic pentameter line in English prosody, had only begun his theme. I agree. It is up to us, in the new dialect, to continue it by a new construc-tion upon the syllables.[32]

When he defines "locality" as a poetic quality related to form, Wil-liams is forced to state his own modernist purposes. As he does so, he repeatedly summons his image of Whitman as the represen-tative of a native countertradition.

Under this challenge, then, Williams abruptly consolidates his notion of Whitman into a set of assumptions that remains rela-tively constant throughout the rest of his career. Unlike his earlier enthusiasm for Whitman's expansiveness, however, Williams' ma-ture appraisal of Whitman centers on Whitman's applicability in a "local" form. Whitman is a failed but invaluable innovator; Whit-man's importance derives from his iconoclastic attitude toward poetic form; to write like Whitman one must follow his example of rebellion against established patterns, even against Whitman's own example. Through the early 1920s, Williams' reading of Whitman shifts slightly from his first interest—in which he is taken with Whitman's liberating tone—to one that stresses more directly the formal implications of Whitman's intuitive "experiments" as anti-dotes to Eliot's "British" formalism. Throughout his career Williams invokes Whitman when he senses a challenge to his nativist aesthetic of idiomatic North American poetry; as he tries to define his own work against more conventional "academic" poetics, Williams summons Whitman to represent an alternative tradition. In fact, Williams calls on Whitman most frequently during specific periods: first at this time (c. 1915–1925) and later while he's composing *Paterson* (published 1946–1958).

At this point, however, in the volume *Spring and All* (1923: the year after *The Waste Land*), Williams seems to have consolidated his adult attitudes toward Whitman. Next to *Paterson, Spring and All* is the most exuberantly Whitmanian of all of Williams' poetic works. In prose pieces shuffled among poems illustrating his argument, Williams insists on the "reality" of the imagination's "flight" among things, in a movement that does not "tamper" with the world nor "move" it. Instead, the imagination makes a "new world" in words. In his discussion of the "dynamizing" force of the imagination, Williams insists on the "separating" power of imaginative language and on the "importance of personality," by which the aesthetic imagination can give the reader a sense of "expansion," "the feeling of completion by revealing the oneness of experience." In *Spring and All* Williams comes closest to a Whitmanian expression of the relations among reader, author, and artwork. The opening statement of the book, for instance, is aggressively robust, challenging comparison with the introductory poems of *Leaves of Grass:*

In the imagination, we are from henceforth (so long as you read) locked in a fraternal embrace, the classic caress of author and reader. We are one. Whenever I say "I" I mean also "you." And so, together, as one, we shall begin.[33]

In short, "what I assume you shall assume." The imagination, by which the individual can "raise himself to some approximate coextension with the universe," is in *Spring and All* a power of liberating identification, impressed on the reader with burly physical metaphors. In this context Williams directly acknowledges the influence of Whitman. In Whitman's insistence on the uniqueness and integrity of individual things, Williams sees a potential for imaginative and assertive individuality:

Whitman's proposals are of the same piece with the modern trend toward imaginative understanding of life. The largeness which he interprets as his identity with the least and the greatest about him, his "democracy" represents the vigor of his imaginative life.[34]

The integrity of the separate thing (or person) is apparently not threatened, but is enhanced, by the identification of it with the speaking self.

The negative urgency of this new interest in Whitman marks a breakthrough for Williams, the beginning of the remarkable decade in which he writes *Sour Grapes* (1920), *Spring and All* (1923), and many of the other poems in his early *Collected Poems* (1931), as well as the seminal prose works *Kora in Hell* (1920), *The Great American Novel* (1923), and *In the American Grain* (1925). The title poem of *Spring and All* recapitulates this sense of breakthrough, as Williams fixes the poem on a dynamic image of growth. Here is the full poem:

SPRING AND ALL

By the road to the contagious hospital
under the surge of the blue
mottled clouds driven from the
northeast—a cold wind. Beyond, the
waste of broad, muddy fields
brown with dried weeds, standing and fallen

patches of standing water
the scattering of tall trees

All along the road the reddish
purplish, forked, upstanding, twiggy

> stuff of bushes and small trees
> with dead, brown leaves under them
> leafless vines—
>
> Lifeless in appearance, sluggish
> dazed spring approaches—
>
> They enter the new world naked,
> cold, uncertain of all
> save that they enter. All about them
> the cold, familiar wind—
>
> Now the grass, tomorrow
> the stiff curl of wildcarrot leaf
> One by one objects are defined—
> It quickens: clarity, outline of leaf
>
> But now the stark dignity of
> entrance—Still, the profound change
> has come upon them: rooted, they
> grip down and begin to awaken[35]
>
> (*CEP,* pp. 241–42)

A generative force focused in the "grass" (like Whitman's leaves and unlike the thwarted vegetation of *The Waste Land*), Williams' growing "thing" emerges unobserved in the squalor of the American landscape (the "new world" in both senses). Unlike the little frogs of the "Pastoral," these growths do not need a poetical gloss. Their profundity is immanent, not transcendent:

> They enter the new world naked,
> cold, uncertain of all
> save that they enter. All about them
> the cold, familiar wind—

Instead of focusing on the "grass," which is amply available in Whitman's more abstracting version, Williams focuses on the emerging definition of outline in the grass, in early spring, as the leaves assert their hegemony and emergent dignity in the blank rubble of the local scene. Whitman's grass had been universalized; Williams' ubiquitous flowers and grasses are particular, in specific times and places. The poem "Spring and All" overtly claims to represent the "thing itself," but it does so by offering that thing in a description that stresses its motion (observe the verbs: the grass "quickens," the plants "enter" the new world, they "grip down and begin to awaken"), as if the "thing" is knowable only as motion or as tendency, not as static fact. The structure of the ending of the poem also enacts this sense of identity-in-motion. The first stanza of the last section quoted above ("They enter the new world naked") locates the leaves in their present scene; the second projects a future for the growth in this clearly defined "new world"; the final stanza ("But now . . .") returns to the immediate scene with a deeper sense of its present motion, because we know where it is tending: toward a season of clarity and of outline.

Similarly, the language of the poem "deepens" the sense of the immediate "thing." The complete single image of the poem works as the vehicle of an enlarged metaphor, the tenor of which is implied by the characteristics ascribed to the unfolding plants themselves; that is, Williams is using the "thing" as a metonymy. Plants are not "naked" when they enter the world, for instance; nakedness is more properly a characteristic of young animals, especially of those who will eventually wear fur or feathers or clothing. One can't be naked unless one can be somehow clothed, nor can one be "uncertain" unless one has a tacit capacity to be certain, nor can plants "awaken" if they do not sleep. Their nakedness, their uncertainty, and their wakening in this poem are metaphorical. These slight displacements in descriptive language make the poem an oblique argument about the relation between Williams' ideally specific observation of "things" ("objects are defined" . . . "clarity, outline of leaf") and the difficult "awakening" (or "gripping down") to a "new world" that is Williams' cultural ideal. If that connection is the "idea," it is embedded in Williams' portrayal of the "thing itself," the growing-motion of the new leaves. Williams has discovered the integrity of the autonomous symbol.[36] (It's remarkable how often Williams returns to these images of seed, leaf, and flower—often to suggest larger "ideas" or emotional recognitions. Even *Paterson* abounds in images of flowers: flowers as images of beauty, immediacy, and growth, as timelessness, as "innumerable women, each like a flower." Williams apparently considered calling the entire poem *Paterson* a "bouquet," the manuscript notes suggest. Instead, he saved that idea and used it in his masterful "Of Asphodel, That Greeny Flower"—a poem originally designed to be part of *Paterson* v.)[37]

The publication of *A Voyage to Pagany* (1928), a novel about an American doctor's travels in Europe, marks the beginning of Williams' concentration on prose fiction throughout much of the 1930s from the Depression until World War II. In the late '30s he returns to poetry, enriching the new verse by an infusion of the social concerns that characterize much of his prose, as in the Stecher trilogy about his wife's immigrant family. *Adam and Eve and the City,* a volume of poems that prefigures *Paterson,* appears in 1934; throughout the late 1930s and early 1940s Williams is apparently mulling over the possibilities of a long poetic project, as he tests the relations between theme and form. Through the rest of his career, he retains a relatively constant opinion of Whitman and of his achievement, an opinion clarified and defined largely before 1921 and strengthened by the continuing "threat" of Eliot's influence to an indigenous American aesthetic. The standards by which to measure antagonists like Eliot, Williams' final images of Whitman and of his "language experiment" seem to derive point for point from H.L. Mencken's discussion of Whitman in *The American Language* (1919), a book Williams calls a "sort of formal liturgy" for himself and for his friends at this early stage in his career.[38]

Potent as an image for Williams and also "incomplete" enough to pose no crippling threat to the imaginative assertion of the newer writer, Whitman seems to have affected Williams through an internalized image of what a vital American poet might do. His prose invocations of Whitman, especially during the composition of *Paterson* I-IV, suggest that Williams needs, if not direct textual help from a study of Whitman's poems, at least the support of a shared image of American poetic possibilities, latent since Whitman's experiments. Whitman himself tacitly appears both at the beginning and at the end of *Paterson,* as we'll see later. First, however, I'd like to pause to look more closely at those images of Whitman—both explained by Mencken—that Williams summons when he works to assert a nativist American tradition to counter Eliot's "conservative" influence.

Remarkably similar to the images of Whitman that other twentieth-century poets have devised as effigies as they try to come to terms with him, Williams' images of Whitman both encapsulate much of the positive Whitman heritage for the twentieth century and also trace, in microcosm, the stages through which other writers have passed as they resist or deflect Whitman's example. Following Mencken's account, Williams' final evaluation of Whitman concentrates first on his "message," by which politics and poetic form are abstractly related, and second on his slangy diction and "democratic" form. For the rest of Williams' career, then, Whitman's influence shows itself most strongly in Williams' two related images of Whitman: (1) in the image of a thematic "pioneer" into new territories—or as a giant who incarnates those territories—which his successors are to explore and to consolidate, and (2) in the image of Whitman as a local settler in a particular place, whose explorations have formal implications for later writers. This doubled commitment toward the "local" scene, Williams often claims, was Whitman's largest contribution to American poetics: (1) in theme and (2) in form or diction. Though qualified by a sense of failure and of incompletion, this doubled image of Whitman is helpful even because of that concomitant weakness, for Whitman's "failure" makes possible—even requires—Williams' own efforts in the same directions.

THREE

Two Whitmans

A Flawed Giant: The Anglo-American Response

LAWRENCE, CRANE, STEVENS, AND OTHERS: WHITMAN THE GIANT

As Williams pictures him, Whitman is always turning his back, either to repudiate the old or to greet the unknown. Eventually the two purposes coincide, but Whitman is important primarily for his negative energy; his assertion of the self is an "attack," in Williams' terms, on literary and social commonplaces.

Self-willed, it was all or nothing with him. It is an attack that had to take a chance of being violently mistaken, an attack directed at the first of all verse verities, measure itself, a revaluation of the underlying principles which carried it. That the whole of it might be outmoded occurred to no one else of his generation.[39]

Although his "rhetorical and long-winded age" eventually compromised his courage, Whitman's attack has the simple and direct force of a flagrant counterassertion. His first gesture of rebellion, the opening of "Song of Myself," already contains his greatest achievement. When Whitman

turned to the American idiom for release, he by the same gesture turned away from an established custom. He was turning toward the unknown future knowing that he did not know its profound implications.[40]

In a similar context, Joel Conarroe describes the modern inheritance from Whitman, the search for an innately American form, as an expansive "turning inward" by the poet. "The action of the poem," Conarroe concludes, "has moved from the external to the internal world, and its point of view becomes a central consciousness in dialogue with its universe"—a remarkably Emersonian inheritance.[41]

For Williams and for other modern writers, to accept this first Emersonian mode of Whitman's example requires the newer writer to come to terms with what Ezra Pound calls Whitman's "message." For writers like Pound, D.H. Lawrence, Hart Crane, and even Wallace Stevens, the most important feature of Whitman's work is the strength of that conceptual base underlying his distinctive diction and form. But if writers who value this first image of Whitman (as pioneer, as giant) respond in general to his "message," they differ among themselves about its content or significance. Agreeing that Whitman projects himself as a giant, they differ about the specific implications of such a projection.

We have seen, for instance, Pound's reactions to the democratic representativeness of Whitman's Composite Individual. Though Pound's estimation of that representative Self changes emphasis in time, that change results less from a direct revaluation of Whitman than from Pound's revised attitude toward the relation of the poet to his culture, an issue Pound consistently infers in Whitman's poems. D. H. Lawrence, by contrast, characterizes the Whitmanian message by emphasizing the ethic of sympathy in *Leaves of Grass*:

Sympathy. He does not say love. He says sympathy. Feeling with. Feel with them as they feel with themselves. Catching the vibration of their soul and flesh as we pass.
It is a new great doctrine. A doctrine of life. A new great morality. A morality of actual living, not of salvation.[42]

Though he eventually faults Whitman for confusing this sympathy with Christian charity, which abdicates the self through a moral "merging" in divine "grace," Lawrence is clearly responding to a spiritually pioneering, self-enlarging image of Whitman. Whitman's work heroically reflects the "sheer appreciation of the instant moment," the moment of the *"pulsating carnal self,* mysterious and palpable," Lawrence writes in 1918.[43] Later he puts *Leaves of Grass* on his list of "great books" and remembers that his first fascination with Whitman had coincided with his own Imagist phase (c. 1914-1918).[44] And still later a more ruminative Lawrence associates Whitman's theme with his form; at times, he claims, Whitman's rhythms are intuitively "perfect."[45]

Though under the Whitmanian spell he can occasionally ring preachy, at his best Lawrence can subsume his Whitmanian political energies into delicately lyrical observations. At its most potent, Whitman's influence helps to intensify that intuitive sympathy of the Lawrentian illumination, "the insurgent naked throb of the instant moment." For one example among many we might point to one of Lawrence's many encounters with flowers. "Almond Blossom," for instance, opens:

> Even iron can put forth,
> Even iron.
>
> This is the iron age,
> But let us take heart
> Seeing iron break and bud,
> Seeing rusty iron puff with clouds of blossom.

And the poem concludes:

> Knots of pink, fish-silvery
> In heaven, in blue, blue heaven,
> Soundless, bliss-full, wide-rayed, honey-bodied,
> Red at the core,
> Red at the core,
> Knotted in heaven upon the fine light.
>
> Open,
> Open,
> Five times wide open,
> Six times wide open,
> And given, and perfect;
> And red at the core with the last sore-heartedness,
> Sore-hearted-looking.[46]

For comparison, one might look at Williams' early poem "The Rose," (1923) first published within a year of both "Almond Blossom" and *The Waste Land.* Here is the whole poem:

THE ROSE

The rose is obsolete
but each petal ends in
an edge, the double facet
cementing the grooved
columns of air—The edge
cuts without cutting
meets—nothing—renews
itself in metal or porcelain—

whither? It ends—

But if it ends
the start is begun
so that to engage roses
becomes a geometry—

Sharper, neater, more cutting
figured in majolica—
the broken plate
glazed with a rose

Somewhere the sense
makes copper roses
steel roses—

The rose carried weight of love
but love is at an end—of roses
It is at the edge of the
petal that love waits

Crisp, worked to defeat
laboredness—fragile
plucked, moist, half-raised
cold, precise, touching

What

The place between the petal's
edge and the

From the petal's edge a line starts
that being of steel

infinitely fine, infinitely
rigid penetrates
the Milky Way
without contact—lifting
from it—neither hanging
nor pushing—

The fragility of the flower
unbruised
penetrates space.

(*CEP,* pp. 249–50)

Though both Lawrence and Williams demonstrate here their affinities with the tenets of Imagism, and though both ostensibly adopt the Futurists' aesthetic of the machine in order to rework those images of mechanism into metaphors of a projective vitality, the differences between the two poems are as evident as the similarities. The two poets handle the relations of flower to machine in different ways, for instance: Lawrence makes the almond branch an "iron" structure from which an unexpected, poignant vitality springs, while Williams takes his rose as the first donée and projects from its edges an image of abstract "geometry." Apparently for Lawrence the Whitmanian "sympathy" informing such lyric moments brings his attention to the static qualities of the observed "thing," person, or flower. In *Studies in Classic American Literature* Lawrence had criticized Whitman for believing his sympathy could let him participate identically in the inner lives of the things or people he encounters; the diction of his Whitmanian poem reenacts his insistence on the ontic otherness of others. Lawrence's poem depends on adjectives ("Soundless, bliss-full, wide-rayed, honey-bodied"), as if the observing self batters at the thing with descriptions of projected emotions. The tacit sadness of the Lawrence poem lodges in these adjectives, because a rhetoric of description presumes some distance from the "thing" described. The observer deliberately uses the blossoms as a metaphor for something else (an organic assertion in an "iron age"): Lawrence's flowers are an unreachable otherness that one can acknowledge and manipulate but cannot comprehend except indirectly, through an adjectival insistence. By contrast, the Williams poem hinges on its verbs—like Heidigger, Williams seems to believe that Being (das Sein) is a verb—as if the message of Whitmanian "sympathy" requires a more organic participation in the internal energies of the "thing." The result, paradoxically, is an ability to see beyond the "thing," to its generative shape. Williams' rose "renews itself in metal or porcelain," as if the "thing" requires observation—imaginative human work—to complete itself in the world. Paradoxically, the flower's strength is its fragility, which makes the flower's presence in the world of fact as exact as that of a steel fiber:

> From the petal's edge a line starts
> that being of steel
> infinitely fine, infinitely
> rigid penetrates
> the Milky Way
> without contact—lifting
> from it—neither hanging
> nor pushing—
>
> The fragility of the flower
> unbruised
> penetrates space.

The transitory presence of the flower, its "fragility," makes it as essentially a part of the world of forms as any construction made of steel or of porcelain, for the moment it exists. This insistence on the "geometrical" and essentialist importance of the flower in the moment it is perceived is the important difference between the Lawrence and the Williams poems. The Imagist form of each poem makes the reader attend to the image "in an instant of time," but it seems to me that in content the Williams poem more clearly realizes that formal commitment to the momentary, the fragile, and the vital. Lawrence uses the Imagist form, but his metaphors describe a process that continues; Lawrence is interested in the continually regenerating Life-Force, and he uses The Moment to illustrate his transitory insight about that continual process. Williams, by contrast, considers The Moment complete in itself; his metaphors of the vertical geometry of the flower's importance emphasize both the expanded significance of the flower and its fragility, its momentary being. Williams' poem, that is, makes the Imagist form and the argument about vitality work together more clearly.

Without pressing the point too strongly, I think it's possible, further, to see in both poems evidence of an Emersonian or Whitmanian belief in the power of physical things to symbolize spiritual truths. "Nature is the symbol of spirit," Emerson declared — though the Emersonian aesthetic presumes that things must be respected in their autonomy before their spiritually symbolic power can be apprehended. (This commitment to the mysterious symbol-generating self-completeness of things distinguishes Emerson's argument about Nature from, say, Edward Taylor's belief that the world is a system of signs, an allegory, about the spiritual world.) The connection with Whitman is clear; section 6 of "Song of Myself" is a good example of Whitman's articulation of the Emersonian ideal. There Whitman first encounters the grass, which becomes his theme:

A child said *What is the grass?* fetching it to me with both hands;
How could I answer the child? I do not know what it is any more than
    he.
I guess . . .

Faced with the mysterious otherness of this crude vitality, Whitman responds with symbol-generating sympathy. He first sees the grass as a sign of himself and than enlarges his participation: "I guess it must be the flag of my disposition, out of hopeful green stuff woven." The natural world can be a symbol of the spirit, but all such allegories return to the Walt-self. Having admitted that the natural thing may be an analogy for a spiritual event, realized through the metaphor-making power of the imagination, Whitman then continues the section by offering a long list of possible analogies for the reality of the grass:

Or I guess it is the handkerchief of the Lord,
A scented gift and remembrancer designedly dropt,
Bearing the owner's name someway in the corners, that we may see and
    remark, and say *Whose?*

Section 6 of "Song of Myself" thus suggests that the grass is finally unknowable *except* as sign or metaphor. When in their poems about flowers Lawrence and Williams ask similar questions about the metaphoric possibilities of "things," each reworks Whitman's gesture—by which "sympathy" generates symbols—but for slightly different purposes. Lawrence adapts Whitman's sympathy in a rhetoric of adjectival paraphrase, but Williams operates at a further level of self-consciousness: he writes a poem *about* this process of extension or projection in sympathy, "so that to engage roses/ becomes a geometry." Both Lawrence and Williams model their approaches to the flowering "thing" on Whitman's symbol-generating sympathy with the grass, but they work that sympathy toward characteristically different conclusions. Both find the Whitmanian sympathy ultimately oversimplified, and both characteristically try to restructure the "flower" into an external form, to make that otherness of the flower's vitality accessible to human response outside the observant self. But Lawrence's adjectives anthropomorphize the flower, making it knowable because it resembles a human being ("sore-hearted-looking"). Typically, Williams makes his flower even more objective, less "sympathetic"; paradoxically, his rose is more knowable as form because its representation is so external, not an anthropomorphic projection but an objective, "geometrical," knowable form.

The pattern in this first category of Whitman's influence is interestingly complex. Both in Pound's satiric ambivalence about Whitman's representativeness and in Lawrence's ultimate disappointment in Whitman for betraying his "heroic message" by an excessive "sympathy," the younger writer treats Whitman as a figure, a personality. Both modernists learn their formal lessons from that figure, more than from Whitman's poems. This first influence of Whitman, that is, leads away from texts, to the "message" or the character behind the poem, as the modern writer copes both with his own attraction toward the Whitmanian message and with his disappointment with Whitman's formal execution. Those poets who respond to this "giant" Whitman often write poems that invoke Whitman in person, either to exorcise his energy or to ap-

propriate it; such poems often use a long enumerative Whitmanian line, as if to evoke Whitman's style and to counter him on his
own formal terms.

Hart Crane's Whitman, for instance, is a personalized image of
American exuberance, wisdom, and pioneering openness to experience. In the "Cape Hatteras" section of his lyric-epic *The Bridge,*
Crane summons Whitman as a personification of place, a Meister-
singer who "set breath in steel," so that Whitman's poems become
a metaphor for the linking power of the Brooklyn Bridge itself.[47]
As he worked on his "epic of modern consciousness," Crane found
the encounter with Whitman ("the Spiritual Body of America")
almost inevitable. He writes in a letter from his home in Patterson,
New York:

The more I think about my *Bridge* poem the more thrilling its symbolic
possibilities become, and. . . . I begin to feel myself more directly con-
nected with Whitman. I feel myself in currents that are positively awesome in their extent and possibilities.[48]

As in the cases of Pound and Lawrence, Crane's uses of Whitman's
"symbolical possibilities" require a "giant" Whitman-figure to embody these attitudes. Thus the Whitman of Crane's "Cape Hatteras" section joins images of geological evolution (the glacial lifting of the Allegheny mountains) with images of the invention of
the airplane (toward "Easters of speeding light," an aerial open
road), until Whitman personifies an ideal vision of America's technological and spiritual possibilities:

> Our Meistersinger, thou set breath in steel;
> And it was thou who on the boldest heel
> Stood up and flung the span on even wing
> Of that great Bridge, our Myth, whereof I sing!
>
> Years of the Modern! Propulsions toward what capes?[49]

Pound had qualified his admiration for Whitman by alluding to
his "crudity," and Lawrence had been dismayed by Whitman's
deathly, self-obliterating mergings. Similarly, Crane qualifies his
ideal vision of Whitman: he makes the arc of Whitman's bridging-
vision the upper half of a circle that the countervailing vision of

Edgar Allan Poe completes. Significantly, Poe's contribution is another half-circle, the underslung arc of a subway in the "Tunnel" section of *The Bridge*. In this descent to an urban Hades under the surface of New York City, Crane makes Poe's under-arc the infernal completion of the circle Whitman's bridging idealism had begun, as if Poe's descent to realist nightmare is the necessary complement for a full vision of American experience. The completion of that circle thus generates the triumphant circling vision of "Atlantis," at the end of *The Bridge*. For Crane, then, Walt Whitman becomes a giant metaphor of positive "symbolic possibilities" in America, though that optimism is not the complete truth. On the whole, within this qualified admiration Crane finds more in Whitman's form to admire—and to appropriate—than do other Moderns who take to his "giant" message.

A strain of submerged Emersonianism runs through the work of Wallace Stevens, as well. Diane Middlebrook has sensitively charted the continuities between Whitman and the Emersonian Stevens, stressing their similarities more than an overt "influence." The concerns both those writers share, Middlebrook argues, are questions of aesthetic identity, involving the creation of a "Real Me."[50] Middlebrook emphasizes Stevens' image of the "giant," whose inclusive size involves metaphors of "nature in the form of a man," another of Stevens' central figures. Tracing these Whitmanian metaphors through Stevens' work, Middlebrook illuminates both Whitman's etiological work toward the "Supreme Fiction" of an ideal Self and also Stevens' reconsideration of those issues Whitman had raised; interestingly, Middlebrook attends specifically to the discontinuities between Whitman's ideal vision and Stevens' meditative argument with that Self.[51]

Like Pound, Stevens recognizes the associations among place, Self, and enumerative style in Whitman's work; if there is a formative lesson to be learned from Whitman, Stevens suggests, it would be implicit in that first Whitmanian equation. And like Pound, further, Stevens works beyond this first admiration to a stylistic qualification of Whitman's worth. Because Whitman so completely identified himself with the things he enumerates, Stevens suggests, Whitman's self is time-bound, defined by transitory events. Thus (as Stevens writes in a letter of 1955): "Whitman is disintegrating as the world of which he made himself a part, disintegrates."[52] What the Whitmanian giant lacks is a power of imagination to help him invent himself past historical contingencies. Implicit in Whitman's rhetoric, Stevens argues, is a belief in a collective identity, a fiction of a "Me" who can engage with others. And yet Stevens worries that the very size of that Self may in fact preclude an authentic private and visionary imaginative experience.

In his early poem "Metaphors of a Magnifico," for instance, Stevens poses the question of a collective identity.[53] Are the soldiers One or Many?—that is the "old song."

> Twenty men crossing a bridge,
> Into a village,
> Are twenty men crossing twenty bridges,
> Into twenty villages,
> Or one man
> Crossing a single bridge into a village.
>
> This is old song
> That will not declare itself. . . .

The "old song" is the philosophical question that modern philosophy inherits from the eighteenth century: do different perceivers see different realities? Do our senses deceive us about the nature of the world? Do they at least deceive all of us similarly? Stevens rephrases the philosophical question as a metaphor of perception (do twenty pairs of eyes perceive twenty realities?) but in such a way as to enlarge the question one step further: would a similarity of perceptions represent a kind of Whitmanian unity, a consolidation of the twenty individuals into one? It is difficult to talk about these questions of perception, reality, and the articulation of reality in senses and words, because we have to discuss the questions within the limitations of our senses and of our words. Thus the "old song" will not "declare itself" easily. But having thus defined the philosophical question, Stevens in the second movement of "Metaphors of a Magnifico" returns to the actual physical scene—the bridge, the village, the men—and restates it, as if equation of perception with the verbal "facts" might prove helpful. But that willed factuality seems to deny the tendency of any image to expand toward meaning on its own terms.

> Twenty men crossing a bridge,
> Into a village,
> Are
> Twenty men crossing a bridge
> Into a village.
>
> That will not declare itself
> Yet is certain as meaning. . . .

At this point, Stevens stops trying to force the visual image to "declare itself"; he submits to the integrity of the image itself, as if in memory, to make the image mysteriously manifest its own significance, if perceived as a different kind of "fact." The poem ends with a detailed consideration of the specificities of the image. Stevens yields, that is, to the concrete/perceptual image, believing in it as completely as he can.

> The boots of the men clump
> On the boards of the bridge.
> The first white wall of the village
> Rises through fruit-trees.
>
> Of what was I thinking?
>
> So the meaning escapes.
> The first white walls of the village . . .
> The fruit-trees . . .

To let the meaning "escape" without pressuring the image to yield its significance is to allow the symbol its integrity—and thus its significance might emerge as symbolic import, verbally as "real" as factual experience. It still is not possible to believe completely in the reality of the world—nor even in our perceptions of the world, nor in memory: once he has submitted to the primacy of the physical image, Stevens admits the world has gotten the better of him; "the meaning escapes." The physicality of physical existence defeats Stevens in this poem; he is left pondering the remembered details of the image, as if in memory. To regard the world without metaphors is finally not to be able to understand even physical phenomena: the physical world needs metaphorical understanding as much as the mind does. The "motive" for metaphor is the desire to clarify both mind and world simultaneously.

The poem that began as a study of perception and identity concludes as a study of the nature of metaphor—because personal and collective identities are themselves metaphors of personal coherence. This association of the issues of identity with the nature of metaphor is, I suspect, the largest single lesson Stevens learns from Whitman. For Stevens, Whitman is important because he realized the self is a metaphor; insofar as his Self resembles other selves, that poetic Self is a "giant."

Twenty men crossing twenty bridges? Or one man crossing one common bridge? Because metaphor is an act of the verbalizing mind, only the verbal ordering of the presentation determines whether experience seems collective or singular. With this Whitmanian argument of Stevens' "Metaphors of a Magnifico" in mind, watch how William Carlos Williams poses a similar problem in "To a Poor Old Woman," a poem from 1935. Here is the whole poem; watch how Williams' title serves as dedication *and* as first line, as if to project us immediately into the "factual" scene of the active poem without distancing the image from the "facts":

> To a Poor Old Woman
> munching a plum on
> the street a paper bag
> of them in her hand
>
> They taste good to her
> They taste good
> to her. They taste
> good to her
>
> You can see it by
> the way she gives herself
> to the one half
> sucked out in her hand
>
> Comforted
> a solace of ripe plums

seeming to fill the air
They taste good to her
                (*CEP,* p. 99)

In Williams' version, the ambiguous nuance of the image resides exclusively in the verbal order of the description. Restating the same observation in three different ways in the second stanza, Williams playfully demonstrates that the emphasis on different units of the sentence changes the denotative sense of the sentence. (Words at the start of a line tend to receive slightly more stress or emphasis than others. Thus "They taste good to her" defines the experience; "they taste good/ to her" emphasizes her, separating her slightly from her experience; "they taste/ good to her" emphasizes the interpreted nature of the experience.) What, then, is the truth of the experience?—or, more precisely, what is the "truth" of the full sentence "They taste good to her"? Twenty men or one man? Stevens had at first tried to withdraw into the sensuality of the image ("the first white wall of the village"), as if to make the image of the world more important than the world, like Whitman describing his largest Self. But Williams at this point returns to the factual scene, to test his various hypothetical verbal orderings more directly against the "facts."

You can see it by
the way she gives herself
to the one half
sucked out in her hand

                .   .   .

They taste good to her

Apparently the "meaning" of the full sentence resides in all the collected possibilities—that is, in all the nuances latent in the full declaration. "You can see it": the poem concludes that language—though distanced from experience because language is innately metaphorical—can be tested in a naive-realistic empirical way. Or more exactly: Williams makes us see the sentence as a verbal "thing." What for Stevens becomes a "Supreme Fiction" becomes for William a self-reflexive "new world" in the poem, a verbal world that more clearly resembles the physical world than Stevens' "fiction" does. The truth of the signifier is in the signified: she sucks half a plum. Williams seems to acknowledge that in the dynamic between language (the shifting image) and experience (the full sentence), he returns for validation to the primary half, to the plum and to the full statement, the articulation of sensual experience. But she sucks only half a plum: perhaps the experience itself, without articulation, is incomplete. When at the end of the poem Williams repeats the integral sentence, "They taste good to her," he reaffirms the power of language to re-create and to complete the experience it describes. By the end of the poem, what had seemed a descriptive declaration has come to seem nuanced and full of possibilities. Language is adequate not because of its denotative or descriptive power but because of its structural possibilities. The final statement comes as a formal rhythmic relief, affirming both the old woman's experience and the power of language to reshape experience.

In "Metaphors of a Magnifico" Stevens had reached his affirmation through a complete (if transitory) submission to an image offered self-consciously *as* an image, as if the palpable and the abstract finally were to be conjoined in the mind's image; in "To a Poor Old Woman" Williams works not by meditating on metaphors about metaphors but by taking primary experience as his first-level "old song/ That will not declare itself" and by working exclusively verbal changes on that experience, until experience and articulation are indistinguishable in the single full sentence. The first time he says "They taste good to her" we understand the sentence as a description; the second time he says the full sentence, at the end of the poem, we hear the larger range of its verbal possibilities. I do not mean that Stevens' argument is more "metaphorical," but that Williams' sense of the metaphorical base of all language makes it possible for him to treat the entire figure as a single integral verbal metaphor. Stevens ends his poem by tacitly asserting the need for metaphor, where the mystery lodges for him, but Williams ends his poem by asserting even more directly the formal complementarity between physical experience (the organic mystery, the half-plum) and verbal experience. Stevens' poem is about abstract metaphor (metaphor-in-the-mind), while Williams' is about metaphor-as-a-process-of-perception. Language does offer a way to share the old woman's experience by remaking it in words, as in a Cubist exercise (Duchamp's "Nude") that structurally dismantles and then reassembles the perception. As in the Lawrence poem, both the Stevens and the Williams poems derive their central problem from Whitman's obsession with the relation between the thing (self) and the idea (America, the large Self). If Whitman's direct equation of the tenor of that metaphor with its vehicle seems ultimately oversimplified to Stevens, nevertheless Whitman did set the question in a way that makes the problem accessible to the modern writer.[54]

Thus for Stevens—as for Pound, Lawrence, Crane, and others—Whitman comes to seem a "giant," both in his comprehensive self-representations and in his large influential example; their common argument with him combines a difficult respect with a necessary qualification about the effects of his gigantism on his style and on the world he generalizes. Further, this tendency to read Whitman as a "figure" whose importance lies in his generous "message" continues through much postmodern and contemporary American poetry. Allen Ginsberg, for instance, meets Whitman at the end of the Open Road, which proves to be a supermarket in California:

We strode down the open corridors together in our solitary fancy tasting artichokes, possessing every frozen delicacy, and never passing the cashier.
Where are we going, Walt Whitman? The doors close in an hour. Which way does your beard point tonight?

And Louis Simpson similarly finds Whitman in the contemporary West (in poems like "In California," "Walt Whitman at Bear Mountain," and "Pacific Ideas"), though Simpson's Whitman is less a Ciceronean guide to the possibilities of the New World than a spokesman of disappointed hope. "Those 'immensely overpaid accounts,'/ Walt, it seems that we must pay them again,"[55] Simpson concludes, speaking for himself, for his contemporary poets, and for modern America.

WILLIAMS AND THE ADOLESCENT GIANT

William Carlos Williams repeats this ambivalence toward Whitman, but Williams works to solve the conundrum by making the "giant" Whitman represent a primary Emersonian stage of necessary reorientation. Williams reads Whitman's first gesture, his representative self-enlargement and his breaking up of iambic form, as a gesture of destructiveness that makes possible the modern writers' subsequent work of "construction."

Williams sketches this volcanic-giant image of Whitman as early as 1917, in his essay "America, Whitman, and the Art of Poetry." "Whitman created the art in America," Williams begins simply. Having established that "rock," Williams associates the social power of *Leaves of Grass* with the revolutionary power of any artwork that is both vulgar—of the vulgate—and paradoxically lasting. Like Pound in *The Spirit of Romance,* Williams likens Whitman to Dante, whose radical construction of an idiom for poetry, repudiating old orders by projecting a "new world" through the finite self, virtually created the modern Italian language.

> There is no art of poetry save by grace of other poetry. So Dante to me can only be another way of saying Whitman. Yet without a Whitman there can of course be for me no Dante. Further than that: there is no way for me to talk of Whitman but in terms of my own generation—if haply such a thing may be.[56]

Pound would make the difference between Whitman and Dante reflect a qualitative difference between their respective cultures (though neither culture sustained its poet). But Williams is more relative, less judgmental, in his comparison of the two older poets. In his appropriation of Dante, as in his use of Whitman, there is something defensive in Williams' argument, a self-ratifying tone that seems an effort to match a "relative" Dante against competing modernist images of Dante—like Eliot's metaphysical visionary or Pound's embittered political exile. For Williams, Dante is the cultural coefficient of America's Whitman: each wrote the vulgate of his culture, discovering the terms appropriate to his surroundings and setting out (through the "dark wood," on the open road), into unknown imaginative territories; each was mystically investigating his own largest Self. And the epic of each poet paradoxically becomes both specific in its referents and visionary in its metaphysics.

The analogy to Dante is helpful because it points to what might appear to be a contradiction in Williams' argument. If Whitman is a giant who repudiates inherited, imposed structures, how can his achievement be weighed against Dante's? How and why should the modern poet use the past—including literary precedents—iconoclastically? The answer is not the Eliotic solution of revisionism, ironically constructing the new from shards of the old. Rather, the answer for Williams lies in his sense of what Whitman discovers when he turns "inland," to his huge diverse self. Beneath the outmoded forms that had conspired to stifle Whitman and Dante, Williams maintains, lay an essential form of appropriateness, a proper formal structure for the particular cultural situation, which each revolutionary poet discovers by an incarnating, pioneering turn. At the end of the journey to specificity, the new writer may arrive at a consubstantial reality that Whitman's poems of nineteenth-century America share with the epics of the ancient Greeks, with Dante's poems of medieval Italy, and with Shakespeare's Renaissance poems.

Back of those aristocratic forms lies the democratic groundwork of all forms, basic elements that can be comprehended and used with new force . . . It is there we must seek.[57]

In Williams' estimation, great poems are contemporaneous because of their specificity. Like his attitude toward the particular (verbal) "place" of the poem, Williams' attitude toward Whitman's gigantism presumes that the latent truth of Whitman's world is not the truth of the modern circumstances. What the modern writer can emulate, however, is Whitman's orientation toward the new world thus encountered: the poet identifies himself with his world, gigantically, then explores "himself." Williams generalizes the pioneer spirit of Whitman ("the characteristic American *position* of the intelligence," the "pioneer turn of mind"), as he pictures other American writers and leaders making the same Whitmanian turn.[58]

From the first Vikings in America, through Christopher Colum-

bus, Père Sébastien Rasles, and other early American visitors por-
trayed in *In the American Grain,* and even through George Washington (the hero of an opera libretto on which Williams worked),
the consistently heroic gesture is this "turning inward," to suspend
one's presumptions, so to let the American locality speak through
the mediating self. In *In the American Grain* Daniel Boone's orientation toward the West makes the characteristic gesture seem
almost mystic. Boone, the "great voluptuary," recognizes the need
for a "new marriage" of the individual and the new world, and his
response, a "life's affirmation" of an organic relation with the land,
makes him a model for all Americans (including Whitman) metaphorically to follow. Whitman looks inward and sees the world;
Daniel Boone descends "to the ground of his desire" and discovers
himself. But the gesture is the same:

Not that he settled Kentucky or made a path to the west, not that he
defended, suffered, hated, and fled, but because of a descent to the ground
of his desire was Boone's life important and does it remain still loaded
with power,—power to strengthen every form of energy that would be
voluptuous, passionate, possessive in that place which he opened.[59]

At times this notion sounds strangely passive,[60] but elsewhere the
movement sounds courageous, even aggressive. Williams makes
Boone's attitude an ideal imaginative encounter with the American
"facts," despite the timidity and repressiveness of his culture. That
attitude is the same imaginative turn toward frontiers that Frederick Jackson Turner calls a psychological and historical characteristic of the North American mind.[61] *In the American Grain* presents this American voluptuousness primarily through Daniel
Boone, but in his ambitious psychohistory of America Williams
does admire the same attitude in other heroic figures. His praise
for Edgar Allan Poe, for instance, makes that writer sound noble
in his individualism, according to the same criteria by which Boone
and Whitman seem heroic: "His greatness is that he turned his
back and faced inland, to originality, with the identical gesture of
a Boone."[62] Though the subject matter of Poe's poems is too
mystically arcane for Williams' taste, the quality of the writing—
the sense of words, of autonymous symbols, of music, of inven-

tion—is admirable, signifying a courageous break with tradition. In *Spring and All,* several years earlier, Williams had explained Poe's turn "inland, to originality," as the result of a "great separation" between the man and his culture:

Poe could not have written a word without the violence of expulsive emotion combined with the in-driving force of a crudely repressive environment. Between the two his imagination was forced into being to keep him to that reality, completeness, sense of escape which is felt in his work—the topics. Typically American—accurately, even inevitably set in his time.[63]

Poe's active hostility toward his world results in a productive imaginative strife between his sense of self and his cultural environment. From this friction, according to Williams, the imagination shoots its sparks: that jump, significantly, becomes a "flare" of "destruction" that must precede the stage of artistic "invention." "Artists," he writes elsewhere, are "vagrants," "brigands" who live "openly," threatening the "walled cities" of science, philosophy, and cultural repression.[64] The American poetic "tradition," appropriately, is a paradoxical tradition of rebelliousness against tradition. The American characteristic is: always to be "at the advancing edge of the art," Williams concludes in 1933.[65]

Like Poe, Whitman the giant is implicitly an agent of destruction, for his characteristic turning-inward or -inland is a turning-from. Just as uranium gives off radical energy as it destroys its unstable form and so makes a new element (as Madame Curie discovers in *Paterson* IV), so Whitman's pioneering is an internal metamorphosis that can generate a "new element" and a reckless energy. In Williams' first image of him, Whitman represents a permanent state of restlessness, a continuous rebellion that must eventually turn even against Whitman himself. From this first mode of Whitman's influence, Williams learns the importance of considering the poem as an inward-tending process[66] that, like the complementary "tradition" of American rebelliousness and reconstitution, falls into two stages. The two-stage paradigm applies both to individual poems and to larger historical movements; in the cultural mode, Whitman is Williams' model of the first ("destruc-

tive") stage. Williams delighted in paralleling two "revolutionary"
aphorisms, one by Thomas Jefferson ("liberalism is not assured
without a revolution every twenty years") and the other by Henrik
Ibsen ("a truth becomes a lie in twenty years"). The problem is
that "men grow away from the quality of language which assured
them stability and which so goes dead."[67] And the solution, appropriately, is a modern attention to language, a new and violent
sense of language-as-attack, to clear the field of the rubble of prior
forms in order to make room for "new constructions."

In his first (giant) mode, then, Whitman is most influential as a
negative influence, a "broom stroke."[68] In this phase Whitman is
a model of destruction for the writer who faces, in the early twentieth century, pressures as potentially stagnating and compromising as those Whitman had faced in the preceding century. Sometimes Williams sees Whitman's destructiveness as a conclusive
dismissal of historical traditions, while at other times Whitman's
destructive energy is simply a gigantic analogue for the work of
others who must "destroy" contemporary forms of traditionalism.
For past forms, carrying evidence of the cultural conditions of their
origins, are no longer applicable for the modern world, with its
new configurations of power, its sciences, its economics. In an interview in 1950 Williams links these metaphors into a single observation about Whitman, tracing his own interest in Whitman back
to 1903—during his medical school days at Penn—and associating Whitman directly with the "pioneer" spirit of Boone and others:

I don't know why I had that instinctive drive to get in touch with Whitman, but he was a passionate man, and the first great poem, "Song of
Myself," was more or less an adolescent poem I think because it was
throwing away any hold the classics had on him. He didn't know where
to go, perhaps, but he didn't know anything about the English language
as taught in England, and he wanted to be himself, and he couldn't contain himself any longer. So he just left off, and he was driven to find a
way for himself, like the American pioneers, we'll say. He had to go. He
didn't know where to go, and he wrote the way he felt.[69]

Like Whitman's assertiveness, the vehemence of Whitman's own
destructive and idealistic energies arises from a rhetoric of aesthetic
self-defence and self-determination.

We must be destructive first to free ourselves from the forms accreting to themselves tyrannies we despise. Where does the past lodge but in older forms? Tear it out. I am not speaking of anything but forms. . . .[70]

Though the rhetoric is violent, the purpose is ultimately constructive. Because it acknowledges the "old dignity" of the past, this "destructive" spirit Williams sees in Whitman finally should let the new writers approach more directly the essential purity and novelty of older forms. Just as we learn from Cézanne how, not what, to see, so in older poems the lesson is not what to write, but how to encounter a world with fresh eyes. This attitude, Williams is quick to explain, is not the dangerously barbaric yawp to which its critics object but derives, rather, from a sense of cultural tradition and of moral preservation more fundamental—because it symbolically repeats the evolution of tribal languages—than conventional historical approaches to the evolution of cultural forms. "Language is the key to the mind's escape from bondage to the past. It is by the breakup of language that the truth can be seen to exist and that it becomes operative again."[71] In a letter about paternity and sonship, Williams writes to his son about his own concern to be part of a poetic "inheritance" or tradition:

I have wanted to link myself up with a traditional art, to feel that I was developing individually, it might be, but along with that, developing still in the true evolving tradition of the art.[72]

As Pound, Lawrence, and others respond to this gigantic Whitmanian "figure," their responses record a pattern of difficult influence, an uneasiness about the rift between the Whitman-figure they envision and the final worth of his achievement. Williams shares this uneasiness about Whitman's "giant" historical shape, but he offers a liberating solution to this difficulty by making Whitman's "gigantic" achievement the "destruction" that anticipates the modern writer's task of "construction." And yet Whitman's exemplary success also makes him another kind of "giant"—a titanic or parental force for later poets, like Williams, to encounter. The catch is that Whitman's example dictates the negative terms on which the new poets will counter him; the "tradition" of rebelliousness anticipates objections. The modernists' chief lesson from Whitman, in this first mode of influence, is therefore paradoxical: "The only way to be like Whitman is to write *unlike* Whitman," Williams concludes.[73] ("He most honors my style who learns under it to destroy the teacher," Whitman had insisted.) That tradition of rebelliousness, adolescent as it may occasionally sound, is the forwarding inheritance Whitman leaves to his followers "ages and ages hence." The journey on the open road that Whitman proposes at his most expansive is the same route as the journey inward: toward an incarnation of the specific place, toward a revelation of a large metaphoric Self, and toward a restructuring of the language of the tribe. This Whitmanian tradition thus defines the motion of the poem as a search for an appropriate form: the new poem will invent both a new giant Self and a place for that Self to inhabit.

If there is no room for us on the outside we shall, in spite of ourselves, have to go *in:* into the cell, the atom, the poetic line, for our discoveries. We have to break the old apart to make room for ourselves, whatever may be our tragedy and however we may fear it. By making room within the line itself for his inventions, Whitman revealed himself to be a worthy and courageous man of his age and, to boot, a farseeing one.[74]

A Simple Separate Person: The International Modernist Whitman

CITIZEN OF A STYLE: WHITMAN IN OTHER LANGUAGES

Whitman is first a thematic giant, but his second significant contribution to modern letters, according to Williams and others, is his ability to stay at home—or at least to make himself at home wherever he might wander. The poet of the particular, the local, and the slangy, Whitman pays attention to the specificities of his place, and that fidelity translates, in many later writers' work, into an unapologetic attention to the specific local details of other places. Whitman spells out his nationalistic message with a synthetic vocabulary incorporating slang, naturalized foreign languages, neologisms generated by new things in the New World; Williams and others adapt that Whitmanian attitude toward style into what Williams calls a "relative" attitude toward diction. In this second mode of influence, that is, Whitman teaches not so much a generalizing message as an individuating style, a personal attentiveness to local details that generates an appropriately "native" diction, which a "simple separate person" might speak.

The process is more complex than it sounds at first. Just as Whitman's diction is not simply mimetic, Williams' insistence on local specificity of diction acknowledges the debased and rigid forms of standardized discourse, but Williams nevertheless insists that the native idiom is the proper first material for a cultural "reconstruction on the syllables." The ambition is not mimetic but proleptic, an effort to say clearly in order to see clearly. (Pound calls this accuracy *virtù*.) Williams shares Pound's moral sense and Eliot's historical purpose to "purify" the language of the tribe, but in this mode Whitman's example returns the poet's attention to a local place and to the issues of "construction" within the native idiom. Thus the pioneer who turns his back becomes the settler who cultivates the new ground; the "open road" becomes the "field" of the contemporary poem. As in "Song of Myself," the democratic giant is also a simple separate person in one place and time. This Whitmanian specificity of observation and of diction requires a different sense of the participating speaking self. The two selves complement each other, of course: the giant needs the separate self to provide information ("things"), while the distinct observing citizen needs the ordering power of the giant (the "idea"). Ultimately each mode of Whitman's influence involves a set of presumptions about the relation between the self and the culture. Taken together, the two modes define a cultural and verbal ideal.

We can recognize this doubleness easily enough in Whitman, who clearly projects his giant Self from his individuated, private self. The local, lonely, carefully lyrical individual who emerges in later Whitman poems (as in the Civil War poems and in the "Calamus" series) occasionally glimmers even in "Song of Myself," when Whitman acknowledges he is consciously offering an image of the Perfect Composite Individual. The Whitman who claims "the scent of these armpits, aroma finer than prayer" both means what he

says and also admits his own magnificent, intimate silliness. Leslie
Fiedler associates this "private" tone in Whitman with a sense of
humor, because he offers these grand egotistic claims anony-
mously: in the first editions of *Leaves of Grass* Whitman did not
even identify himself until halfway through the first poem (later
called "Song of Myself").[75] "Both in and out of the game and
watching and wondering at it," Whitman assumes both perspectives, that of the democratic giant and that of the separate citizen,
within the same poem. His dual tone is a formal vehicle for his
political and philosophical ambition: to reconcile the One and the
Many in a dynamic synthesis appropriate for the American nation
on the brink of civil war.

It is difficult—perhaps ultimately arbitrary—to distinguish
Whitman's role as giant from his role as private citizen. In general,
the distinction separates the idea of poetic form conceived as gross
structure or theme or gesture from the idea of poetic form as diction, syntax, and rhythm. Whitman's influence as a giant is easier
to identify: "he established the art" in America through his magnanimous formal gestures and through his first metaphorical association of giant Self and private historical self. But to try to
locate Whitman more specifically, Williams has first to portray
Whitman's model as prophetic and then to propose the specific
modern continuation of that model (paradoxically both in and out
of the tradition). Just as Whitman's "private" tone is often subordinated in "Song of Myself," so this second mode of influence—
his effect on style, or on an attitude toward style—is harder to
articulate. In a sense Williams "completes" Whitman more obviously in this second mode, where Whitman is less strongly dominant. But because gesture and style are intimately related in Whitman, I think it would be arbitrary to distinguish too finely here.
Whitman's gift was his ability to unite gesture and style (that is,
his identification of his giant Self with his personal self). To work
toward a clearer conception of that private and stylistically influential self, therefore, it might be helpful to look at the pattern of
responses to Whitman among a few poets—all writing in foreign
languages—who have been influenced by that equation of politics
and style (One and Many) in Whitman's work—to see how those

writers have associated the structural-and-political influence from the "locally" stylistic influence.

This pattern differs slightly from the pattern of responses to Whitman among the Anglo-American modernists. Writers in non-English-based languages and in other cultures have had to address more directly the question of Whitman's effect on the diction, syntax, and vocabulary of poems; the application of such stylistic concerns is the second mode of Whitman's influence. Pound the North American can address Whitman as a North American forerunner writing in the same idiom and facing similar cultural difficulties. The problem is somewhat different, say, for a Spanish poet—or for a poet in Hispanic South America. In fact, Whitman's work toward a nationally appropriate poetry parallels the development of a national literary consciousness in several emerging countries in the nineteenth and twentieth centuries. For some writers in those countries Whitman's influence has been more strictly stylistic, fixing on Whitman's creation of an indigenous diction; others adapt Whitman's style in order to emulate his attempt to create a new national myth to represent an emergent nation for world citizenship. Like Fenimore Cooper in the Leatherstocking novels, Whitman worked deliberately to invent a new mythic history for North America, personifying the myth in a single character (Cooper's Natty Bumppo, Whitman's "Myself"). In the nineteenth century several European countries passed through this stage of national artistic self-consciousness (with Grieg's Peer Gynt in Norway, Walter Scott's legendary Britons, Dostoyevsky's "soil-bound" Slavic heroes, Wagner's Teutonic titans. Even the young Yeats admired Whitman's theatrical sense of his representative "second self.") In the twentieth century, third-world countries have undergone similar processes of national artistic individuation, and for writers in those countries the analogy with Whitman has proved strongly helpful. Whitman's work is also attractive to writers in a subculture within a dominant culture: for black writers like Imamu Baraka in North America, Whitman's rhythms and slang have been liberating formal models, sometimes with radical political implications.

Thus the phase of colonial-linguistic rebelliousness that Whit-

man represents for the nineteenth-century United States makes him
a formative analogue for other writers working through the transition from colonialism to emergent nationalism in other literatures. In *The Wretched of the Earth* Franz Fanon plots a general
process by which writers in a colonized culture can use its arts to
shape its emergent nationhood by redefining attitudes toward native tradition. The process involves a deepening enthusiasm for the
textures of local language and experience: its first stage actively
distinguishes local experience from the manners and language of
the dominant "imperialist" culture, and its second stage distinguishes between authentically formative folk art and a narrowly
sentimental interest in the historical forms of native custom. Not
a direct assault on "imperialist" values, this nativist countertradition evolves first through an abstractly collective political commitment and then through a more personal commitment to the vitality of local experience (conceding "your flesh and blood" to it and
"your own self to others," Fanon insists). Fanon quotes René
Char's restatement of the process as a fusion of subjectivity and
objectivity in the native work: "the poem emerges out of a subjective imposition and an objective choice. A poem is the assem-
bling and moving together of the determining original values, in
contemporary relations with someone that these circumstances
bring to the front."[76] Fanon does not discuss Whitman, but in
these phases of a developing national literary consciousness, Whitman's work in nineteenth-century North America has seemed an
impressive analogue—indeed, a direct influence—for many subsequent writers.

Whitman's example functions both in the first general transition
(beyond the imitation of imperialist models) and also in the individuating second movement (beyond a descriptive, folkloric sense
of local tradition). In the five movement, Whitman is significant
because he rejects inherited formal structures in politics and in poetics, and in the second movement because he represents himself
as a single participating man speaking in a local idiom. The influence of Whitman thus works through the relations between the
two separate images of Whitman; the practical application of his
model in the new work depends on which elements of Whitman's

work, those of public message or those of private craft, the new poet chooses to emphasize. Whitman may be the historical-political poet (the giant, in Pound's reading): in that case the political form generates the literary gesture. Or conversely, Whitman may be the symbolic-lyrical poet in his landscape, in which case the style or gesture generates the form.

It would be restrictive to associate these images too directly with Fanon's two stages of cultural transition, though Whitman *is* often helpful politically or thematically for the first transition and stylistically for the second. That equation is somewhat complicated historically, however, because of the different dominant ("imperialist") traditions which the modern colonial movements resist. In Hispanic America, for instance, the early-twentieth-century continental models already included some Whitmanian, late-Romantic stylistic tendencies. Once again the question arises: how does a poet break from a tradition of rebelliousness? The paradox both Williams and the Hispanic writers face is that by overtly trying to break from the tradition, one joins the inherited tradition: the Romantic conundrum again.

At the end of the nineteenth century Whitman enters Hispanic American poetry through the first image. The collectivist Whitman, appropriate to Fanon's first stage of colonial individuation, becomes a contributing voice in Spanish American *modernismo* through the work of José Martí, who hears Whitman lecture in 1887 in New York. That same year Martí publishes an essay ("The Poet Walt Whitman") that introduces a "dynamic and delicate" Whitman to Hispanic readers. A leader of the Cuban struggle for liberation from Spain, Martí—like Georg Lukács and other subsequent Marxist critics—insists on the ideological bases of literary forms. In Whitman's example Martí recognizes a "vast fiery love" that takes form as "the mystery of suggestiveness, fervor of uncertainty, flaming prophetic word." In a circle of mutually reinforcing enthusiasms, therefore, Whitman's passionate sense of the word informs his political vision: "Then just imagine what an extraordinary effect this language, charged with animal vitality, would have when it celebrates that which will unite humanity!" [77] Martí's essay recommends Whitman's politics both through its intensity and through its timing; it coincides with the loosening of Portuguese and Spanish power in the Americas, in a process that led toward Brazil's independence from Portugal in 1889 and toward the collapse of Spanish hegemony in the Caribbean by the Spanish-American War of 1898.

Though Martí's 1887 essay introduces Whitman as a vigorous available model, not all of the subsequent Whitmanian influence on Hispanic *modernismo* is so apocalyptic. The most representative work of the movement, in fact, seems largely influenced by the French Symbolists and Parnassians. After the delicacy and exoticism of Mallarmé, Verlaine, and the Gallic Poe, the poems of the *modernistas* tend to be mannered formal pieces—synaesthetic, subtly musical, occupied by swans and tubercular princesses. When this dominant style overlays Whitman's "message," the results are a surprising hybrid, an invigorated Symbolism and a mellowed Whitman—as in this famous Rubén Darío poem of 1890:

> En su pais de hierro vive el gran viejo,
> bello como un patriarca, sereno y santo.
> Tiene en la arruga olímpíca de su entrecejo
> algo que impera y vence con noble encanto.
>
> Su alma del infinito parece espejo;
> son sus cansados hombros, dignos del manto;
> y con su arpa labrada de un roble añejo,
> como un profeta nuevo canta su canto.
>
> Sacerdote, que alienta soplo divino,
> anuncia en el futuro tiempo mejor.
> Dice al águila: " ¡Vuela!" " ¡Boga!" al marino,
>
> y " ¡Trabaja!" al robusto trabajador.
> ¡Asi va ese poeta por su camino
> con su soberbio rostro de emperador!

> The old man lives in his land of metal.
> He is handsome as a patriarch, quiet and holy.
> He has a high olympian furrowed forehead
> that challenges and conquers with a noble enchantment.

His soul is a mirror onto infinity, and
his tired shoulders deserve the mantle;
his lyre is carved from an ancient oak;
he sings like a modern prophet.

He is a high priest of divine help,
announcing a better future;
he tells the eagle "fly!" and the sailor "sail";

he tells the hearty worker "work!"
And so the poet passes on the open road,
with the radiant face of a king.[78]

For writers at this end of the political spectrum of *modernismo,* Whitman is exemplary because his private emotion is so dominant that it assumes public significance. Rubén Darío acknowledges that he takes his first image of Whitman from Martí's, but Darío changes the emphasis slightly, reading Whitman less as a passionate revolutionary prophet and more as a Romantic bard who celebrates the mysterious possibilities of the world. As elder, patriarch, high priest, bard, and prophet, Whitman in this "land of metal" is a spiritual leader because he has a special relation to the spiritual cosmos: he finally resembles an exemplary theocratic king, in a subordinated system of power. Perhaps the poem suggests that Whitman's democratic power replaces that of a king—but his tone of command, and the power he has to make things happen according to their own natures, locate that democratic power in him. He is not so much the vehicle of spiritual power as its origin. Darío characterizes Whitman as that mystical force that makes the inevitable happen, in politics, poetics, and metaphysics; his power is musical speech, apparently attuned to idioms appropriate to eagle, sailor, and worker. Darío's argument is democratic, but the poem's images are hierarchic, as if Whitman is to bring old forms to life in the New World. Similarly, though the diction here is high-spirited and exclamatory, the form in Spanish is an un-Whitmanesque sonnet: again, through his delicate force Whitman apparently re-empowers old forms.

As these images of Whitman suggest, however, Spanish mod-

ernism's two images of Whitman can be reconciled without Whitman's loud paradoxes. Late in his career, in the year Pablo Neruda
is born, Rubén Darío publishes his *Songs of Life and Hope,* in which
that cerebral-sensual poet rebelliously works to integrate the Spanish cultural tradition with the Indian landscape, in order to define
the integrity of Latin American experience against the threats of
Saxon and continental models. This new aspect of *modernismo,*
corresponding to Fanon's movement toward the second, liberating
stage of an emergent nationalism, has been somewhat awkwardly-
called *mundonovismo:* New-World-ism, or the Return to America.[79] In this new movement, Whitman's importance comes directly from his diction, not—as earlier in Darío's work—from his
mystical "message." Darío's famous poem "To Roosevelt" (1905),
for instance, admits that it needs Whitman's "voice" to articulate
its new claims, but once Darío appropriates that voice, he turns it
vigorously against its own generating context, using Whitman
"relatively" to articulate another America in contradistinction to
Whitman's "corrupting" United States.[80] This new America "tiem-
bla de huracanes" and "vive de amor" ("trembles with hurricanes"
and "lives in love"):

> hombres de ojos sajones y alma bárbara, vive.
> Y sueña. Y ama, y vibra, y es la híja del Sol.
> Tened cuidado. ¡Vive la América española!
> Hay mil cachorros sueltos del León Español. . . .
>
> Y, pues contáis con todo, falta una cosa: ¡Dios!

> O men with Saxon eyes and barbarous souls, [this America] lives.
> And dreams. And loves, and moves; it is the daughter of the Sun.
> Beware! Long live Spanish America!
> And the thousand lively cubs of the Spanish Lion!
>
> For though you have everything, there's one thing you lack: God.

In Chile in the 1930s, Pablo Neruda similarly recognizes the need
to distinguish a South American poetic voice from its European
and North American antecedents—and also from simple historical
sentimentality. Oddly, the pressure to distinguish South American
possibilities from European models seems to drive Neruda toward

a North American model, Whitman. The result in Neruda's work is a nationally generous voice that specifically celebrates the Chilean landscape and people. In loose-joined nationalistic poems, Neruda celebrates iguanas, artichokes, tomatoes, copper, and village ceremony—but his central focus is always the observing historical self as it internalizes its place, working the local details toward a new synthesis. Like Whitman, Neruda lists what he experiences; he is learning from Whitman's style, though what he includes in his own lists is physically different:

> . . . sólo yo no existo,
> la vida corre
> como todos los ríos,
> yo soy el único
> invisible,
> no hay misteriosas sombras,
> no hay tinieblas,
> todo el mundo me habla,
> me quieren contar cosas,
> me hablan de sus parientes,
> de sus miserias
> y de sus alegrías,
> todos pasan y todos
> me dicen algo,
> y cuántas cosas hacen!:
> cortan maderas,
> suben hilos eléctricos,
> amasan hasta tarde en la noche
> el pan de cada día,
> con una lanza de hierro
> perforan las entrañas
> de la tierra
> y convierten el hierro
> en cerraduras,
> suben al cielo y llevan
> cartas, sollozos, besos,
> en cada puerta
> hay alguien,
> nace alguno
> o me espera la que amo,

y yo paso y las cosas
me piden que las cante,
yo no tengo tiempo

. . . I do not live alone,
life runs
like all the rivers,
I am the only
invisible man,
there are no mysterious shadows,
there is no darkness,
all the world speaks to me,
they all want me to tell things:
I talk about their relatives
and their miseries
and joys,
they all pass by and they all
say something to me,
and so many things happen!
Lumberjacks chop wood,
steeplejacks climb wires,
late into the night people knead
the daily bread,
with an iron spike
they drill into the innards
of the earth
and change the iron there
into locks,
they rise to the sky and carry
letters, sobs, kisses;
in every port
there is someone,
someone is born,
or the one I love waits for me,
and I pass by and whatever
they ask me to, I sing about:
I just don't have enough time
                    (from "Invisible Man")[81]

In the startling diversity of his career, Neruda, who inherits the Spanish modernists' two related images of Whitman, is difficult to characterize. He moves restlessly from the surrealist-*modernista* intensity of his *Twenty Love Songs and a Song of Despair,* to the broad inclusiveness of the *Canto Generale,* to the elegant simplicity of the *Elemental Odes.* But in this "impure" poetry Neruda consistently works to fuse the collective man with the private sensual self. For all the formal diversity of his poems, the integrity of Neruda's career consists in this steady ideal of fusion, just as he works to fuse the two images of Whitman the *modernista* tradition bequeaths him. In a 1967 interview Neruda even takes up William Carlos Williams' distinction between the Whitmanian and the Eliotic poetic traditions. Neruda accounts for the "neglect" of Whitman by North Americans:

Many of the American poets just following Eliot thought that Whitman was too rustic, too primitive. But he was not so simple—Whitman—he's a complicated man and the best of him is when he's most complicated. He had eyes opened to the world and he taught us about poetry and many other things. We have loved him very much. Eliot never had too much influence with us. He's too intellectual, perhaps, we are too primitive. And then everyone has to choose a road—a refined and intellectual way, or a more brotherly, general way, trying to embrace the world around you, to discover the new world.[82]

Neruda is unapologetic about his appreciation for Whitman; the influence first appears at the same time Neruda turns from early continental symbolism and returns to Chile, to "elemental" themes and to chanting Whitmanian lists held together by the centering integrity of a single self. In addition to appreciating Whitman's diction, Neruda clearly responds to the radically democratic principles informing Whitman's style, principles Neruda regards as the nineteenth-century corollary to his own communism; Neruda's politics are more sensual and emotionally generous than theoretical. Appropriately, Neruda's most direct encounter with Whitman happens in the context of Neruda's *Elemental Odes* (1954–1957), among poems addressed to salt, watermelons, magnolias, parrots, and knitted socks. One of the most memorable of the twentieth-century pacts with the older poet, Neruda's "Oda a Walt Whit-man" is a poem that ranks beside Federico García Lorca's ode to Whitman in his book *A Poet in New York* (1929–1932). The two odes differ widely, from the hominess of Neruda's spoken voice to the luminous lyricism of Lorca's invocation, but both poems share an admiration for the comradeship of Whitman and for his "voz perfecta [decir] las verdades del trigo" ("perfect voice [to speak] the truths of the wheat").[83]

Neruda arrives at his optimism directly. His ode recalls Whit-man as a somatic memory; Whitman's presence as a poetic influ-ence is assured through Neruda's immediate "physical" contact with him, a contact continuous since Neruda's youth.

> toqué una mano y era
> la mano de Walt Whitman:
> pisé la tierra
> con los pies desnudos,
> anduve sobre el pasto,
> sobre el firme rocío
> de Walt Whitman.

> I touched a hand and it was
> Walt Whitman's hand;
> I walked across the earth
> with naked feet,
> I walked on the grass
> on the dependable dew
> of Walt Whitman.

The first half of Neruda's poem details this revelatory presence ("tu/ me ensenaste/ a ser americano": "you/ taught me/ to be an American"), recalling Whitman's lessons of fraternity and cultural inclusiveness and restless forward motion. After detailing this openhanded, sympathetic inheritance, Neruda ends his poem in the present tense, making Whitman himself available as a harvest of hard-earned joy. The simple, the needy, and the oppressed

> se congrega cantando
> bajo

la magnitud
de tu espaciosa vida:
entre los pueblos con tu amor camina
acariciando
el desarrollo puro
de la fraternidad sobre la tierra.

gather together singing
in the largesse
of your spacious life:
they walk with your love through the cities
caressing
the pure unfolding grassy leaves
of brotherhood on earth.

Purified of specific physical details, the poem reclaims some of the specificity of Whitman's diction in the metonymic images Neruda uses to carry his abstract argument: what is "elemental" about this ode is not its language, things, or people, but its attitude to Whitman, who seems an "element" of imaginative physical life. Whitman's "message" is a palpable "thing" in this world. From Whitman Neruda learns the importance of the "elemental," both in vision and in diction.

Lorca, by contrast, begins his address to Whitman with present-tense verbs and with specific, nightmarish "things." Lorca's Whitman asserts himself not against active suffering, as in Neruda's version, but against static death, in a landscape of blight and urban desolation. Physical materials that should suggest an organic connection with the world seem perverse and constraining:

Por el East River y el Bronx,
los muchachos cantaban enseñando sus cinturas,
con la rueda, el aceite, el cuero y el martillo.
Noventa mil mineros sacaban plata de las rocas.
y los niños dibujaban escaleras y perspectivas.

       . . .

Nueva York de cieno,
Nueva York de alambres ye de muerte.
¿Qué ángel llevas oculto en la mejilla?

¿Qué voz perfecta dirá las verdades del trigo?
¿Quién el sueño terrible de tus anémonas manchadas?

   Along the East River and the Bronx,
the young men were singing, naked to the waist,
among the wheels and the oil, the leather and hammers.
Ninety thousand miners scrabbled at silver in the deep rocks,
and young boys drew ladders and distant perspectives.
                    .   .   .
   New York of garbage,
New York of cables and death.
What angel is in you, hidden in your cheek?
What perfect voice to speak the truths of the wheat?
Who can tell the terrible dream of your soiled anemones?

Among the surreal modern challenges to the Whitmanian message
of organic connectiveness, emotional and linguistic and cultural
perversities surround the figure of the potentially joyous Whitman,
with his "barba llena de mariposa . . . . barba luminosa y casta"
("beard full of butterflies . . . . luminous and chaste beard.") If
there is hope in this ode, it lodges in Lorca's occasional shift from
present-tense declarative verbs to subjunctive:

   Agonía, agonía, sueño, fermento y sueño.
Éste es el mundo, amigo, agonía, agonía.
Los muertos se descomponen bajo el reloj de las ciudades,
la guerra pasa llorando con un millón de ratas grises,
los ricos dan a sus queridas
pequeños moribundos iluminados,
y la vida no es noble, ni buena, ni sagrada.

   Puede el hombre, si quiere, conducir su deseo
por vena de coral or celeste desnudo.

   Pain, pain, dream, change and pain.
That's the world, my friend: pain, pain.
Under the village clock the dead rot,
the battle goes on, crying, with a million grey rats,
rich men give dead little sparks

to their mistresses,
and life is not noble, nor wholesome, nor holy.

    But a man could, if he wanted, guide his desire
through the vein of the coral, or the body—naked and celestial.

This song of contingent praise reaches Whitman where he sleeps on the banks of the Hudson, while America "se anega de máquinas y llanto" ("drowns in its machines and tears"). And where Neruda had concluded with the collective voice of the needy in Whitman's organic song, Lorca concludes with a single voice, that of a black boy who sings to the sleeping Whitman and announces "la llegada del reino de la espiga" ("the heavenly world to come in a leaf of grass.") Neruda's collective Whitman becomes a friend or a harvest, a personal organic immanence, but Lorca's sense of re-empowerment is more transcendent and apocalyptic, more like the Lawrence-Pound Whitmanian "message" that America ignores. Both see Whitman latent: for Neruda, that latency is accessible to individuals, while for Lorca that power is a possibility the culture ignores, available only to the culture as a whole.

Lorca and Neruda respond to different possibilities tacit in Whitman's example. Neruda reads Whitman's forms as joyously egalitarian; the essential Whitman lives in the bond between the immanent private self and the collective, linguistic, Whitman-harvest. The connective here is "touch." Lorca, stressing the nightmarish public circumstances, makes Whitman connective in a more cerebral mode, in a countersong: he is that coherent, vital force technological America historically needs and neglects. Each of these images of Whitman, Neruda's immanent touch and Lorca's transcendent call, can signal a cultural regeneration; for both Neruda and Lorca, Whitman's power to "connect" is a future possibility that his style—more than his giant "message"—makes possible.

Latin poets in the latter half of the twentieth-century continue to observe this relation between Whitman's form (politics) and his style (aesthetics). Pedro Mir in the Dominican Republic uses Whitman's enumerative style ironically, for an overt political re-orientation, in his "Countersong to Walt Whitman: Song of Ourselves," while in Spain Miguel de Unamuno in his essay "Adamic

Song" points to that style as proof of Whitman's "pure" lyricism.[84] Among more contemporary writers, Octavio Paz in Mexico relates the historical idealism of Whitman the collectivist to the Utopian innocence of Saxon America:

> Whitman never had consciousness that he was dreaming and always considered himself a poet of reality. And so he was, but only insofar as the reality he sang was not something given, but a substance shot through with the future. America dreams itself in Whitman because America itself was a dream, pure creation.[85]

Conversely, the Argentinian Jorge Luis Borges—although he too uses Paz's metaphor of Whitman's doubling dream—emphasizes the internal relation of Whitman's personal self to the giant ideal in *Leaves of Grass*. Only after Whitman had negotiated that private correspondence, Borges writes, could he recognize that that internal relation also links him with others in brotherhood. Borges first offers this reading of Whitman in 1918, and he continues to elaborate the image for over fifty years,[86] perhaps because the theme reinforces several of Borges' other thematic obsessions. For Borges in 1975, Whitman's magnificent "experiment" is the effort of a single lonely New Yorker "in a kind of divine humility, in a kind of god-like modesty . . . to think that he was Everyman, and so, he wrote those poems."[87] In both versions—Paz's oneiric collection and Borges' psychological projections—Whitman's style is more significant than his innocently radical theories: in one version Whitman's style reveals latent democratic political convictions and in the other latent brotherhood. Thus the two versions converge.

It is possible to see this doubled reading of Whitman continue through the reception of Whitman in other languages and cultures, as well. In Italy, Fascist writers during Word War II embrace Whitman for his vigorous nationalism, while Cesare Pavese—virtually as an act of political resistance—advocates Whitman on the basis of his delicate, objective craftsmanship. It seems odd to think of Whitman as a formal influence on a writer as intensely hermetic as Pavese, but in his essay "Walt Whitman: The Poetry of Poetry Making" Pavese addresses the apparent paradox by reading Whitman as a brooding, willful formalist, a kind of proto-Stevens:

He did not succeed in his absurd attempt to create a poetry adapted to the democratic and republican world and to the characters of the newly discovered land—because poetry is one—but as he spent his life repeating this design in various forms, he made poetry out of this very design, the poetry of the discovery of a world new in history and of the singing of it. To put the apparent paradox in a nutshell, he wrote poetry out of poetry-making.[88]

The history of Whitman's reception in Russia poignantly repeats this doubled tradition (one Whitman for an aristocratic or bourgeois European culture, another for a proletarian or colonial culture). Early in the twentieth century, a bourgeois European-Russian Whitman lapses with the decline of Czarist Russia, and a Whitman of Bolshevik enthusiasm replaces him. Ivan Turgenyev had translated Whitman early in the 1880s, making him sound sweetly generous; the spiritual inclusiveness of Whitman's lists apparently appealed to the fundamentally conservative Slavophiles of the late nineteenth century. (By 1879 Turgenyev the "European" novelist was mending his fences with Tolstoy and Dostoyevsky, after feuds about the "decadent" influence of European literatures on Russian art.) Even throughout the 1920s, Russian poets continue to call Whitman the "American Tolstoy"—an analogy Tolstoy himself accepted, for the stylistic similarity he thought it suggested.[89] After the Bolshevik Revolution, poets and theorists reaffirm this version of Whitman, though they change its emphases to make Whitman's democratic politics sound not Czarist or Slavophile but aggressively socialistic; to emphasize the difference between the two readings of Whitman, theorists often defined this "New World" Whitman against the "aristocratic" and "half-French" Poe. Thus Vladimir Mayakovsky follows the "political" Russian tradition of reading Whitman, applying Whitman's principles of native language to Russian life and Leninist politics. The poems that result are "Whitmanian" insofar as they are Soviet in content and nativist in diction. Mayakovsky's tonal self-confidence predates the Bolshevik revolution, to be sure; he calls his first book, from 1913, simply *I,* and in his second (a long poem called *A Cloud in Trousers,* 1915) Mayakovsky virtually cannibalizes Whitman—with the hungry assertiveness of his style, with his conjunctions of disparate materials, and with his sensual iconoclastic joy. The enthusiasm centers around his compelling self: **"И/ чувствую/ 'Я'/ для меня мало./ Кто-то из меня вырывает-ся упрямо."** ("I feel/ my/ 'I'/ is too small for me./ A second body pushes aggressively through me!"). When the Soviet Revolution offers him an external metaphor for his grand assertiveness, however, Mayakovsky's work takes a firmer, more generous form. Like other futurists of the 1920s, Mayakovsky admires Whitman's textured democratic radicalism, insisting that future translations of Whitman should be less "sweet and melodic," more "harsh and rough." Like Whitman, Mayakovsky can tend toward hero-worship when he displaces the personal self as the centering force in a poem or in a culture; where Whitman had admired Lincoln, Mayakovsky admires Lenin. And like William Carlos Williams, Mayakovsky eventually focuses his Whitmanian enthusiasms in a long "triadic" line. Mayakovsky even expands his progressive, Trotskyist vision of the future into the United States, which he visits in 1925. In his poem on the Brooklyn Bridge, Mayakovsky uses the metaphor of the Whitmanian bridge as Crane does, as a span between past and future. But where Crane finds in the Whitmanian perspective a vision of a golden American past, half of the truth, Mayakovsky sees an objective, gloriously technological future for all:

> Я горд
>> вот этой
>>> стальною милей,
>
> живьем в ней
>> мои видения встали—
>
> борьба
>> за конструкции
>>> вместо стилей,
>
> расчет суровый
>> гаек
>>> и стали,

Если

    придет

        окончание света—

планету

    хаос

        разделает влоск,

и только

    один останется

        этот

над пылью гибели вздыбленный мост

I am proud

    of this

        long stretch of steel,

because upright on it

        my visions are made real—

a struggle

    for construction

        instead of for ornament,

a strict organization

    of bolts

        and steel.

And even if

    the end of the world should occur——

if nothingness

    should

        crush this planet,

what remains

    would be

        this—

rearing above the rubble of destruction: this bridge.[90]

In his painfully restless search for absolutes, Mayakovsky embraces Whitmanian individualism, then the collective aesthetic power of drama—then Bolshevism, then Futurism. Despairing finally of

movements and of generative possibilities for political art, he committed suicide in 1930.

This tendency of poets in colonial or newly nationalistic countries to read Whitman as a "separate citizen" whose sense of brotherhood makes him a metonymic figure for a whole nation emphasizes the simple separateness of Whitman's style and makes his
stylistic representativeness the secret of Whitman's larger applicability. Thus this "colonial" interpretation of Whitman works against
the North American modernist image of a giant who collects his
country's diversity in a dominant abstract metaphor. For North
Americans, Whitman's message precedes his form. The Saxon
Whitman is a model of larger structural possibilities (Pound's discovery of enumeration as a technique is more important than what
he actually enumerates in his lists, for instance), but the Latin version of Whitman returns the issue of structure to questions of
idiomatic diction and vocabulary. This distinction is nowhere so
clear, perhaps, as in the distance between the Whitman-figure of a
dominant "imperial" culture and the Whitman-figures of its colonies that share a common language. The comparison of Lorca's
mystical singer (in Spain) with Neruda's political hero (in Chile)
is a good example. The distinction obtains equally well in the relation between the Whitman whom the French value—a "mythic"
and philosophical poet—[91] and the Whitman whom French colonial writers need. The Symbolists read him as a mystic; in the
French Caribbean, by contrast, Aimé Césaire assumes Whitman's
diction, his politics, and his personal involvement in the details of
his place, to inform his moving long poem "Return to My Native
Land" (1956).

Ironically, the distinction between the imperialist and the colonial Whitmans extends even into English-based languages. In England, the mythic, mystic lyrical reading of Whitman has seemed
dominant, for poets from Tennyson to contemporaries. (Whitman's delicate sense of place influences the evocative descriptions
in Basil Bunting's autobiographical *Briggflatts,* for instance, though
Bunting *is* interested in Whitman's form, and Whitman's in-stressed
enthusiasm for the mysteries of animal life influences several of

Ted Hughes' best poems about animals.) But in the English colonies—especially in the twentieth century—Whitman's structural and political implications, his return to "local" conditions of diction and of form, dominate his reception. Exploring the stylistic applicability of Whitman's nativist aesthetic, for instance, the Scots poet "Hugh MacDiarmid" (Christopher Grieve) moves Whitman's local sense into Scottish locales and Scots diction. Thus MacDiarmid uses the methods of Whitman's nationalistic North American poetry to articulate his own violent contempt for American-style capitalism. Surprisingly, MacDiarmid's use of Whitman is not ironic, neither toward Whitman nor particularly toward North America. Rejecting the sentimentality of Whitman's passive mystic-democratic absorptions, MacDiarmid emphasizes the "poetry of fact" and of scientific specificity in Whitman, making Whitman's democratic thinginess seem a forerunner of Marxist materialism. When he adapts the Whitmanian model, MacDiarmid aspires to write a national literature that can speak internationally. MacDiarmid calls his purpose not nationalism—though he is a Scottish nationalist—but internationalism, or *Partikularismus*. For such an ambition, Whitman's diction and form are more useful than his overt "message"[92]—and MacDiarmid uses Whitman's own metaphor of the grass to turn Whitman's style against his naive politics:

> This renewed impetus
> Toward the local and the vernacular
> Implies a changing conception of culture,
> No longer a hothouse growth but rooted.
> If all the world went native
> There would be a confusion of tongues,
> A multiplication of regionalisms.
> *Partikularismus,* however,
> Is hostile to nationalism
> And friendly to internationalism.

As the cases of Neruda and MacDiarmid illustrate, sometimes Whitman's literary nationalism contributes in the work of later writers to a local and vernacular movement for an international identity, often with an anti-American inclination. In this sense,

Whitman helps those writers who want to move beyond Fanon's goal of aesthetic and cultural independence. And their use of Whitman clarifies the distinction between the political implications of Whitman's giant Self and those of Whitman's "simple separate person": his mode as giant tends toward democratic nationalism (collectivity), while his mode as individual citizen tends paradoxically both toward particular attention to place and toward a spiritually broader concept of what is humanly "collected." The paradox is that the specificity of this second mode is both individuating in perceptions and verbal tactics *and* collective in an essential sense.

WILLIAMS AND THE PARADOX OF THE LOCAL

This apparently paradoxical expansiveness of the "local" possibilities for poetic diction is an important lesson Williams learns from his reading of Whitman. During the years just after World War I, while he is coming to terms with Whitman (especially in contradistinction to Eliot), Williams is opening the material of his poems to immediate experience and is expanding his rhythms into the looser pace of spoken American English. Both developments move the poems toward a more conversational, personal tone. Even as casual readers we are familiar with Williams' aesthetic of the intimate "glimpse" in his shorter poems, in those moments when Williams registers with wonder the apparently incidental detail.

So much "depends upon" Williams' famous wheelbarrow (1923), in fact, that that poem never explains exactly what *does* depend on it, beyond the minute observational joy the poem recreates. After our first reading we ask: just what does "depend on" these apparently insignificant details? When the poem refuses to answer that question in expected terms, we return to the details themselves, and to their verbal depiction, for a different sort of answer. What finally depends upon these sensual and verbal details is immanent:

THE RED WHEELBARROW

so much depends
upon

a red wheel
barrow

glazed with rain
water

beside the white
chickens.
  (*CEP,* p. 277)

The piece contains no verb but the editorially introductive "de-pends"; the rest of the poem, however, flickers with the sense of a large unspoken verb "is." Composed like a still-life painting and attentive to color (red, white) and to texture (glazed), this Imagist piece works structurally through a series of progressively more specific observations: from the rhetorical abstraction of the first couplet, to the generic object of the second, to its qualities (in the third), to its relation to a sentient world (in the fourth). Each stanza contains itself in rhythm and in vowel sounds (like the a's in couplet 3, the i's in couplet 4), as if to assert the integrity of each phase of the observation. Each phase is a category, in se-quence: from abstraction (the grammar of couplet 1), to inactive, processed material (the wheelbarrow), to more active organic ma-terial (rainwater), to living creatures (chickens). The sequence sug-gest that the farther one departs from abstraction (couplet 1) the closer one approaches vitality. The grammatical abstraction in the opening couplet separates physical things from their immanent significance (the couplet contains no nouns); in 2 and 3 the full names of inert things are still divided (wheel/barrow, rain/water); but in 4 the noun (chickens) has its own line. The chickens are simply there and are simply "white." The least qualified and least acted-upon of the things in the scene, the chickens are fully sepa-rated from their adjective; occupying the last line, their name seems to be the destination of the entire linear sequence.

This short poem thus seems to be a straight line from abstrac-tion to mysterious vitality. And yet our sense of the importance of that scene is provoked by the first couplet ("so much depends/ upon"); the "abstraction" of the framing language is what makes the scene seem immanently important. Perhaps the straight-line effect toward vitality is something of an illusion. Because the conscious framing of the scene in the rhetoric of the first couplet *makes possible* the sense of immanence, the poem makes a circling return, from abstraction to vitality and back, as if to assert a complementarity. Formally the poem reinforces this sense: the poem moves forward rhythmically by a curious verbal effect of echoes or of half-returns. The first line of each stanza (3 or 4 syllables) is longer than the second, qualifying line (2 syllables), so that the poem extends and then gathers itself at each stage (4/2, 3/2, 3/2, 4/2): thus the rhythm calls attention to the integrity of each "thing" or category of the sequence. And further, the abstraction (couplet 1) and the vitality (couplet 4), apparently the two extremes of the linear spectrum, share a metrical subtlety (4/2 . . . 4/2). They are united by the made "thing," the wheelbarrow (3/2, 3/2), in a process like that by which the mind is joined to the world through the objectification of a perception, in a "thing" (the wheelbarrow, the poem).

Thus the poem makes an argument larger than its immediate observation, but it does so through the specific verbal tonalities of its description. The immediate perception is neither qualified nor allegorized; in fact, the poem makes a deft case against allegory in favor of immanence as a way to "read" experience. The smallness of the scene makes for a close, almost personal tone, purified of willfulness—and yet in its specificity the poem is remarkably "objective."

The argument of "The Red Wheelbarrow" is Emersonian, but it would be stretching the point, I think, to designate strict literary-historical antecedents for Williams' sense of wonder at the world or for the self-confident tone of the poem. Even the adjective "Emersonian" here presupposes a literary precedent I do not mean to claim too strongly.[93] What Williams does learn from the Emerson-Whitman model, however, is the association between such personal verve and the universality of local detail. The link between the outer and the inner worlds is the imagination, which seizes words as its bridging medium. Williams' exuberance and personal vitality of perception become issues of historical note only when he formalizes his theory of the imagination on the basis of that connection—that is, when he begins to explain how the private imagination is to work through the "new world" of the poem.

Williams' sense of "local virtue" intensified, we recall, about the time of the Armory Show in 1913; during the same time that Pound makes his "pact" with Whitman, Williams begins to move from the formal stiffness of his early poems toward the liberated Whitmanian suppleness of some of the poems in *Al Que Quiere!* in 1917. By 1918 the threat of Eliot's popularity hurries Williams' sense of urgency. As he retrospectively identifies Whitman as the root of an alternative tradition, Williams takes the terms of Eliot's fractured, allusive associativity and rewrites them into his own nativist countertradition: "The poetic line, the way the image was to lie on the page was our immediate concern."[94] This refocused attention to the "local" particulars in relation both to the landscape of the American scene *and* to the "field" of the new American poem makes Williams realize he needs Whitman in his second mode (Whitman's specificity as an individual, his use of the native idiom)—needs him, that is, and needs his failure, too.

This "local" assertion is not provincial but parochial, reminding us that we live in a specific place and time. Empirically, therefore, if we can reach a universal truth we can do so only through the evidence the sensational world provides. The poems of Whitman, the pictures of Steiglitz, the paintings of Marcel Duchamp and others in the Armory Show, all taught Williams that the materials of the artwork itself were the field for the modernist aesthetic battle over "the way the image was to lie on the page." But unlike Whitman's hieroglyphic reading of divine meanings spelled out in the materials of the world, Williams' "local assertion" is not transcendent; he uses the local details to register, in a new world of the imagination's words, the individual's perceptions and imaginative encounters with the physical world, through a kind of immanence. In his lists in "Song of Myself," Whitman usually does not claim to be recording experience. When he lists "gneiss, coal, long-threaded moss, fruits, grains, esculent roots," Whitman is alluding to things, not claiming to encounter them directly but enumerating what he abstractly "contains." In order to meet Whitman's second mode of influence on his own modernist terms, Williams reverses Whitman's primary relation to the outside world. For Whitman the abstract democracy is all-important, and the Composite Individual is the detailing spirit of that democracy; Whitman needs details to prove this abstraction. For Williams, the private democrat himself, the smaller self, is more often the primary fact of the poem. Thus the opening lines of Williams' *Paterson* focus on the individual task of the writer in a more limited and urgent way than the hyperbolic "I celebrate myself" of Whitman:

> To make a start,
> out of particulars
> and make them general, rolling
> up the sum, by defective means—
> Sniffing the trees,
> just another dog
> among a lot of dogs. What
> else is there? And to do?
> The rest have run out—
> after the rabbits.
> Only the lame stands—on
> three legs. Scratch front and back.
> Deceive and eat. Dig
> a musty bone
>
> (*P*, p. 3)

After this introduction of the artist-as-dog, digging a musty bone in the soil of the particular place, *Paterson* recognizes both the circularity of the effort "to make a start" and also the advantage of this apparently arbitrary limitation:

> For the beginning is assuredly
> the end—since we know nothing, pure
> and simple, beyond
> our own complexities.
>
> (*P*, p. 3)

Over this image of the dog, digging into the local earth and thus beginning Paterson's encounters with the particulars of place and of self, Williams superposes the image of Paterson as a separate person, a "nine months' wonder, the city/ the man, an identity," as if the effort to "dig down," limited by the recognition of one's own boundaries, were simultaneously the gestation of a baby and a citizen's encounter with the specific details of his city (an "identity"). This "interpenetration, both ways" is not so far-fetched if we consider the gestation of a baby a "descent," the beginning of an aggregative process, like the growth of a city, which includes in its final state all the stages through which it has passed. In the poem, in the pregnancy, in the city, and in the poet's gradual discovery of a local idiom, ontology recapitulates philogeny.[95] Like Whitman, who modeled *Leaves of Grass* as "a gigantic embryo or skeleton . . . for native models,"[96] Williams shapes his poem *Paterson* as the life and body of a single man (Paterson, also the city and the poem). His life begins in this "Preface," which works in two directions. The journey goes down and in, "from mathematics to particulars," and yet at the same time the poem starts an outward cycle, like the water cycle or like the retentive progress of evolution:

> divided as the dew,
> floating mists, to be rained down and
> regathered into a river that flows
> and encircles:
>
> shells and animalcules
> generally and so to man,
>
> to Paterson.
> *(P, p. 5)*

Evolution carries the life-stuff through the "particulars" of less organized forms toward the man who is also a "city" of related organs, and then that man returns to study those stages of development, self-consciously recognizing his history in them. In a similar cycle, water flows as a river past the city Paterson to the sea, disperses and rises, rains, and eventually returns to the place in which it has human likeness (Paterson, the city, the river, and the "verbal" falls). These cycles in the introduction to *Paterson* make clear that the quest of the poem is a journey of self-discovery for Paterson the separate person—but to discover himself he must examine those stages of the cycles that have produced him, the man/city. Like the dog, he has to dig in the ground of his local field to discover the "old bone" of his origins. Like Whitman's universal-izing expansion of himself across the landscape, so that to "read" the landscape is to find him, Williams' overture to *Paterson* makes the task of the poem a quest of self-discovery, and like Whitman's representations of himself as a "simple separate person," Williams' Paterson undertakes this large quest through a specific exploration into the details of his place. In the process of "digging" into the local ground, the poem makes a "start" toward individual devel-opment, toward a recognition of historical roots in the city of Paterson, N.J., and toward a poetry that can record its own quest for an adequate form. Just as Gaston Bachelard's Poet of Spaces can look into himself and find the world, or into the world and find himself,[97] so *Paterson* begins with images of the water cycle, of a baby's gestation, and of a dog's digging into the local ground: all beginnings of a quest toward a "discovery" of something end-less, a new sense of the public implications of the private self. In Book I of *Paterson,* the quest moves through the history of the city, and Williams includes prose sections of narrative history, an-ecdotes, and legends to make us see the city historically as well as geographically.[98] In these "local" discoveries Paterson discovers his "own complexities."

In Williams' estimation, therefore, Whitman generates a "local" self by inventing a "local" idiom, and his call to his readers toward the open road, as new pioneers to continue his work, is clearly a form of parentage, of continued "generation." In *Paterson,* a poem whose name suggests a line of generation (pater-son), Williams begins his journey inward with the image of a cycle of renewal and of promise—but the cycle is endangered by the state of the "loam" into which the vegetable "seed" of hope falls. The process of generation and of verbal transmission is perilous at the start of *Paterson:*

> (The multiple seed,
> packed tight with detail, soured,
> is lost in the flux and the mind,
> distracted, floats off in the same
> scum)

(*P*, p. 4)

This "seed" is the seed of hope for a new poetic language; it is also the "seed" that produces the baby who is Paterson. Like the plot of Sterne's *Tristram Shandy* (a book Williams cites as an innovation in the direction of modern objectivism), the story of Paterson's life is a narrative tending toward his own birth (at the end of *Paterson* IV).[99] In the works of Sterne, Whitman, Joyce (in "Oxen of the Sun" and parts of the *Wake*), and Williams himself, the objective self-consciousness of the central character in the artifact emphasizes the "process" of the hero's emergence and thus the process of creation of the artwork itself, in the act of making its own "world." The poem itself is a cycle.

It is important to recognize from the start the cyclical nature of Williams' quest in these introductory images to *Paterson,* because the circular movement suggested in the "Preface" makes Paterson's "descent" into particularity seem clearly one stage of a process that continues beyond his immediate encounters with his local materials. Digging into the locale, we discover universal phenomena, which are important in part because they enrich our perceptions of our local habitats. Williams' argument about place, that is, presupposes that the local is important both for itself and for the larger discoveries the local discoveries make possible.[100] In 1944 Williams writes to Horace Gregory in terms that directly relate this local sense to the generative water cycles at the start of *Paterson:*

Just as the city depends, literally, both for its men and its materials on the country, so general ideas, if they are to be living and valid, to some extent depend (at least for their testing) on local cultures. It is in the wide range of the local only that the general can be tested for its one unique quality, its universality. The flow must originate from the local to the general as a river to the sea and then back to the local from the sea in rain. . . . It is the poet who lives locally, and whose senses are applied no way else than locally to particulars, who is the agent and the maker of all culture.[101]

Because he lived "locally," exploring his America with an eye for the specific detail, Whitman is a model for such attentiveness; the specificity of his poems in effect "created" his culture for history. The applicability of Whitman's cultural realizations, however, involves the "democratic groundwork of all forms," as Williams had concluded in 1917.[102] (Admittedly, this personal inclusiveness is Whitman's weaker side, as he himself had seemed to sense: he interpolated the most personal information in "Song of Myself"— "now thirty-seven years old in perfect health" and so forth—years after he first published the poem.)

Given these assumptions, however, two difficulties immediately arise. First, how can Whitman, the giant-pioneer model for Williams, be also a model of a local "simple separate person"? For Whitman the relation of the giant and the private self is proleptic: the giant is an ideal to which we should aspire. But because Williams' use of specific "things" is different from Whitman's, the relation of objective giant to observing self in his work changes too. Thus the second question follows from the first: if the local materials are important largely for the evidence they provide in the poet's approach to a general truth, isn't one set of local materials as good as another? Isn't Williams really compromising the importance of the particular place?

In a sense the two questions answer each other. As we have already seen, Whitman is Williams' model for the giant who incarnates his place by recognizing it within himself; his "giant" self opens out by turning inward, toward his own experience and toward a new generative destruction of old forms, toward new stylistic freedoms. In this iconoclastic movement he opens new territories for subsequent generations of writers, who follow his lead and complete what he only began. Significantly, however, what Whitman "began" was a structural and stylistic attention to the details of his local scene. Despite his own metaphors of journeys and of adventures, his contribution in a "giant" mode is, finally, a new imaginative orientation toward the familiar things of the world. Facing the expansive panorama of Jacksonian America, Whitman extends himself imaginatively across the continent, expanding his poetic line to include what he encounters and what he discovers about himself. The process of his growth, though it tends toward the universal, is a close attention to the names in each locality, especially to the jargon and slang by which the brawny American language registers its "things." Throughout "Song of

Myself," Whitman identifies himself with the world he perceives. Finally, he leaves the world he has created in the poem. At that moment of disappearance, he directs his followers to continue his track by paying attention to his influence as it is—as he is—manifested in the things (and names) of the world they behold anew. "If you want me again look for me under your bootsoles." Like Whitman's movement from mathematics to particulars, Williams' *Paterson* works both down (or in, to local details, prose history, the personal self) and out (or up, to "make a start/ out of particulars/ and make them general"). The "accidental place, therefore America" is where the individual finds himself and where he must pioneer to discover whatever general significance is possible.

Thus the second question, whether Williams does not finally compromise the autonomy of the particular place, speaks to the issues raised by the first question. Williams does relativize the importance of the specific locale, and in so doing he follows the examples of Whitman, Boone, and others, who "turn inward" toward the local in order to "break through" to a general truth embedded in local detail. Whitman's pioneering spirit turns away from a "direct" approach toward a universal. "We must make anew! of old particulars," Williams insists. That is, "discovery" or "invention" in a poem will be the discovery of new formal combinations for received materials. The "new world" of the poem will be familiar in its elements, but "new" in its forms.

The poem is related to reality in that it supersedes the particular, being made up of nothing else, by its *form*. Thus it connects the past with the present; and thus we know we are alive; for seeing particulars all about us, and being instructed by the poem that the past was no different, we get our sense of continuity and the world becomes real to us. PROVIDED that we find ourselves able today to recombine the particulars of the past into the poems as those in the past composed them.[103]

Quoting from John Dewey ("the local is the only universal, upon that all art builds"), Williams expands the significance of the "local" scene by making it, in the texture of its details, an analogy to the this-ness of the past. Like Whitman's use of physical "things" in words, Williams' "experience" of the immediate things of the

world corresponds to Dewey's definition of art as an "experience":
the artwork bridges between one set of local experiences (the artist's) and another (the reader's, in another time or place). Dewey's
argument in *Art as Experience* (1934, when Williams read it) thus
makes the artist self-conscious about the medium he uses as the
physical vehicle of this communication; at its best, art is a "local
assertion." Art translates an "essence" from one locality to another,
but that essence is more physical than abstract; it is a distillation
more than a concept, an "essence" in an almost pharmacological
sense. Dewey concludes:

> The term "essence" is highly equivocal. In common speech it denotes the
> *gist* of a thing; we boil down a series of conversations or of complicated
> transactions and the result is what is essential. . . . All genuine expres-
> sion moves, in this sense, toward "essence." [104]

Through its local pride, a work of art can express what Williams
calls a "radiant gist." ("Poetry," says Ezra Pound, "consists of gists
and piths.") It does so, moreover, by remaining firmly anchored
in things—or in Dewey's vocabulary, by staying true to its nature
as physical, mediating experience: "all art is local."

Local and important. In Dewey's argument, art records that aesthetic quality, that sense of this-ness, that permeates certain experiences. The material of aesthetic experience is human and social.
The artist, therefore, is the person who "makes" a culture by affirming its local reality and who thus gives the culture permanence
and historical significance. Dewey considers this ratification of a
culture, in its locally unique secrets, the highest function of the
artwork:

> The individuals who have minds pass away one by one. The works in
> which meanings have received expression endure. They become part of
> the environment, and interaction with this phase of the environment is
> the axis of continuity in the life of a civilization. [105]

Without intrusive rhetoric, Dewey makes art the formative continuity of a culture, a history of experience: the objectively expressed artwork becomes part of the "environment" or "local condition" that will affect those who come later. This enlargement of

the concept of "location" to include the important artworks of a place is important for Williams' idea of the formal objectivity of the new poem's language, for it seems to validate his claim that a poem can create a model "new world" through the lay of its syllables.

Dewey's argument clears the ground for Williams' attempt to make Paterson, New Jersey, stand verbally integral and complete in the objectification of his poem *Paterson*. The words of the poem, the "local material" of the poem-city Paterson, become "things" in a new world. Like Dewey, Williams recognizes the importance of the artist in fixing a culture in history. In his essay "Against the Weather" in 1939, Williams specifically repeats the argument and terms of Dewey's *Art as Experience,* and he cites Dewey as proof of his claims. The artistic imagination simultaneously particularizes and universalizes, compacting "things" into an "essence" that is not philosophical but is a new "physical reality," distilled and connotative.

That—all my life I have striven to emphasize it—is what I meant by the universality of the local. From me where I stand to them where they stand in their here and now—where I cannot be—I do in spite of that arrive! through their work which complements my own, each sensually local.[106]

Later, shortly before the publication of *Paterson* I, Williams associates Dewey's argument with Whitman's depiction of his America, and the conclusions he draws point toward the culture's essential need for poetry: "No world can exist for more than the consuming of a match or the eating of an apple without a poet to breathe into it an immortality." Elsewhere in 1944, Williams pointedly compares his own sense of the "universal in the particular" to Eliot's "fatal blunder" of thinking that "place is always and only place."[107]

Whitman's importance in this historical argument is that he was the first American, in Williams' estimation, to address the "local" situation that was America: he gave us the sensual "essence" of that place. In his construction of a self and of its circumstances, he is the first American writer to give America a reality (in the poetic line, in the poem, and in history); in Dewey's terminology, he "experienced" his America and communicates the "essence" of that experience through a detailed language of things, projecting through art toward the local conditions of other places. (As he was drafting *Paterson* Williams read with interest Arthur Schlesinger's account of the intellectual life of nineteenth-century America; in *The Age of Jackson* Schlesinger also describes the culturally fixative effect of Whitman's attempt to invent a "new social myth.")[108]

Though Whitman's attempt seems directed more toward reshaping his contemporary society than toward establishing its reality in history, his final achievement, in Williams' view, is more historical than political; Whitman often did not know the implications of his intuitive discoveries. But unlike Whitman the idealizing democrat, Williams is at times skeptical of the ability of capitalist democracy to respect a "pluralistic realization of place." Like subsequent Marxist critics, Williams is unwilling to separate the artifact from the cultural context in which it was made. Such historical placement involves a necessary political connection between objective and subjective realities, as Georg Lukács argues: "Content and form of truly artistic works cannot be separated from the soil of their genesis just from the standpoint of aesthetics. It is precisely in works of art that the historicity of objective reality receives its subjective as well as its objective shape."[109] To put the argument in Dewey's terms: the artwork records not only the facts of a culture, but the experience of the individual within that culture, made accessible to later individuals. Dewey, Lukács, and Williams agree that this culturally fixative power is especially important in the art of a democracy, which claims to value the experience of its individuals.

It is no coincidence that this argument about aesthetics and historicity arises in this context, in a discussion of the position of an "epic" poem in a democracy. For democracies have a special relation to time: the absence of atemporal continuities in a democratic culture forces its social forms—and its arts—to account for the vicissitudes of change in time. Thus the arts in a republic—especially in a democracy—need to replace the vertical sense of changeless time (in a class structure) with a horizontal sense of time as development; especially the verbal arts in a democracy must accommodate to this tension between transcendent truth and sequential change. Following this pattern in the works of historians and artists from the pre-historicist social theoreticians of Athens, through Machiavelli and Hobbes, and into the writers of the modern world, J.G.A. Pocock concludes that in the verbal forms of democratic societies

time so conceived differs from the time of the physicist or metaphysician in being filled with—indeed, composed of—a rich texture of the acts, words, and thoughts of personal and social beings; and in stating the continuities and recurrences and occurrences of which it consisted, theorists encountered problems which compelled them to recast their thoughts in terms of process, change, and discontinuity.[110]

Pocock presents the problem as a conflict that generates positive, adaptive results: a more fluid definition of "history" and a more open, less definitive structural model for poetics. But conversely, Alexis de Tocqueville states the same case negatively, specifically about North America, when in *Democracy in America* (1835) he claims that poetry suffers here because language in such a cultural form tends to love evolutionary change, slang, and large synthetic abstraction, as means to counteract the democracy's confusion of the "Real" and the "Ideal."[111] Williams is sympathetic to both interpretations of the effects of democracy on the language—and so on the poem's timing and diction. The philosophical ideal of an abstract "Democracy" appeals to his sense that the culture needs a model for that "pluralistic realization" he demands for the poem. And yet democracy as a contemporary social form is stultifying: it "distrusts all elevations of the realization of intense place" and "sets a premium on placelessness."[112]

　　Williams tries to satisfy both ends of the conundrum of democratic historicity through his insistence on the "universality of the local," a concept that honors historical change by making historical specificity a vehicle toward an ideal synchronicity of different places. (In *Paterson*, too, as we will see shortly, he pursues two different sets of "timing" or of organizational structures, one "improvisational" and one fixed.) Unlike Whitman's democratic and finally homogenized universality, Williams' "local pride" claims to respect the differences between persons and places. On the one hand Williams seeks a common denominator of place, historical or contemporary:

Why do I live in the town in which I was born? . . . Because one clarity is like another. To know all towns of greater or less degree to which I may go.[113]

And yet Williams rejects the effort of abstract science or history or philosophy, which in their pursuit of Truth often deny the absolute that is a living and developing common characteristic of a group of individuals. Thus Williams tries to join democratic historicity with "scientific" objectivity, while avoiding the dangers of both extremes. And just as he tempers his suspicion of democracy by considering it a philosophical, not an exclusively political, principle, so Williams longs for a "practical" science he can claim as a paradigm: he wants to use the solidity of the new scientific truth as a model for the new poetic.

To avoid appearing to contradict himself, Williams enthusiastically turns to the "new" science, as an analogue to his theories about a "universal-local" truth. In his assertion of "location" as a complex and integral form of universality, Williams repeats almost verbatim what he'd read in A.N. Whitehead's philosophical interpretation of Einsteinian physics: according to the theory of relativity, the apparent unity of a perceptual field is the result of the individual person's "unity of bodily experience." "Every location," Whitehead concludes, "involves an aspect of itself in every other location."[114] Anywhere is everywhere. Or as Williams paraphrases the application of the Einsteinian principle: "We live in one place at a time but far from being bound by it, only through it do we recognize our freedom."[115]

This dual sense of place makes the local scene seem an objectification of the "unknown" that universally underlies all knowledge. The "mode by which all the prelogical is made known to us, the unknowable," Williams says, is "objectified" in one place and time, and the observer, acknowledging that we cannot know the un-

knowable, realizes that we can intuit that unknown only by beginning *"within* a certain tacitly limited field of human possibility to
seek wisdom." [116] In his second mode of influence, Whitman offers
Williams a helpful historical analogue through Whitman's "simple" and "separate" process of physically encountering the known
in order to intuit the unknown. Throughout Williams' poems and
prose, this search for the "impalpable *something*" that "inhabits the
real" [117] works through the urge to encounter the local scene itself,
metonymically. In a sense both tasks are identical. The fusion of
place-bound observation with that sense of organic mystery and
beauty in the commonplace and in the man-made pervades all of
Williams' work, both in the long poems like *Paterson* and *Asphodel*
and in shorter pieces like "Between Walls" (1934):

> BETWEEN WALLS
>
> the back wings
> of the
>
> hospital where
> nothing
>
> will grow lie
> cinders
>
> in which shine
> the broken
>
> pieces of a green
> bottle
>   (*CEP,* p. 343)

The tone is mild, restrained and attentive; the quiet joke is that
where one would expect to see shreds of green grass in the hospital grounds, one finds instead shards of green glass "where/
nothing/ will grow." The poem suggests, however, that the joy of
surprised recognition in perception is qualitatively the same
whether one observes grass or glass, pastoral lushness or urban
grit. This aesthetic of the "glimpse" does not naively accept the
shattered mechanical urban landscape of walls and cinders and glass;
the poem notes that the scene is immured behind a public building, that the land is sterile, and that the cinders simply "shine,"

whether or not anyone observes them. Nevertheless the imaginative eye may deftly catch the glimpse of a difficult beauty in such a scene, even while the observer regrets the difficulty. In "Between Walls" Williams balances forces of consolidation (institutions like a hospital, igneous cinders) against forces of diversity (shards of broken glass). What shines is the scattered detritus of the broken bottle; what matters, what carries significance, is the Many, not the One. "Between Walls" (1934) is Williams' populist and urban and antiformalist version of Wallace Stevens' "Anecdote of the Jar" (1919).

Because the "things" in these shorter Williams poems appear "locally," the poems can capture that mysterious sense of significance surrounding apparently unimportant details. Seeking a perspective by which he can objectively judge and also subjectively participate in the scene, Williams follows Whitman through his "local pride" of diction to a new sense of the impalpable embedded in the real, and to a new method of registering that mystery formally. To generalize ideas responsibly, Williams needs a distanced and objective ("giant") point of view, but to observe things locally and to record them specifically, he needs also the perspective of a "simple separate person." The mode of the giant is Whitman's latent "message," and the mode of the individual citizen is his stylistic specificity. Just as Whitman dramatically equates the giant Self with the historical, individuated self, Williams through his images of Whitman acknowledges the need for such a relation: ideology and style are finally inseparable. After he has reached this association, however, and has invented verbal strategies that let him explore the relation in shorter poems ("To Elsie," "The Red Wheelbarrow," and so on), Williams has yet to develop new stylistic techniques to realize that discovery more fully within the order of a longer poem. That work will be the task and the theme of *Paterson*.

PART II

Reading Williams

FOUR

A Relative Formalism:
Relativity, Metrics, and the Separate Self

Throughout his adult career William Carlos Williams maintains that the lessons he and his contemporaries have to learn from Walt Whitman's example are both appropriate and urgent; Williams is equally outspoken about the ways his images of Whitman influence his own work. As we've seen, this influence is neither textual nor specific; rather, it works through Williams' internalization of his two dominant images of Whitman. Although his opinion of Whitman remains relatively constant, he does seem to use Whitman intermittently. Williams alludes to the giant and to the private Whitman during several specific periods of his life, calling on Whitman at those times when he needs to assert that his own work continues an indigenous American experimental tradition in poetry.[1]

After his first adult enthusiasm for Whitman's expansiveness (c. 1914–1925), Williams consolidates his reading of Whitman into several steady assumptions: Whitman is a failed but invaluable innovator; his importance derives from his iconoclastic attitude toward poetic form and from his self-conscious "materialism"; to write like Whitman one must follow his example of rebellion against established patterns, even against Whitman's example. As we've seen, in his early essay "America, Whitman, and the Art of Poetry" (1917) Williams had invented a Whitman to use as an analogue to Dante because, like Dante's, Whitman's work fixed his culture in time. Thus Whitman is "our rock, our first primitive," whose work is generative because it demands a new completion in new cultural circumstances. For Williams in 1917, Whitman is "above all a colorist—a mood man," though this limitation (Whitman apparently depicts his own moods as cultural norms) does not seem troublesome.[2]

By the early 1930s, however, Williams is less concerned about enjoying a liberty of tone and more concerned about clarifying his ideas of poetic form. Still longing for the confirmation of a tradition, Williams tries to enlarge the applicability of the Whitmanian model—but by now the freedom of Whitman's associative form has come to seem problematic. Williams' ingenious response is to redefine what it might mean to belong to the "tradition" Whitman had begun. Somewhat vaguely characterizing the Whitmanian "tradition" by its rebelliousness, its formal experimentation, and its necessary incompleteness, Williams postulates a Whitmanian line of American poetry in order to associate his own restless formal experimentation with the paradoxical stability of such a tradition.

Thus Williams' allusions to Whitman shape a chronological pattern, a pattern of apparent need. First he invents a thematically important Whitman, about the time of World War I; near the beginning of World War II Williams revises that image to make a stylistically generative Whitman. In general, the earlier version resembles the "giant" of Pound's Whitman; the second version involves that more private Whitmanian citizen whose particularity can imply larger concerns, as in "To Elsie." That is, in the later version Williams invents a new Whitmanian style by mediating between objective observation and personal revelation. Coincidentally, that mediation is the central theme of *Paterson;* appropriately, Williams invokes his "second" Whitman especially during the late 1930s and the 1940s, while he is at work on his "lyric epic." In an essay of 1939 he stresses Whitman's "message" of "freedom," with the qualification that such freedom demands a new sense of "structure"; in letters from 1939 through the early 1950s he less formally emphasizes the same attitudes.[3] In 1947 Williams repeats his premise that Whitman's "Song of Myself" is the cry of a man breaking through the barriers of constraint IN ORDER TO BE ABLE TO SAY *exactly* what was in his mind. The first dominant assertion of the necessity for a new form in America. And by that, as an American, he spoke for the world.

Though this praise sounds as if it values Whitman chiefly for his thematic breakthrough, Williams now sees Whitman's lasting "heritage" as a commitment to formal innovation. The structure of Whitman's line is his great discovery, Williams insists; on that basis Williams calls Whitman a "hero," even a "progenitor."[4] In his *Autobiography* (1951) Williams characterizes Whitman as an aggressive pioneer. When Whitman "turned his back" on established forms, he was "turning toward the unknown future."[5]

Later, about the time of *Paterson* V, Williams returns for the last few times to this image of Whitman: his "message" is "freedom" (1959), and "Song of Myself" is a "great" though "adolescent" work (1960).[6] Throughout all these essays, Williams argues that Whitman's experiments are both signal and incomplete ("scattering himself broadcast. That was his form, but it ended there"). Around 1955, to coincide with the hundredth anniversary of the first *Leaves of Grass,* Williams wrote several essays to commemorate that "revolutionary blast."[7] The specific implications of Whitman's distributive form, he says in those tributes, are still latent, the formal origins of an American poetic that is always "in the act of being created."[8] These allusions to Whitman during Williams' planning of *Paterson* suggest that he needs the support of an image of American formal possibilities, even if by negative exemplum; it's important that these allusions evoke a forefather who is both useful and flawed. Appropriately for the argument of *Paterson,* Williams believes Pound's story that Whitman learned his need for "freedom" because of a thwarted romance (the "affair of the southern Nancy").[9] And the example of his compensatory freedom persists as potential: "it is and was meant to be only a beginning which we were enjoined to carry on to new inventions— because the secret in it was the same as the secret of a bud that will unfold later into a leaf or flower."[10]

Taking the example from Whitman's break with formal tradition, Williams models his own line not on Whitman's enumerative line but on a more general attitude toward poetic form that Whitman was the first to assert and that seems historically analogous to the modernists' ambitions.

Formally his great contribution to us which constitutes our major heritage from him is in the break he instituted with traditional forms of the poem. He returned us to the elements of the art—which he associated more or less successfully in his best work but only in a tentative manner.[11]

What Whitman did best, Williams continues, was "to abandon all the staid usages of writing a poem and thus [to] bring the sense of unassociated elements of composition. . . . He abandoned formal associations in the body of a poem with a purpose: to make the line free (as he thought)." Williams accepts Whitman's "freedom" as first premise but then he asserts the need to impose a "relative" order on the "unassociated elements" Whitman had freely allowed into the line.

From the 1920s on, Williams works to enlarge the scope of the poem's "composition"—not only within the single neo-Whitmanian line but also within the poem's larger structures. Williams' poem "St. Francis Einstein of the Daffodils" (written in the early 1920s but first published in book form in *Adam and Eve and the City,* 1934) is probably the most famous example of Williams' "composing" those "unassociated elements" in order to make the poem "free" but "measured." The poem's overt occasion is Einstein's celebrated visit to the United States in 1921, and Williams begins simultaneously with a quotation from Einstein as he disembarks (" 'Sweet land' ") and with the arrival of spring. Here is the full poem:

ST. FRANCIS EINSTEIN OF THE DAFFODILS

*On the first visit of Professor Einstein to
the United States in the spring of 1921.*

'Sweet land'
at last!
out of the sea—
the Venusremembering wavelets

rippling with laughter—
freedom
for the daffodils!
—in a tearing wind
that shakes
the tufted orchards—
Einstein, tall as a violet
in the lattice-arbor corner
is tall as
a blossomy peartree

A Samos, Samos
dead and buried. Lesbia
a black cat in the freshturned
garden. All dead.
All flesh they sung
is rotten
Sing of it no longer—

Side by side young and old
take the sun together—
maples, green and red
yellowbells
and the vermilion quinceflower
together—

The peartree
with fœtid blossoms
sways its high topbranches
with contrary motions
and there are both pinkflowered
and coralflowered peachtrees
in the bare chickenyard
of the old negro
with white hair who hides
poisoned fish-heads
here and there
where stray cats find them—
find them

Spring days
swift and mutable
winds blowing four ways

> hot and cold
> shaking the flowers—
>
> Now the northeast wind
> moving in fogs leaves the grass
> cold and dripping. The night
> is dark. But in the night
> the southeast wind approaches.
> The owner of the orchard
> lies in bed
> with open windows
> and throws off his covers
> one by one
>
> (*CEP,* pp. 379–80)

From the start of the poem, then, Einstein is a type of Columbus—and also a type of Botticelli's Venus, rising from the sea to
a vernal landscape. Primarily, in its title and in its opening section,
the poem associates Einstein and his work (insofar as his arrival
represents also the arrival of his ideas in America) with Saint Francis of Assisi and with the spiritual hope of his *Little Flowers.* Just
as Einstein is the "patron saint of the United States" because both
his work and the U.S. share a fascination with unity (matter-as-
motion), so St. Francis is the patron saint of verbal unification and
communicability, because he found a "common stem where all [are]
one and from which every paired characteristic branches".[12] Because
the vehicles of these two metaphors (Einstein, St. Francis) are thus
related, the tenors of the metaphors (Einstein's physics in relation
to modern America, and St. Francis' spiritual unification in relation to animal and vegetable life) are tacitly related, physics and
metaphysics. Because of Einstein's liberating influence on our concepts of space and time, the arrival of the theory of relativity in
America promises a flowering spring of abstract—spiritual—unification. Like the effects of Proust's Bergsonian "duration" on
modern poets' sense of association and of timing in the sequence
of images in a poem, and like St. Francis' effect on our concepts
of the organic world, Einstein's discoveries occasion a new encounter with the physical world.[13] If we realize that time is a relative relation between matter and velocity, then our concepts of

sequence (matter-in-motion) must change. And if we see that matter is timed energy, then Einstein's theory changes our concept of the autonomy of the single physical "thing"—and thus our understanding of the relations and similarities between things changes, too. Accordingly, we must adapt our concept of metaphor (the trope of similarity). Thus

> Einstein, tall as a violet
> in the lattice-arbor corner
> is tall as
> a blossomy peartree

The imaginative freedom that can let Williams represent Einstein in these apparently contradictory comparisons within four lines is also an associative freedom of form, a "relativity" that Einstein and St. Francis and Whitman, in their own ways, make possible. (The referent is Einstein's body; recall that in Whitehead's paraphrase of the principles of relativity, such associations are valid—are both "relative" and true—because a "unity of bodily experience" reconciles them.) Having thus set his terms, Williams can focus the rest of the poem not on the person of Einstein but on the effects of his arrival (his "idea") in America. The rest of "St. Francis Einstein of the Daffodils" works through a series of self-contradicting "paired characteristics," bound together because of abstract concepts (Einstein) and because of their simple verbal juxtapositions (St. Francis). Although the daffodils are "free" and the wavelets "ripple with laughter," a "tearing" wind "shakes" the orchards. "Side by side young and old/ take the sun together." Peartrees of two colors blossom by day, but the poem ends on a foggy evening. "The "northeast wind" moves the fog, but the "southeast wind" approaches. A dead black cat named Lesbia is buried in the garden ("All flesh they sung/ is rotten/ Sing of it no longer"), as if the ancient past (in the Catullan tradition of "Vivamus, mea Lesbia," recalling Campion and Swift and others) were well forgotten, but within a few lines an old man hides poisoned fishbones "where stray cats will find them," as if those antivitalistic forces that thwarted past liveliness (and desire and poets) still persist. Through all these paired images, Williams playfully constructs a doubled world in which things are challenged or complemented by their opposites; the duality is as characteristic of human history ("Lesbia") and of insentient life (the trees) as it is of the weather. Even Williams' adjectives repeat this dialectical or recombinatory effect (the "Venusremembering" waves, and so on), in the poem's diction. In this dualistic world, the unity both Einstein and St. Francis can offer is a binding energy, a "freedom/ for the daffodils!" And the poem ends on an image of incipient human freedom:

> The owner of the orchard
> lies in bed
> with open windows
> and throws off his covers
> one by one

The uncovering of the restless owner suggests a personal liberation (he is physically free of his blankets and is able to handle them "one by one") and also a social liberation because of that new personal freedom (because he is the "owner" of the orchard, the image suggests that this new sense of unity might even free him from domineering concepts of ownership). The owner ends the poem as naked (uncovered) as Botticelli's Venus, so that the final effect of Einstein's visit—and of the poem—has been to uncover the individual man in his somatic integrity and to signal him as the locus of experience and of hope in the vernal "new" world.

The poem does not articulate these ideas so much as allude to them, primarily through the analogy Williams suggests in his deft title. In the "construction" of the poem, Williams abuts separate images abruptly, to suggest a latent argument through their juxtaposition. Because of the "relativity" of these independent but juxtaposed truths, the construction through successive images demands that the reader reconstruct a sequenced argument by following the shared third qualities that associate the separate images. Einstein relates matter and light in a conceptual unity; St. Francis relates flesh and spirit in the unity of the Word; Williams aspires to a similar synthesis, a "relative" associative unity for the juxtaposed images of his poem.

In "St. Francis Einstein" Williams is clearly trying to claim the

central premise of modern physics (as he understands the popularized versions of relativity) as an analogy, to ratify his new ambitions for the modern poem's structure. But he handles Einstein as
he handles Whitman; in his letters Williams even describes Einstein in the same terms he saves for Whitman, associating physicist
and poet because their works remain "incomplete."

When Einstein promulgated the theory of relativity he could not have
foreseen its moral and intellectual implications. He could not have foreseen for a certainty its influence on the writing of poetry. . . . [we need]
some sort of measure, some sort of discipline *to free* from the vagaries of
mere chance and to teach us to rule ourselves again.[14]

Just as he reinvents Whitman as a literary predecessor, Williams
uses Einstein to personify a theoretical justification for his own
sense of the practical need for a new "measure," a new construction "upon the syllables." This "measure" affects not simply the
pace or rhythm of the separate poem, but also the structure by
which a poet associates separate perceptions, in what Emerson
called a "meter-making argument." As the example of Whitman
had helped Williams in the historical problem by allowing him to
conclude that "anywhere is everywhere," so the example of Einstein helps in the formal poetic problem by allowing Williams to
consider the specific place of the poem "relatively," with confi-
dence that its local imagistic truth can expand toward a more universal symbolic significance.

"St. Francis Einstein" is an example of Williams' attempt through
juxtaposed images to make the whole lyric poem the integral vehicle of his measure. In *Paterson* Williams further enlarges the
principles of "construction" in the poem; there he associates not
only images but entire sections of prose and verse, juxtaposing
those larger "compositional elements" so that each unit—lyric or
paragraph—can be complete and also can comment in context on
neighboring sections. This larger application of the principles of a
"relative" composition helps Williams to organize complete poems
structurally, but the metrical problem of the separate line still be-
devils him. By Book I, section iii of *Paterson,* he finds a possible
metrical solution, and with the section beginning "The descent

beckons/ as the ascent beckoned," Williams arrives at the long triadic line, a measured combination of quick-paced shorter lines in an inclusive, unified phrase. That form, which Williams uses repeatedly after *Paterson* II (1948), is the form that (as he tells John Thirlwall in 1955) "most influenced" his life's work.[15] Broken in two places to make a descending-step with three unit-stresses ("variable feet"), the triadic line seems hard to define except by analogies: it is like musical phrasing, like descents and renewals, like the valence-changes of radioactive uranium. When Williams uses the form in many of his longer later poems, the form seems especially flexible for meditations on the "relativity" of time and of memory. It is one line but it looks like three; thus the triadic line is a metrical solution to the problem of formally reconciling the One and the Many. Whitman had worked on the problem tonally and politically, Einstein scientifically, St. Francis spiritually. In the triadic line Williams approaches the problem metrically, through a "relative" division of time into a diverse-but-unified movement through a "place," the poem.

> The (self) direction has been changed
> the serpent
> its tail in its mouth
> "the river has returned to its beginnings"
> and backward
> (and forward)
> it tortures itself within me
> until time has been washed finally under
> (*P*, p. 233)

(These lines also echo Williams' early poem "The Wanderer," as if to draw attention to the change-and-continuity in Williams' handling of similar themes; the self-reflexive, "curved" time of the relativity theorem changes one's sense of one's own development through time.)

From the late sections of *Paterson* through the rest of his later poems, Williams often makes the meter of his poems similarly suggestive, as he adapts conventional metrical systems as if to recall them and to call attention to the "relative" changes he works on those conventions. His use of triple rhythms and of Sapphic dactyls, as in many of the poems in *Pictures from Brueghel* (1962), for example, may originate in his discovery of the possibilities of the unified triple beat of the triadic line.[16] In effect, the triadic line itself is an extended dactyl, a single line composed of three "variable" feet (each containing one to four syllables and one or two distinct stresses). If the tripartite line is an extended dactyl, then each line contains two separate caesurae, like the "ancient divisions" that Williams hopes the "new invention" of *Paterson* I will reorganize.[17] In both the particular Sapphic dactyls and in the general tradic line, Williams sees that the triple form carries certain tonal possibilities innately; it is no coincidence that Williams' poems in these triplet forms often involve tones of retrospective understanding and of a stately joy. Triple meters, in English usually dactylic or anapestic, seem "inevitably to have something vaguely joyous, comical, light, or superficial about them," Paul Fussell generalizes in his detailed study *Poetic Meter and Poetic Form*.[18] Though he has little positive to say about Williams' notion of the "variable foot," Fussell does recognize in much of Williams' work a powerful use of the triple meter to express a saltatory gaiety:

> In Brueghel's great picture, The Kermess,
> the dancers go round, they go round and
> around, the squeal and the blare and the
> tweedle of bagpipes. . . .
>
> *(CLP*, p. 11)

On the other hand, as Fussell explains, triple meters can equally well convey a "certain degree of passion and seriousness." This combination of gaiety and passion does not sound paradoxical when we consider Williams' work at its best. As we've seen, the form suggests a tonal unity-in-diversity that corresponds to Williams' Whitmanian desire to reconcile the One (universal and serious) with the Many (particular and frisky). To keep his tone from becoming repetitive, Williams does occasionally vary the triadic line: the occasional fourth line that grammatically opens or closes periodic sentences, giving them a sense of completion and of inevitability, both prevents the triple line from sounding formulaic and also slows the pace of the quicker one-third-lines. This shortened fourth line lends the whole section a tone of retrospection and of control underlying the apparent spontaneity. Admittedly, criticism of Williams' triadic line can rapidly become impressionistic. We feel retrospectively the propriety of the phrasing, but formal analyses of the effects seem to find an inevitability of form only after the fact.[19] Because we hear the appropriateness of the voice, we recognize that the basis for this new measure is American speech: basically trochaic and dactylic, heavily accented, slower and more Germanic than Latinate British English.

Besides using his famous triadic line, Williams also experiments with a varying iambic or dactylic beat in the single line; that is, in some poems he suggests a regular measure just enough to make us conscious of the diversions from and returns to that implied norm. The dactyls of these lines from Book I of *Paterson,* for instance, are not regular but are frequent enough to suggest a metrical endoskeleton for the poem:

> Plaster saints, glass jewels
> and those apt paper flowers, bafflingly
> complex—have here
> their forthright beauty, beside:
>
> Things, things unmentionable,
> the sink with the waste farina in it and
> lumps of rancid meat, milk-bottle-tops: have
> here a tranquility and loveliness
> Have here (in his thoughts)
> a complement tranquil and chaste.
>
> (*P,* pp. 38–39)

In these lines, too, the implicit theme of poems like "Between Walls"—the displacements the modern imagination must make to discover the modern beauty—becomes a more dominant theme, as Williams describes how the perceiving mind ("his thoughts") both discover *and* invent the "tranquility and loveliness" of the world's "Things." The metric of these lines is subtle; Williams is using measure "not to intensify but to control," Denis Donoghue concludes, "to test the feeling as it meets the edge of language."[20]

This restless inventiveness, the search for a new measure, which occupies Williams for the rest of his career, relates to Williams' consistent appraisal of Whitman as a forerunner whose achievements are valuable but flawed.[21] Because he could not intellectually consolidate the terms of his early—intuitive—discoveries, Williams argues, Whitman is finally a "magnificent failure," whose later career is a record of adolescent self-parody; the measure of his lack of discipline is the increasingly iambic, almost fixed beat of his line. Whitman recognized that freedom was the first premise of the new poetic, and later he also saw that such freedom requires some metrical discipline. What Whitman did not understand in his later poems, apparently, was how to control his freedom from within his materials.

Williams' criticism of Whitman here is neither exact in its claims nor specific in its reference. It is not even particularly accurate. For the candid, understated, and poignant glimpses of camp life in *Drum-Taps* (1865), for instance, Whitman earnestly adopts a new form and a new tone, reticent in the face of suffering. Had he attended to those poems, Williams could have found evidence of Whitman's formal flexibility. In Whitman's self-representations as an army nurse, Williams might also have seen an analogy to his own work as a poet and a doctor; he might also have been able to make the case for Whitman as a proto-Objectivist, influenced by Mathew Brady's Civil War photographs just as Williams was by Alfred Steiglitz's pictures. Williams doesn't read the shorter Whitman poems attentively, however. Relying more on assertion than on illustrated argument from specific poems, Williams characterizes Whitman as a dissenter whose formal rebellion was co-opted by his initial successes. What the modern writer can still learn from Whitman's troubled model is that same belief in the importance of the line as a unit of metrical and social measurement, the same rebellious tone toward established verities, and the same urgency of invention that characterize Whitman's earliest and best work. "What we have wanted" for the modern writing, Williams claims, "is a *line* that will allow us room in which to develop the opportunities of a new language, a line loose as Whitman's, but *measured* as his was not." Without measure, no verse is "free," for "verse is measure—that is the only permissible term."[22] Accordingly, Williams develops a "relatively stable foot, not a rigid one," a line descended from Whitman's but informed by the rhythms of contemporary speech, "a language full of those hints toward newness."[23] The locomotive's broad, regular rhythms had sounded in Whitman's line; the modern line should follow the rhythms of the automobile—swifter, lighter, less continuous.[24]

Williams' theoretical definition of the Modernists' program is as deliberately vague as his characterization of Whitman and of Whitman's "failure." That vagueness is deliberate, he claims, because "it cannot be *said* what we are and what we do. It can only be proved by our creation of formal configurations that we *were* and so remain. This is the work of the poet."[25] Despite his willful uncertainty, Williams is clearly applying the "relative" and local appropriateness of Whitman's second mode of influence to the internal structure of the modern poem itself. Williams' "local pride" within the poem's "measure" means simply an appropriateness of construct—an attention to the poem as a made thing or as a composed "place." Pound insists on a free verse that takes its formal measure from the shape of the utterance's meaning, and Williams agrees at least in part. The "new" measure will arise organically from the contingencies of the context, but—perhaps paradoxically—the new and relative form must also be "measured." The new self makes a new place in the modern poem—and "metric then is mapping," concludes Charles Olson, who elaborates Williams' idea some years later.[26]

Accepting Einstein's principle that we know time only as movement through a place, and relating that principle to Whitman's idea of the poem as a "body" or a place (America), Williams devises his new metric. The timing of the new poem will be "relative," and it follows that the self who speaks it will also be relativized. No longer a fixed, enlarged "giant," the speaking self whom Williams' new metric implies is individual, smaller, more local, and associative in a newly private way. Like Whitman he links his perceptions in ordered lists, though not horizontally; he resembles the second Whitman, the "simple separate person" whose personal experiences imply large cultural generalizations tacitly. The new self does not "celebrate" himself so much as offer his perceptions (images) humbly and objectively, letting them speak for themselves.

This general theme is clearly Whitmanian—the relation of public and private selves—but Whitman's influence is so open and pervasive that we tend to forget its specific, original causes. Whitman was the first American poet to ally politics, in a large sense, with the necessary form of the poem; he was also the first to join the joy of free personal perception with a corresponding exuberance of diction and of form. "The greatest poet," Whitman stressed,

> has less a marked style and is more the channel of thoughts and things without increase or diminution, and is the free channel of himself. . . . He swears to his art, I will not be meddlesome. I will not have in my writing any elegance or effect or originality to hang in the way between me and the rest like curtains. . . . What I tell I tell for precisely what it is.
>
> (*LOG*, p. 717)

To Williams, the Whitmanian form—joyously free of European influence but ultimately mannered—does seem to hang like a rich curtain between the speaker and the reader. Whitman's "principle of choice," in Susan Sontag's definition of literary "style," remains markedly consistent. In his own shorter poems Williams affects an apparently "transparent" style, an apparently effortless transmission from experience to expression. This "transparency" is the cause of what James Wright calls Whitman's "delicacy."[27] For Williams, that ideal transparency Whitman had claimed requires a "relativized" self that is usually more restricted, more lonely, and more observational than the ostentatiously participatory "I" of Whitman. Williams' poem "Danse Russe" (1917) illustrates how Williams' "relative" self participates more personally in the life of his place:

DANSE RUSSE

If when my wife is sleeping
and the baby and Kathleen
are sleeping
and the sun is a flame-white disc

in silken mists
above shining trees,—
if I in my north room
dance naked, grotesquely
before my mirror
waving my shirt round my head
and singing softly to myself:
"I am lonely, lonely.
I was born to be lonely,
I am best so!"
If I admire my arms, my face,
my shoulders, flanks, buttocks
against the yellow drawn shades,—

Who shall say I am not
the happy genius of my household?
                    (*CEP,* p. 148)

"Danse Russe" works through an extended if-then grammatical sequence, as if the conclusion of the poem were immediately contingent on the preceding details. But the self of the Williams vignette—obviously the emotional center of the poem—enters the poem syntactically through the "if" clauses ("If when my wife is sleeping," "if I in my north room," "If I admire"). Those subordinate clauses, in the larger section of the poem, gradually narrow the focus—from other people (wife, baby, Kathleen), to the place (sun, trees, room), through the man's external image (in the mirror), to his song-and-dance and eventually to the specific parts of his naked body. That is, the poem narrows, excluding the facts of the rest of the world (paradoxically by naming them), until the final if-clause fixes attention on the most intimate details of the man's body, observed and specified. The lonely revealed self in this poem is the locus of interest, but this individual self is important in a quieter, more contingent way than Whitman's Self is important in "Song of Myself," where Whitman appears more assertively participatory. Even when he presents himself as a simple separate person, Whitman is still arguing to prove a point. Whitman wears his intimacy publicly, as if there were no difference between one side of the Transcendentalist metaphor (the self-reliant giant Self) and the other side (the suffering private self). Williams is still working within those Whitmanian terms, but he does not share Whitman's presumption that such an equation—between the public Self and the private self—is self-evident. The individual self in the Williams poem is difficult to reach; it needs to be isolated from its surroundings and from its associations in order to be addressed; the temptation toward a narcissistic celebration of the exclusive private self (in the mirror) needs to be faced and superseded, before the man reveals his essential physical and emotional self. Only at that point does Williams take, with a difficult joy, the step that was Whitman's first leaping premise. When Williams surprisingly concludes "Who shall say I am not/ the happy genius of my household?" he seems vividly to reverse the isolating movement of the rest of the poem, as he moves from an intensely personal intimacy (his naked flanks) to the suddenly self-conscious and objective celebration of his public function in his context. The end seems a jump in perspective, from the personal to the public.

In fact, though, that "jump" oddly continues the poem's emotional momentum. Just as Williams claims that the specificity of the simple separate person—or of the particular "thing" or of the purified word—can lead to a "universal" recognition of the abstract truth immanent in a discrete unit, so in "Danse Russe" he leads through a process of individuation and divestiture, until at the most intimate point of the poem he "breaks through" to an objective recognition of his own centrality in the spiritual life of his household. He is a "genius" in the sense of a *genius loci:* at the heart of the local is an informing essence, indistinguishable from the details of its appearance. Insofar as the poem is a linear experience, the "step" beyond the most private is the "leap" into universality. But these linear descriptions of the poem deny the sense of joyous revelation, of inevitability and of depth, that the ending provides. Williams is the "happy genius" of his place exactly because he dances naked, because he self-consciously enjoys and sings that self-reflexive knowledge of his identity. The conscious intimacy of the self-representation apparently leads him to the larger truth, through the linear movement of the poem (and through the purposiveness of the if-clauses, which tend us strongly toward the

main clause). But in a more profound sense the objectified intimacy of the main clause *is* the idea in the thing: we have arrived
where Whitman began, in an equation between the private self
and the public circumstance.

Thus the two Whitmanian perspectives, that of the separate citizen and that of the giant or informing spirit of place, are novelly
linked in "Danse Russe." That association does not happen until
the end of the Williams poem, however. Even then it comes as a
joyful surprise, separated from the rest of the poem by the only
stanza-break, as if the difficulty of arriving at that reciprocity produces the unexpected and surprised joy of its realization. The terms
are originally Whitman's, but the new resolution of those terms is
recognizably Williams'. Beyond this exuberance, the early lesson
Williams learns from Whitman, Williams has taken the Whitmanian injunction against "style" one step further. In order to elaborate on Whitman's "incomplete" beginnings, Williams admits an
erotics of style, a focusing consciousness of language as a flexible
medium, for his deceptively simple effects. Whitman's disavowal
of style, his insistence that the "perfect user of words uses things,"
begets Williams' quest of completion, a quest that takes him beyond the ambitious generalizing of Whitman into a more direct
acknowedgment of the words themselves as "things," with which
he can re-present an object or an event "for precisely what it is,"
simultaneously an external and an internal phenomenon.

I do not mean to stress this Whitmanian influence too insistently, for fear of reducing Williams' achievements in directions
that even predate his appropriations of Whitman. As we've seen,
Williams takes Whitman as a retrospective model to justify his
own commitments to "local" consciousness of the physical place
(America, Paterson, the household) and of the verbal "place" of
the poem. As he defends his choice of Whitman for this role, Williams gradually discovers the appropriateness of Whitman as a formal model. Williams' developing attitudes toward that model, toward his two images of Whitman, and toward a possible fusion of
those two perspectives, are the course of Whitman's "influence"
on Williams. Oddly, Williams develops this "influence" in some
sense after the fact. Williams chooses Whitman as an appropriate

model because Williams needs to invent a tradition to join. Within his definition of that tradition, however, Williams can claim to join the Whitmanian tradition by working independently of it. For the rest of this essay, I'd like to look more directly at Williams' independent work, especially at his own modern epic poem *Paterson,* in order to see how he carries these issues from his chosen "tradition" into his modern epic "place." Those ambitions for which Williams retrospectively adopts Whitman as his forebear are the terms of his independent completion of implicitly Whitmanian goals. The early "Danse Russe" represents some of the stylistic techniques Williams develops in this quest to reconcile the One and the Many, implication and specificity, giant and citizen. The key, for Williams, is that paradox at the heart of Whitman's poetry: the giant Self can convey delicate perceptions *because of* its grandeur, and conversely the personal self can be "objectified" into a representative or metonymic significance *because of* its specificity. These new ambitions require a new "relative" concept of form—a new sense of structure (form or style conceived broadly) and of diction (form or style conceived "locally")—that can make the most private utterance an "objective" phenomenon, and vice versa, by making words themselves seem both objective and connotative.

FIVE

Williams and the American Beauty: The Objective Use of Words

Objectivity and Things

"No ideas but in things": when Williams summarizes this first necessity for modern writing, he is talking about the need for two kinds of objectivity, both toward the world and toward words. His belief in the power of words when they're used objectively, that is, stems from a fundamental belief in the power and significance of objective things in the physical world. In his axiom Williams is not advocating literal-mindedness, nor "Naive Realism," nor even what Wallace Stevens calls the "anti-poetic." Rather, Williams assumes that "things" are important because if we can see them clearly, empirically, we can more clearly define our relations to the external world (and paradoxically to our inner selves). Williams is arguing for a Whitmanian ideal, a perfect use of language by means of a clean and efficient use of "things" within words. Whitman called things our "dumb beautiful ministers," because they "furnish" their "parts toward the soul." For the same reason, Williams wants to write poems that can liberate things to be both physical and metaphysical, vehicles of both an objective truth and a subjective revelation.

The first commitment of Williams' objectivity, therefore, involves an attention to objects outside the self; frequently in the shorter poems, Williams recognizes a particular history or energy in a place or object or plant he observes, as the self recognizes the nonself outside it. But this movement is different, for instance, from a Romantic movement of the imagination, by which Wordsworth can see a pile of stones and on the basis of that evidence can project a history—like the story of Michael the shepherd whose son broke faith with the past. Though Wordsworth does claim in "Michael" that a similar event did in fact occur, his poem establishes the poet's personal association with the object (the stones) and creates a narrative history on the basis of both that observation and that imaginative association. (Things in Romantic lyrics often provoke this associativity in narrators: Wordsworth's ruined abbey and collapsed fence, Coleridge's sooty film in "Frost at Midnight," Keats' Grecian urn, Blake's sunflower, Whitman's star and lilac.) Williams' objective sense of the external object, by contrast, makes his imagination not project but introject. His use of history is more direct and, at the same time, less personally associative. Like Rilke, Williams tries to see the indigenous history of the thing *in* the thing (not in memory or feeling), and so to remake a "history" for the thing within the restructured "world" of the poem.

In "The Yachts," for instance, Williams tells essentially two different poems (1935: *CEP* pp. 106–7).The first, in the opening seven stanzas, is pure observation ("The Yachts/ contend in a sea which the land partly encloses"), filtered through an admittedly personal sensibility but nevertheless relying on objective presentation to register the "thing." The diction is sometimes metaphorical, but the metaphors seem designed more to convey the external reality of the thing than to associate the thing with some abstract conceptual or emotional argument ("Now the sea which holds them/ is moody, lapping their glossy sides.") When the wind dies and then revives, the poem begins again ("The yachts/ move, jockeying for a start"), but in the course of the race, in the final four stanzas, the narrative assumes a social context and history, "until the horror of the race dawns staggering the mind." The struggle of the contending yachts against one another and against the sea suggests a social and economic conflict underlying the scenic upper-class event, the race of the sleek yachts. Unlike Wordsworth,

Williams infers a tacit history in the object, not an associative history projected from the imagination or memory of the observer. Throughout *Paterson,* too, the poet's dialogue with the history of the place (the prose in smaller typeface) is distinct from the personal history and associations of Dr. P. (in verse). (Williams seems to have learned this use of prose materials from Marianne Moore's use of quotations in her lyrics, from Pound's use of allusions in the *Cantos,* and from Nathaniel West's use of fictional letters in *Miss Lonelihearts,* 1933).[28]

What obscures our perception of the objective, natural, experiential thing is not the innate limitation of individual perception, but our arbitrary restrictions on our verbal abilities to articulate what we do experience; we simply do not see the world clearly, because corrupt forms of language and outmoded conceptions intervene between us and the world. From the 1920s through the rest of his career, Williams seems obsessed with images of clarification, of connection and synthesis, of doubled "revelation" (from the outside in and from the inside out). Though he has been misunderstood because of his apparently "anti-poetic" bias, I think it should be clear by now how much Williams' belief in the importance of "things" in poetry is part of a larger argument about the proper use of "things" for the liberation of perception.

Works like "Spring and All," "The Rose," and "To a Solitary Disciple" (1917) emphasize the relations between the external, objective configurations of things, with which the imagination should keep faith, and the internal configurations which the modern imagination will also "reveal" or "construct" in a mediating form. As "To a Solitary Disciple" illustrates, a scrupulous attention to the geometry of facts is essential to the imagination's grounding in the external world.

TO A SOLITARY DISCIPLE

Rather notice, mon cher,
that the moon is
tilted above
the point of the steeple
than that its color
is shell-pink.

Rather observe
that it is early morning
than that the sky
is smooth
as a turquoise.

Rather grasp
how the dark
converging lines
of the steeple
meet at the pinnacle—
perceive how
its little ornament
tries to stop them—

See how it fails!
See how the converging lines
of the hexagonal spire
escape upward—
receding, dividing!
—sepals
that guard and contain
the flower!

Observe
how motionless
the eaten moon
lies in the protecting lines.
It is true:
in the light colors
of morning

brown-stone and slate
shine orange and dark blue.

But observe
the oppressive weight
of the squat edifice!
Observe
the jasmine lightness
of the moon.
(*CEP*, pp. 167–68)

The disciple is "solitary," I presume, because he or she is not distracted by convention or by socially determined modes of per-

ception. The outside facts are significant but not because of an
observer's ability to construct fictions about them nor because in
a realistic self-sufficient way they are adequate materials for art.
Rather, the disciple needs specifically to notice the objective detailed facts in order to recognize accurately the implications of what
he sees. The poem opens with a rejection of metaphor, association, and private interpretation of the scene:

> Rather notice, mon cher,
> that the moon is
> tilted above
> the point of the steeple
> than that its color
> is shell-pink.

The "facts" about this scene are formal, almost geometrical—not
associative, emotive, or impressionistic. (The angle of the moon's
ascent is more important than the moon's "shell-pink" color.) As
the poem continues, the attentive imagination looks and looks and
then continues to look, even after the thing itself has been exhausted as an object of perception; then the imagination pivots
and continues, beginning its own invention as a continuation of
the shape of the physical thing it has been observing. The imaginative assertion takes its impetus from the angle of the steeple, but
it constructs, appropriately, an answering shape that comes to resemble a mental flower. Williams' "idea" in the "thing" is a geometry that answers the "literal" geometric forms of the thing
with a completing, fulfilled, abstract geometric form; just as the
human eye pivots and reverses the image it sees, on the retina, in
order to carry the image to the brain, so the imagination pivots
and projects the image of the "thing" in order to understand it for
what it is. The poem admits that the imagination makes images or
symbols from items of experience in order to organize perception,
but then the speaker seems to suggest that sometimes such symbols can obfuscate, instead. As the disciple's eye follows the line of
the steeple, it sees a crucifix:

> Rather grasp
> how the dark

> converging lines
> of the steeple
> meet at the pinnacle—
> perceive how
> its little ornament
> tries to stop them—

The lines "converge" into a cross because of our tendency to make abstract truths (like fixed religious dogma and symbolism) to represent our truths, to make them sharable and common. And yet such a use of predetermined symbols presumes that the truth of the symbol precedes the particular occasion. We are tempted therefore to see the thing (crucifix) and to associate it with a fixed, predetermined truth; what we miss in this use of the symbol is an encounter with *this* building, *this* steeple, *this* place. Whitman, for one, had tried to avoid this standardization of symbols. In section 6 of "Song of Myself," for instance, Whitman had presented the grass first of all, as the central mystery. In order to comprehend that mystery Whitman finds eventually he has to resort to metaphorical associations: the grass is the flag of his disposition, the handkerchief of the Lord, and so on. The mysterious *thisness* of the grass, however, precedes Whitman's metaphorical extrapolations. Similarly, in "To a Solitary Disciple" Williams insists that as the imagination works to construct an abstract understanding of this particular scene, the observer must not assume that a symbolic truth precedes the truth of the particular literal thing. The "little ornament" of the crucifix on the steeple—that received cultural icon—"tries to stop" the movement of the imaginative eye. But

> See how it fails!
> See how the converging lines
> of the hexagonal spire
> escape upward—
> receding, dividing!
> —sepals
> that guard and contain
> the flower!

And this poem of advice concludes on a preferential judgment. The speaker clearly finds the flower of the imagination as graceful

and as lasting as the cruder facts of the perceived world. Nevertheless, this imaginative "flower" is visible only because the imagination has stayed true to the "shape" of things as they appear.

> But observe
> the oppressive weight
> of the squat edifice!
> Observe
> the jasmine lightness
> of the moon.

Between these two alternatives—the literal building or the mental
flower—Williams ultimately values the moon-flower more. He ex-
presses this preference both aurally and rhythmically: heavily
stressed consonantal stops for the physical version ("oppressive
weight," "squat edifice"), clear open vowels and sibilants for the
imagination's construct ("Observe/ the jasmine lightness/ of the
moon.") These last three lines, taken as a syntactical unit, make a
line of perfect iambic pentameter—we don't necessarily recognize
it but we sense its consoling metrical regularity—as the imagination paradoxically returns to perception both a sense of traditional
reassurance (in the rhythm) and (in the image of the jasmine) an
organic freshness that not even the physical world, with its squat
edifice, had offered. The poem that began with a rejection of metaphor and association (in a gratuitous, personal sense) returns at
last to metaphor—now conceived as the necessary "shape" of the
"thing" as the imagination perceives and completes it. If we can
see the "flower" that the steeple's shape makes in the mind, then
we can metaphorically attribute "jasmine lightness" to our imaginative perception of the moon.

Throughout his career Williams fixes on that pinnacle of the
steeple, where learning and precise observation can find the accurate shape of things and where the constructions of the imagination touch and answer the shape of things in the world. That point
of contact is the "intersection of loci" (in the essay on Marianne
Moore), the "flame" that "jumps the gap" between inner and outer
worlds (in "Della Primavera Trasportata Al Morale"), the "hole in
the bottom of the bag" through which the imagination escapes

into its "secure world" (in *Paterson* V), the points of intersection of the threads of the Unicorn tapestries (again in *Paterson* V),[29] the "bridge" and "tightrope" and "marriage" that in its largest ambitions *Paterson* as a whole attempts to represent (as we'll see in the next sections).

As structural technique and as theme, this principle of intersection—between the physical world and the mental—is central to Williams' work. The ambition is especially urgent because the alternatives, according to Williams, are deadly processes: either Eliotic traditionalism, fantasy, and associativity, or a direct transcription of the external world's verities, a copying of "the oppressive weight/ of the squat edifice." But the modern imagination does not register the nuances of the external world simply in order to represent them mimetically, nor is the "new world" the imagination shapes a haven in which to escape from vulgar experience. (In any case, in anti-Freudian works like *Spring and All* Williams shows why such an escape would be illusory). Rather, the imagination answers—in words—nature's self-sufficient world with a world of its own device, a world of language, in which verbal energies mediate between external and internal forces. "A poem is a complete little universe," Williams writes in *Paterson*. "It exists separately" (*P*, p. 224). How this commitment to a scrupulous attention to the literal world results in a belief in the power of words to make a "complete little universe" is the subject of our next section.

Objectivity and Diction

In a 1947 essay entitled "Revelation," Williams states directly his basic proposition about the duality of the mind and the world: each is distinct, each in its way unknowable. One studies the things of the world for the evidence their "geometry" may afford the imagination, and one learns to know oneself, often, by triangulating against objects outside the self. The converting medium between the mind and the world is the imagination, which uses various "objective" media (words, paint, stone) for articulation. In the essay "Revelation" Williams makes the objectivity described in the preceding section the vehicle for a subjective "revelation" like that of Mallarmé.

The objective in writing is, to reveal. It is not to teach, not to advertise, not to sell, not even to communicate (for that needs two) but to reveal, which needs no other than the man himself. . . . Reveal what? That which is inside the man.[30]

"Life becomes actual," Williams generalizes elsewhere, "only when it is identified with ourselves"—that is, when the imagination links us actively with the world. The imagination can lead the individual out of the isolate personal consciousness and into a border-territory, like Hawthorne's realm of "romance," where the self and the nonself can meet in an observed, represented object. Such an attitude clearly requires a certain detachment in the workings of the imagination, a detachment that comes from an awareness of the materials, words for instance, which the imagination seizes to shape its new forms. This jump between fact and emotional reality is constantly new, constantly in the process of being created, and artistic work that "bridges the gap" is "real":

It is new, immediate. It is so because it is actual, always real. It is experience dynamized into reality.[31]

For poetry "has to do with the crystallization of the imagination—the perfection of new forms as additions to nature." Such an attitude requires that the self purify, objectify, its observations. Then the self can "expand" beyond personal identity, toward that "new" border-territory of clarity. That expansiveness, the imagination's paradoxically self-realizing power beyond the private self, once again recalls Whitman's democratic largeness-and-intimacy:

No man could suffer the fragmentary nature of his understanding of his own life—

Whitman's proposals are of the same piece with the modern trend toward imaginative understanding of life. The largeness which he interprets as his identity with the least and the greatest about him, his "democracy" represents the vigor of his imaginative life.[32]

That imaginative or "democratic" expansion of the self is the basis for Whitman's participatory sense of the life around him. But Williams reverses the Whitmanian pattern. Where Whitman's work is transcendental and trans-substantiating and metaphoric (I = you, you = I), Williams' is immanent, trans-signifying, and metonymic. Or to put it more simply: as in "Danse Russe," Williams' private self implies the larger self (household or nation or external perspective), reversing the Whitmanian pattern. For Williams, the imaginative impulse comes as often from the particularly observed thing, or from the individual self, as from the demands of the larger public world for articulation. The imaginative "enlargement" toward significance—as at the end of "Danse Russe"—is the modern imagination's understanding of that discrete smaller unit, an understanding that jumps the gap, in words, between the internal and the external worlds.

Whitman presumed such a contact and celebrated it from the start, often by beginning with the larger Self and then moving back toward intimacy. Williams longs for that ideal connection—he does not presume it—and therefore he works to construct it by working its terms backwards, from the small to the large.

> As birds' wings beat the solid air without which none could fly so words freed by the imagination affirm reality by their flight. . . .
>
> Sometimes I speak of imagination as a force, an electricity or a medium, a place. It is immaterial which: for whether it is the condition of a place or the dynamization its effect is the same: to free the world of fact from the impositions of "art". . . . and to liberate the man to act in whatever direction his disposition leads.[33]

Here Williams states clearly his double purpose. The imagination is objectified in words, which jump between inner and outer worlds. As they do, they both "free the world of fact" from the restrictions of conventional perception and also "liberate the man." Clear sight and purified words, through the imagination, free both the world and the individual: thus the importance of objectivity in our encounters with the world, and thus the importance of "objectivism," or of objective verbalism in our use of words, to keep that medium free from smudge, contamination, traditional associations, convention, "art." Rilke calls this pure power the "angel" who returns us to the earth, while Wallace Stevens calls it the "necessary angel" of the compelling physical world. Typically, Williams describes the same power with a metaphor of "birds' wings," described both organically and aerodynamically: Williams' metaphor associates the Romantics' descriptions of the imagination as "organic" with the modernists' interest in mechanical forms. The imagination "frees" both the organic private imagination (like Wordsworth's) and the mechanized public modern world.

Williams' "objectivism," the "verbalism" he praises in works by Joyce, Moore, Stein, and others, is an application of these principles of theory to matters of style. Verbal Objectivism transfers the poet's attention from the objective reality of the external world to the equally objective, active contingencies of his verbal construct, the poem. "A work of art is important only as evidence, in its structure, of a new world which it has been created to affirm," Williams writes in "Against the Weather" (1939). Thus the poem "in its structure" makes a "new world" for the poet, who resembles Christopher Columbus in his approach to the literal New World. Because it fixes the ephemeral geometries of the imagination, the world of the poem is distinct both from the world of things and from the internal world of the observer. Though their geometries may be related, the aesthetic third term is not a "copy" of inner or of outer worlds: the words of the modern poem are "purified," "scrubbed clean," so that the poet can "engineer" or "build" a "new place."

In his essays and poems, especially those written after the mid-1920s, Williams often insists on the machinelike purity and precision of words for the modern poem. His famous description of Marianne Moore's method is a good example of this aesthetic commitment:

With Miss Moore a word is a word most when it is separated out by science, treated with acid to remove the smudges, washed, dried, and placed right side up on a clean surface. Now one may say that this is a word.[34]

If the poem is a "small (or large) machine made of words," as Williams defines it elsewhere, then the poem's individual units—words, phrases, rhythms—should fit as efficiently as mechanical cogs: the poet should purify the words and should engineer the poem "objectively," "scientifically." Paul Valéry had postulated a similar ideal, the poem's machinelike transmission of energy, when he defined the poem as "une sorte de machine à produire l'état poétique au moyen des mots."[35] Both machine and poem transmit energy by changing the form it takes, and by channeling it to use for deliberate purposes (for instance, to produce "the poetic state" efficiently.)

To illustrate his point about words as "things," about the modern artist's self-conscious use of materials, Williams liked to tell a story:

> Alanson Hartpence was employed at the Daniel Gallery. One day, the proprietor being out, Hartpence was in charge. In walked one of their most important customers, a woman in her fifties who was much interested in some picture whose identity I may at one time have known. She liked it, and seemed about to make the purchase, walked away from it, approached it and said finally, "But Mr. Hartpence, what is all that down in this left hand lower corner?"
>
> Hartpence came up close and carefully inspected the area mentioned. Then, after further consideration, "That, Madam," said he, "is paint."[36]

The beginning of the modern artist's self-conscious use of the artistic medium, Williams concludes, marked the "transition of a work of art as a copying of nature to the thought of it as the imitation of nature." Later in his *Autobiography* he returns to this "objective" attitude toward the medium of the artwork, once again claiming to find the most important experimentation of this kind in the work of post-Cézanne Expressionist and Cubist painters:

> It is in the taking of that step over from feeling to the imaginative object, on the cloth, on the page, that defined the term, the modern term—a work of art, what it meant to them. . . . This is a hard climb, it was for me—a hard thing to accomplish, but it is that which must be accomplished before sentimentality can be abolished and the thing itself emerge, liberating the man.[37]

When the "thing" is thus liberated, the human is liberated: Williams' "scientific" objectivity has a humanistic ambition. This commitment to the objectivity of the medium led Williams toward a concern with "the way the image was to lie on the page," by expansion of the image to include that which was "implied in the materials, respecting the place I knew best. . . . finding a local assertion—to my everlasting relief."[38]

In this period—beginning shortly before World War I and intensifying throughout the 1920s—Williams and others applied the "modern term" to their own work and eventually formulated a theory of "Objectivism," which stressed the importance of the objective world, of the poet's personal "objectives," and also of the mediating, "objective" properties of the word. The Objectivists (notably Williams, Louis Zukofsky, Charles Reznikoff, and George Oppen, later Kenneth Rexroth and then Basil Bunting in England) argued that the poem,

like every other form of art, is an object, an object that in itself formally presents its case and its meaning by the very form it assumes. Therefore, being an object, it should be so treated and controlled—but not as in the past. For past objects have about them past necessities—like the sonnet—which have conditioned them and from which, as a form itself, they cannot be freed.[39]

The poet, therefore, must work with the "object" of the poem, with words construed as "things," to make a new thing "consonant with his day."

Williams even published his *Collected Poems, 1921–1931* with the Objectivist Press, run by Zukofsky and funded by Oppen. His affinities with the Objectivist group, which even at its most active was only loosely a "movement," reflect nevertheless a consistent attitude throughout his work, even after his associations with the other poets in the group had somewhat diminished.[40] We should be careful, however, not to take Williams' homiletics here too literally. Even while he claims the poet should scrub words clean to reveal their essential denotative character, Williams is arguing through a submerged metaphor—a poem *is* a small machine—in an argument not all that different from Eliot's theory of the "objective correlative."[41] A poem and a machine do share certain characteristics (both transmit "energy," both are governed by rules of engineering or syntax, and so on). But a poem is identical with a machine only in a metaphorical sense. That is, in his advocacy of a "purified" native idiom, even in this statement of the word's objective purity, Williams assumes that all poetic language is fundamentally metaphorical.[42] Williams berates those whom he calls "Puritans" for their insistence on seeing something else (abstract Truth) when they look at physical things. But Williams' own use of the metaphor here assumes that all poetic language—all language chosen to be in a poem—has an ability to suggest an abstraction arising even from the expression of immediate literal "facts"; apparently the word's appearance in the context of a poem endows it with a Benjaminian aura that makes a reader begin to think metaphorically.

The difference from the "Puritan's" concept is that Williams claims his abstraction should be unpremeditated, immediately pertinent, and defined by its context. Williams' sense of "generality" is related more to construction than to conceptual abstraction. Now, the substitution of a word's primary category of meaning for another category, the exchange of fields of reference for a word, is the process we traditionally call "metaphor." (The word in ancient Greek means literally "transport" or "transfer"; in modern Athens to ride in a crosstown bus, or in a truck, is to travel in a "metaphor.") Though Williams may call the process "intersection," "construction," "objectivism," or "verbalism," the process is clearly metaphorical, a transfer or overlapping of meanings for a word, as he carries the word into new contexts. This procedure lets us read "ideas" in "things" because of the overlapping of the connotations of certain words used to depict the thing. (In *Finnegans Wake* Joyce carries the process one step further, into pure verbalism. Both terms of his metaphors are verbal, without primary denotation of a "thing": thus the wild and abstract Joycean pun.)

William Carlos Williams' significant discovery here is to make a complete poem the vehicle of a single integral metaphor, the tenor of which is not stated but implied, so that the whole poem is a single enlarged metonymy, one half of a metaphor of which the other half is not overtly given. Denise Levertov, one of the most gifted and influential followers of Williams, succinctly explains: " 'No ideas but in things' does not mean 'no ideas'. . . . It means

that poetry appears when meaning is embodied in the figure."[43]
The "objectivity" of the poet's words can make possible this use
of the whole poem as a metonymy, because through such
"scrubbed" words the poet can control the associations of words
within the poem, to suggest the metaphor's other side without
stating it directly.

This procedure sounds like Williams' description of Marianne
Moore's method, and although Williams does learn much of this
"objective" aesthetic from Moore's example, his elaboration of the
aesthetic differs, slightly, from Moore's. As they work to enact the
theory in specific poems, both poets discover that a certain prosiness, even a potential chilliness, threatens to enter the poem because of this "objectivity" of tone, of observation, and of diction.
Moore begins her poem "Marriage," therefore, by inviting that
possibility in order to dismiss it:

> This institution,
> perhaps one should say enterprise
> out of respect for which
> one says one need not change one's mind
> about a thing one has believed in,
> requiring public promises
> of one's intention
> to fulfil a private obligation:
> I wonder what Adam and Eve
> think of it by this time[44]

After the polysyllabic and impersonal theorizing of the first eight
lines, the droll and personal speculation that follows comes as a
refreshing surprise. Here Moore invites the possibility of prosiness
or of chilliness in order to dispel it; she then continues the poem
largely as a dialogue between Adam and Eve. The conversation is
widely allusive, with Adam quoting Trollope, Pound, and Daniel
Webster, among others, while Eve cites the Bible, Shakespeare,
and the founder of Mount Holyoke College. These unfootnoted
allusions, given in quotation marks in the poem, in effect provide
the ballast of otherness, the "transfer" or "tenor" that a metaphor
requires. Thus Moore manages to write a strongly "metaphorical"

poem without using conventional metaphors. In his own application of the "objective" aesthetic, Williams tries at times to use this allusiveness as a model (in much of *Paterson,* for instance, though his allusions in that poem are directed, less wide-ranging). Williams' response to the tonal challenge is usually more structural, more conventionally metaphorical: he chooses and arranges his "objective" details so that the image can be cleanly independent and yet can still suggest abstract configurations of meaning. The "naked," "uncertain" green shoots of vegetation in "Spring and All" are a good example of this effect, which sometimes only narrowly escapes anthropomorphism. When he has the technique under control, however, Williams can make the combination of objectivity and suggestiveness seem hauntingly appropriate. Some of my favorite examples are Williams' short sketches of flowers, in lines and phrases that register the essence of the separate flower clearly but that nevertheless—because of that lucidity—can suggest emotional or narrative or metaphorical possibilities. The "solitary" scent of orange blossoms; the "eternally/ unready" forsythia; the "tingling" leaves of early spring; the "greeny" petals of the pale and woody asphodel: in these examples, all from *Pictures from Brueghel,* the observation is accurate and the diction is objective, and yet the descriptions are suggestive enough that they seem almost-metaphorical, without drifting toward the pathetic fallacy.

When he calls for an "objective" use of words, then, Williams is working to shed the word's former associations (literary, historical, or personal), in order ultimately to give the word a greater contextual suggestiveness within the poem. When W. B. Yeats, by contrast, entitles a poem "The Secret Rose," he implicity requires the alert reader to add depth to that image by supplying wide-ranging associations. The word "rose," in Yeats' context, carries implications of Blake's sick rose, of the allegorical rose of alchemy, of the rose upon the rood of time, of the mystical rose of the Rosicrucians, of Ireland, of Tudor England, and so forth.[45] Especially in his early and middle poems, Yeats' flowers strike literary roots.[46]

For Williams, the flower in the poem aspires "objectively" to register the mental energy a rose in the world, objectively seen, provokes in the mind. In a poem entitled "The Rose" (1939), for instance, Williams begins without even description. Here is the full poem:

THE ROSE

First the warmth, variability
color and frailty

A grace of petals skirting
the tight-whorled cone

Come to generous abandon—
to the mind as to the eye

Wide! Wider!
Wide as if panting, until

the gold hawk's-eye speaks once
coldly its perfection

(*CEP,* p. 369)

The poem opens almost within the flower itself, not with Whitmanian sympathy but with observation so detailed that one is uncomfortably uncertain whether the point of view is that of an observer or that of the rose:

First the warmth, variability
color and frailty

The poem then continues like a stop-action film of a rose opening, in motion. As the flower unfolds, its dilation comes to sound erotic, generous, and warmly feminine. Simultaneously, the reader's relation to the rose changes, as we become less the observer and more the potential lover:

Come to generous abandon—
to the mind as to the eye

Halfway through "The Rose" this slight shift, like the pivot at the steeple of the "Solitary Disciple" poem, reminds us that this "rose" is somehow both physical and mental: it is visible "to the eye," as a physical thing, and yet it is also visible "to the mind." Its metaphorically erotic accessibility, its "generous abandon," makes it seem almost-abstract. That is, the more we see the rose as itself, opening, the more it invites us into a relation with it, a relation that partakes both of the physical and the mental, as sexuality does:

> Wide! Wider!
> Wide as if panting, until

Until what? Until the flower fully opens? Until sexual engagement? Until we go so deeply into our observation of the flower that we lose ourselves? Until we go so deeply into the flower visible "to the mind" that we see its essence *as* a conceptual flower, in the mind? Just who is seducing whom here? In all these possibilities, we expect somehow more largesse and warmth (the fullness of the flower, the sexual conjunction, the nature of the image fully revealed "to the mind"), but when the rose does finally open, at the end of the poem,

> the gold hawk's-eye speaks once
> coldly its perfection

The literal "hawk's eye" is, presumably, the sexual stamen-and-pistil organs of the flower, not fully visible until the bud has opened. That is, this image does complete the movement of the poem, in terms of the literal figure (the opening flower) and in the erotic undertones (the petals open toward the stamen-and-pistil, the sexual organs of the plant). This ending also metaphorically completes the pattern of the poem involving the rose "visible to the mind": we are looking at the flower, and at the end the flower seems to be looking at us, with its "eye," as if in a perfect reciprocity. But to call that part of the flower a "gold hawk's eye" also seems to shift perspective. As at the end of "Danse Russe," the journey into specificity, into relation with the specific thing, surprisingly leads to a displacement, to an objective and distanced point of view, like a hawk's. The "erotic" heat and motion of the description lead to a "perfection"; but it is a "cold" and objective perfection, reachable only through the heat of the rose. That is, at the center of the specific rose *and* at the clitoral apex of this "erotic" experience *and* at the heart of the image visible "to the mind," we find an access to a keen objectivity, an essentiality. The rose concludes the poem, looking at us and speaking its "perfection," as if this sudden objectivity liberates both the "thing" (rose) and the observer. The bond between the rose and the observer/lover seemed to be erotic, but by the end that bond is not so much erotic as abstract, the image visible fully "to the mind." Sex is both intensely personal and oddly impersonal, abstract: thus Williams uses the submerged metaphor of eroticism to describe the way this mental image of the rose similarly mediates between subjectivity and objectivity, just as Marianne Moore had written about "marriage" in an objective-and-yet-personal way.

The "rose" in this short Williams poem mediates between the private experience of viewing a rose and the public experience of seeing through a hawk's eye, objectively. At the intersection of the private and the external experiences is the image of the rose "visible to the mind," in the word/thing "rose." Just as Elsie's name appears only once in "To Elsie," as if to unite the objective and the subjective worlds she incarnates, so here too Williams uses the word/thing "rose" to show how the personal and the impersonal realms can be joined, in a name.

Through this mediation, Williams argues, his use of the word or of the image "rose" is "objective," intended to suggest an "idea" by presenting the "thing itself," an opening rose. A rose is a rose is . . . a "rose." Words, too, are things: the things of the poem's world, which is neither the physical world of organic roses nor the internal world of unsharable mental images of roses. Williams' word "rose" is self-consciously a word, a unit of measured denotation, and the measure by which it mediates and transmits meaning is a central concern of Williams throughout his career. For Williams the test of metaphorical depth in a poem is not whether historical or cultural or emotional associations can be supplied through the use of a word in a poem. Rather, Williams wants directly to bring into the poem the mental energy that an objective encounter with a rose might arouse "to the mind." From that direct objective encounter, registered objectively in "scrubbed" name, a cleaner and newer sense of the metaphorical significance of the "thing" should arise. Thus the ambitions that make Williams require an objective sense of physical vision for himself (as described in the preceding section) are the same ambitions that make him work toward an "objective" diction for his verse.

POEM

The rose fades
and is renewed again
by its seed, naturally
but where

save in the poem
shall it go
to suffer no diminution
of its splendor

(*PB*, p. 39)

Objectivity and Systems

In a Williams poem, especially one as self-reflexive as *Paterson*, words are objective units of signification. They register discrete objects or imaginative energies within the world the poem shapes, without relying for their importance on the associations readers bring to the text. (There are notable exceptions: sometimes Williams does use mythic and historical figures to carry clusters of conventional cultural information, but he tends to use such figures typologically, and often in recombinative identities. The figure of "St. Francis Einstein" recalls St. Francis and Einstein and Venus and Columbus: the "idea" he personifies is a "new" idea, a synthesis of traditional associations.) Thus the poet "cleans" words and uses them "locally" in the "little universe" of the poem. Accordingly, Williams' insistence on the "local" fidelity of art relates as much to his techniques as to his theme—for the poet "locates" the words and lines and sections in space and time, in a poem that is a distinct "place." J. Hillis Miller characterizes the dynamic: "The word is given positive reality by the fact that it names, but the independence of the fact from the word frees the word to be a fact in its own right, and at the same time 'dynamizes' it with meaning."[47]

The surgical purity Williams describes, however, does not suggest that words register only their dynamic surfaces. Free from restrictive historical associations, objects and words in Williams' constructed "world" reflect on each other in context, acquiring "historical" significance within the limited specific "history" Williams constructs in the lyrical sections and in the reordered historical facts of the prose sections. In *Paterson* the illusion of sequential, experiential time diminishes, but the illusion of historical depth intensifies, for the word echoes in its appearances through the poem, giving a sense of the hidden relations among objects that appear superficially distinct. Williams' shorter poems had concentrated on the moment of revelation: the rose expands to a hawk's-eye perfection, the green plants break through, the man dances naked. But The Moment in those poems is counterhistorical, out-of-time. A city, by contrast, accretes; it does not bloom. Having mastered the art of the illuminated moment, Williams still needs to find a compositional way to make an art of continuity and of connection, without sacrificing the integrity of the purified word. His further theme, therefore, is the emergence of the language of the larger poem itself, in its attempt to represent the historical development of the place (Paterson: city, man, and poem).

The assertion that there are to be "no ideas but in the facts" relates to the theme of a man as a city, in *Paterson,* by means of this connecting theme of the poem's self-conscious search for its own language. The objective use of words, the scraping clean of words from arbitrary associations, leaves the writer free to "build" the city of new relations on the page. Williams' theme of "locality" in a cultural mode is also the theme of the "language," converted to formal terms. Thus he writes that Marianne Moore, who "despised connectives," shapes a poetry in which words show their "edges," arranged in an "edge-to-edge" contact with other words, just as the articulation of a culture in an artifact "fixes" the culture for history, and just as the things of the outside world abut each other to form abstractly "geometrical" structures.[48] The effort of all these "objectifications" is to provide a mediating structure between tradition and democratic historicity, between fixedness and randomness, between exteriority and interiority, between gigantism and privacy. The "Preface" opens *Paterson* by stating one side of the problem,[49] in prose:

> "Rigor of beauty is the quest. But how will you find beauty when it is locked in the mind past all remonstrance?"
>
>   (*P*, p. 3)

That question states the problem in terms of the private self. The "Preface" then quickly shifts to verse and represents the poet-as-dog, digging in the loam, as if to remind us of the countervailing problems of the public self. That abutment, without explanatory bridge, is typical of this "edge-to-edge" effect in the new Williams work.

The largest effort of *Paterson* is this attempt to marry in language the general with the particular, the giant (male and inner world of private beauty) with the landscape (female, external, "loam"). In his essays Williams also draws the analogy at length, in terms of craft. While discussing Marianne Moore's poem "Marriage," Williams arrives at his pivotal discovery that the modern poem should be a collection of intersecting loci forming a web — a constellation of knots important both for its structure and for its opacity. On the one hand, the poem has its shape, the grid of intersections:

Poetry has taken many disguises which by cross reading or intense penetration it is possible to go through to the core. Through intersection of loci their multiplicity may become revelatory. The significance of much reading being that this "thing" grow clearer, remain fresh, be more present to the mind.

On the other hand, though it may sound paradoxical, the weblike poem is important because its "open" structure, made of familiar elements, can let the light of the luminous background, both the inner light and the familiar culture from which it arises, shine through—like the effect of Moore's quotations and like the Beautiful Thing of objective being that Paterson's medical work enables him to see closely. Marianne Moore places words edge-to-edge, omitting conjunctions and transitions, and yet the poetry that results is an "inevitable connective":

Marriage, through which thought does not penetrate, appeared to Miss
Moore a legitimate object for art, an art that would not halt from using
thought about it, however, as it might want to. . . . The interstices for
the light and not the interstitial web of the thought concerned her, so it
seems to me. Thus the material is as the handling: the thought, the word,
the rhythm—all in the style. The effect is in the penetration of the light
itself, how much, how little; the appearance of the luminous background.[50]

From these two compositional elements, the object with its edges
and the contact of its edges with the perimeters of other objects,
Williams derives a formal ideal for the modern poem, an ideal that
approximates a definition of marriage in a linguistic mode. Each
word or element is discrete and independent and purified, but the
composition (marriage) of the elements can embody a holistic
unity. In his insistence on the integrity of things Williams continues a commitment he had made long before, with poems like "The
Red Wheelbarrow." In earlier—shorter—poems, the single figures in their "peculiar perfections"[51] are the full vehicle of the implied metaphor; the mute objects of the physical world express a
tacit language or a numinous meaning the poet apprehends and
restates. In *Paterson,* the "objects" of the long poem's world (discrete sections of prose or of verse) are similarly integral and self-
contained, awaiting the action of a reader to apprehend their significance and relations. Where Whitman had expanded his orders
of meaning concentrically around a central Self, Williams diffuses
the edges of his orders of meaning, making them overlap—like
Venn diagrams or Joycean puns.

Thus throughout *Paterson* Williams works to reach from the
sleeping giant who "dreams" the present, to his female counterpart, whose plentitude is the world's richness. The foremost thematic tension in *Paterson* is also its structural problem: to reconcile
the (male) "dream," or principle of contraction and unity, with
the (female) "bloody loam," or principle of expansion and multiplicity. The poem intends, Williams writes, to produce "by multiplication a reduction to one"—for the inner world is sometimes
luminous but inaccessible, the outer world sometimes lovely but

chaotic. Williams proposes several metaphors to describe this ideal reconciliation: the "radiant gist" (in physical/imaginative terms), the "song" or "intersection" (in imaginative/structural terms), the "tightrope" or "marriage" (in structural/thematic terms arising from the poem's physical images). To walk the tightrope, to marry, to connect: the pressured repetition of these metaphorical ideals suggests the intensity of the problem. The inchoate connection *will be* the language of the poem itself. Thus the theme is also the structuring principle of *Paterson:* the "tightrope" and the "marriage," for instance, are images of binding, and as repeated metaphors they also function throughout *Paterson* to bind the whole poem together. I'd like to look at each of these two metaphors a bit more closely, to see how they function *as* metaphors—and then to ask how they accomplish the "structuring" that is Williams' formal challenge for *Paterson*.

The "tightrope" is the more overt figure of connection. In the opening movements of Book I, the Whitmanian giant lies beside his bride, the mountain, and between them the river runs. Simultaneously the Passaic River, the mystery of language, and the potential for destruction and regeneration in its divisive roaring, the river geographically separates and thus defines "male" and "female" worlds, city and landscape.

> From above, higher than the spires, higher
> even than the office towers, from oozy fields
> abandoned to grey beds of dead grass,
> black sumac, withered weed-stalks,
> mud and thickets cluttered with dead leaves—
> the river comes pouring in above the city
> and crashes from the edge of the gorge
> in a recoil of spray and rainbow mists—
>
> > (What common language to unravel?
> > . . combed into straight lines
> > from that rafter of a rock's
> > lip.)
>
> A man like a city and a woman like a flower
>
> (*P*, pp. 6–7)

The attempt to bridge the Falls at the head of the river is metaphorically a linguistic attempt, in the figure of the "tightrope"; just
as Williams aspires to "comb" into a "line" the tangled water of
the river, so the tightrope-walkers over the Falls negotiate a "line"
across the nonverbal power beneath them. The "tightrope" is Williams' metaphor of the process of metaphor, a "transfer" or "exchange."

The poem *Paterson* is the tightrope Williams/Paterson walks.
Williams jokes about this ambition and even denies, at times, that
such an attempt can succeed; in the first appearance of Sam Patch,
for instance, a bridge-builder named Timothy B. Crane has built
an arc that failed, occasioning Patch's first dramatic jump across
the Falls. Crane's "bridge" here should probably remind us of Hart
Crane's problematic and Whitmanian epic *The Bridge* (1930), a different bridging attempt toward a similar ideal.[52] Like Crane's poem,
Tim Crane's attempt to bridge the gap is apparently a loosely organized, unstable construct, compared in Book I with the more
compact, robust, leaping, organic connection Sam Patch makes:

> These were the words that Sam Patch said: "Now, old
> Tim Crane thinks he has done something great; but
> I can beat him." As he spoke he jumped.
>
> There's no mistake in Sam Patch!
>
>   The water pouring still
> from the edge of the rocks, filling
> his ears with its sound, hard to interpret.
> A wonder!
>
>   (*P*, p. 17)

In *Paterson* III, iii, at the depth of his discouragement after the
flood of his city, Paterson doubts even the effort to "build bridges."
This failure of "engineering" seems to refer both to Eliot's "frame-
work" *and* to Crane's "aerodynamic" hope:

>   The seepage has
> rotted out the curtain. The mesh
> is decayed. Loosen the flesh
> from the machine, build no more

bridges. Through what air will you
fly to span the continents? Let the words
fall any way at all—that they may
hit love aslant. It will be a rare
visitation.

(*P*, p. 142)

Even in this section, however, the effort to "go down" results in a crossing, of sorts: though bridges fail, the spectacular efforts by Patch and Paterson to cross the Falls still seem heroic, because the need to bridge the gap in some way is still urgent. "The Falls let out a roar as it crashed upon the rocks at its base," Williams recalls in his *Autobiography*. "In the imagination this roar is a speech or a voice, a speech in particular; it is the poem itself that is the answer."[53] That roar, sounding also the threat of mute death, rushes beneath the speaker and floods to the unregenerate, indifferent sea.

In this context, the metaphorical tightrope-walkers of the poem, and those who leap the gap to cross, are the heroes of Williams' *Paterson*. Each major figure, in his own way, walks the line between two worlds, threatened by a silence that is also a roar beneath him. Patch leaps the notch; Harry Leslie walks a tightrope; Marie Curie links science and human generation; Noah Faitoute Paterson combines a city and a man ("Noah" for his "ark," "Faitoute" for the massiveness of his task,[54] "Paterson" because he is both city on the river and citizen). Even Book V of *Paterson* presents various "Madonnas" who link the human and divine realms, because each bears an Incarnation that is the Word objectified in flesh: the Unicorn joins animal and mythic worlds, Sappho links passion and aesthetics, the figures on the tapestries bind present and historical time in an artwork.[55] All these figures serve as metaphorical "bridges," models for Williams' effort in the poem to "marry" the mind to its surroundings. In Williams' original drafts to *Paterson* III (Buffalo mss.), the history of the tightrope-walkers in the city was to be the prime object of Faitoute's search in the library, but the history of the city's fires and floods (in the historical events that eventually replaced the tightrope-walkers as the object of his search) signals even more effectively the threat of dissolution that a failure to make adequate "forms" metaphorically implies.

Similarly, from his first notes toward *Paterson* I Williams proposes the theme of "marriage" as a binding metaphor of the binding power of language. To establish the proper "marriage" of individuals, or the link between mind and world, or the "edge-to-edge" contact of words, is the most important function of the "new" form, Williams notes to himself. "To marriage: no ideas but in things. Metaphor is a marriage—right and free" (Yale mss.). The "marriage" theme recalls that story of Whitman's discovering his poetic identity by compensation, after what Pound called the "affair of the southern Nancy." The story involves a marriage prohibited because of social prejudice; Pound had made it an allegory of American sterility and historical discontinuity, but as Williams retells it the central issue is one of freedom, as Whitman associates his incipient poetic identity with a compensatory internal "marriage."

Whitman took it from his Creole sweetie, whom he wanted to make his wife until his friends and relatives prevented him from marrying a "nigger," prevented his happiness, took it over into the field of letters. Freedom, was what he understood. That alone.[56]

Williams carries this metaphor wholesale into *Paterson,* in the "marriage" motif of the opening books. It appears in the first section's separation of the slumbering giant from his female counterpart, in Mrs. Cumming's tedious marriage, and in the poem's images of a "first wife" whose attributes are constancy and an ideal, wise beauty. In all these figures the desire the woman feels—and rouses—must be transmuted into language (an "interpenetration, both ways") because some obstacle frustrates the encounter. (Paterson is geographically separated from Garret Mountain, Mrs. Cumming drowns herself to escape her husband's "false language," the crowd in the city dies "incommunicado" because "Marriage comc[s] to have a shuddering/ implication," Doctor P. knows the "first wife" only through the memory of a photograph.) "Divorce," a "sign of the times," makes for a debased language—the "bud" is broken from the tree (p. 18)—but it also generates Paterson's obsession to "say" his world accurately, as a metaphor which "*is*" a marriage.

In this "divorced" cultural situation, "marriage" is the formalization of a binding power—like a tightrope, like a metaphor—and the poem, in its bridging attempt, is an epithalamion. Robert Lowell, who calls *Paterson* "our 'Leaves of Grass,'" suggests in a review of *Paterson* II that Williams in that book consistently hopes for a marriage that never happens.[57] He sustains that hope through all five books of *Paterson* and through much of his other work, from *Kora in Hell* (1920) to *Pictures from Brueghel* (1962). In the fifth book of *Paterson* Williams arrives at the realization, implicit from the beginning, that the strength of that marriage appears most strongly in the effort to achieve its union. That the marriage theme is the language theme ought to be clear: despite contemporary difficulties, the roaring glossolalia of the Falls is a sign of a wild verbal and erotic power.

> The giant in whose apertures we
> cohabit, unaware of what air supports
> us—the vague, the particular
> no less vague
>
> . . .
>
> We sit and talk,
> quietly, with long lapses of silence
> and I am aware of the stream
> that has no language, coursing
> beneath the quiet heaven of
> your eyes
>
> which has no speech; to
> go to bed with you
>
> (*P*, p. 24)

The landscape of the Falls is both a riddle and its answer:

> the answer is
> the language. It is
> without meaning
> That is the riddle.
> (Yale mss.)

In its other forms, the ideal marriage of mind and fact (counter-
pointing modern "divorce") is the riddle of the Falls, "the riddle
of a man and a woman," "a marriage riddle" (p. 105). Several times
in *Paterson,* Williams sets the question ("in the Joycean mode"),
most memorably in the library sequence of Book III, section i. In
that interlude, the marriage motif relates directly to the theme of
the Falls' voice and indirectly to the theme of the city's purifying
destruction by fire and flood. For "indifference" propounds a riddle:

> What end but love, that stares death in the eye?
> A city, a marriage—that stares death
> in the eye
>
> The riddle of a man and a woman
>
> For what is there but love, that stares death
> in the eye, love, begetting marriage—
> not infamy, not death
>
> .   .   .
>
> Sing me a song to make death tolerable, a song
> of a man and a woman: the riddle of a man
> and a woman.
> What language could allay our thirsts,
> what winds lift us, what floods bear us
>   past defeats
> but song but deathless song ?
>
> (*P,* pp. 106–7)

With the articulation of this mystery of love, then, a matrimonial
song rises from the river's roar, a song of the hermeneutically circular question:

> The rock
> married to the river
> makes
> no sound
>
> And the river
> passes—but I remain

                         clamant
                         calling   out   ceaselessly
                         to the birds
                         and clouds
          (listening)
                         Who am I?

                                        —the voice!

                  —the voice rises, neglected
                  (with its new) the unfaltering
                  language. Is there no release?
                                        (*P,* pp. 107–8)

"There is no direction," Paterson confesses at the start of his quest
in Book I, section ii. "Whither? I/ cannot say. I cannot say/ more
than how" (p. 18). And in his notes Williams declares the insolu-
bility of the question:

                  I ask no answer
                  to my riddle
                  only that it be reported

                  is all I propose
                                  (Yale mss.)

The paradox is that while he thematically declares this "marriage"
is the first requirement of the new poetic, Williams is writing a
marvelous poem of complaint about his failure to achieve such an
ideal verbal "marriage."

   So the "tightrope" and the "marriage" motifs are both thematic
and structural "systems" in *Paterson.* A man is a city and a city is
a man, Paterson, and both are complex organisms, composed of
such systems. Each system regulates a theme or argument that
seems self-contained yet incapable of sustaining life without the
context of other complementary patterns. Like the digestive, ner-
vous, and reproductive systems of the body—or like the govern-
mental, social, and economic networks of a city's "organism,"—
the "systems" of *Paterson* both perform with apparent self-com-

pleteness and also contribute, by their interrelations, to the larger composition. We may read discrete patterns of imagery related to tightropes, marriages, flowers, aesthetics, and so on, as those arguments work through the poem, yet the separate themes depend on each other for their larger coherence, history, shadows, and textures.[58] Thus, as we have briefly seen, the theme of marriage contains an argument about the nature of metaphor; the marriage metaphor is also related to the theme of the role of proper economics in the new world (in a late section of the poem linking "credit" with the "radiant gist" of Marie Curie's radium). The interconnectedness of these systems suggests that Williams is concerned to invent a structure (style conceived broadly) that could be both fixed and improvisational, just as he had worked out a diction (style conceived more locally) that was both objective and connotative.

This interconnectedness is not only Williams' overarching theme, that is, but also his principle of construction. The early drafts of *Paterson* reveal Williams at work to refine the intersecting "edge-to-edge" effect in each section of his poem. Often in these drafts Williams seems to have decided early which elements would go into each section, but he seems uncertain in what order to arrange the discrete blocks of prose or of verse, and he often cuts down long sections to a pith or a suggestive gist, instead of drawing conclusions and indicating connectives within the poem. Through several drafts Williams works to order those self-contained units so that their interrelations can become clearer—more tacit, more suggestive—in a holistic figure.

Because we've been discussing the "marriage" theme here, we might look, for example, at that section of the poem in which the lovely "first wife" lyric appears:

> and then   .   .
> the last, the first wife,
> present! supporting all the rest growing
> up from her—whose careworn eyes
> serious, menacing—but unabashed; breasts
> sagging from hard use   .   .
>
> (*P*, p. 13)

Williams decided early what the elements in the section would be; he finished the elements as separate lyrics, then began to recombine and to braid them. In the final version, ten pages of diverse text separate the introduction of this first wife ("I remember/ a *Geographic* picture, the 9 women/ of some African chief semi-naked/ astraddle a log") from the conclusion ("there is a first wife"). Between the introduction and the conclusion come the story of Mrs. Cumming, the first appearance of Sam Patch ("A wonder!"), Patch's demise (in prose: "Speech had failed him. He was confused. The word had been drained of its meaning.") Then, finally, comes an interlude with Doctor Paterson alone. Walking through the city, Dr. P. observes a specific "thing," a green bud broken from its branch:

> a bud forever green,
> tight-curled, upon the pavement, perfect
> in juice and substance but divorced, divorced
> from its fellows, fallen low—

And Paterson generalizes from this sign:

> Divorce is
> the sign of knowledge in our time,
> divorce! divorce!
>
> (*P,* p. 18)

This generalization leads Paterson to think about other signs of marital and linguistic divorce: "two halfgrown girls" he sees, who are uncertain of their cultural and sexual identities; Mrs. Cumming; Sam Patch; disenfranchised American Indians: all victims of a "fall" from linguistic order. In effect, Paterson here enumerates a series of subsequent "wives," in inadequate unions, as if by showing us their inadequacies he can postulate an ideal. He considers that ideal briefly in geographical metaphors but quickly personifies the abstraction, when he returns to the thought of that "first wife," who then reappears in the poem, the more luminously important because we had been away from her long enough to recognize the danger of her absence. This time she appears not visually but philosophically ("Which is to say, though it be poorly/

said, there is a first wife/ and a first beauty"; p. 22). By separating
the sections of this longer (first wife) lyric, Williams adds a connotative, contextual depth to the independent image.

Shuffling, rearranging, editing, Williams finally settles on an order here that can allow the structure to suggest the interpenetrat-
ing significance of discrete particulars. The ordering is not simply
improvised (as many critics of the poem claim); rather, Williams
works in a deliberate, twofold method of composition. Though
the individual sections sound like improvisation, one of Williams'
favorite techniques, the sequence is nevertheless an externally
structured whole. That process of doubled construction resembles
the ideal of verbal objectivism as Roy Harvey Pearce characterizes
it: the process begins with the realization that "to invent is at once
to find by making and to make by finding."[59] "Constructed" in
its larger orders and "organic" in its immediate (local) pieces, *Paterson*'s structures share that Whitmanian doubleness that also influences Williams' tone. Williams "structures" a shape with his
largest patterns of images, and he "improvises" within the separate
sections, in their lines, their associations, and their pace.

Finally, before we leave this question of "marriage" and of com-
binatory structures in *Paterson,* one possible difficulty remains. A
potential danger in this proliferation of metaphors about metaphor is that the connotations of different figures may work
against one another. One example of the problem might be the
apparent incompatibility of the "sexual" figures (city = male, landscape = female) and the "tightrope" metaphor. The combination
of the two sets of metaphors suggests that somehow the tightrope-
walkers must reconcile not only the abstract tenors of the metaphors (city/landscape, unity/diversity), but also the physical vehicles. They must bring male and female together, either in a sexual
conjunction ("marriage" or parenthood, by which the child shares
traits of the giant-father and the flowering mountain-mother), or
in a more internal conjunction (a kind of androgyny: "male" and
"female" are separate parts of a self Paterson needs to reconcile or
to conjoin). Insofar as the poem is a public gesture—reshaping
the relation between the external world of the culture and the in-

dividual life—then the association between the two terms must be external, a "marriage" between two participants, to witness the bonding publicly. But insofar as the poem is an individual's quest—to reconcile different parts of the self—then the association must be internal, a reconciliation of "male" and "female" tendencies within the single psyche. Williams seems to want it both ways. We've seen several examples in which the "marriage" motif functions in the poem, both as theme and as structuring metaphor. But Williams offers also examples of the internal conjunction of those erotic forces, with images of androgyny and of sexual exchange. One of the tightrope-walkers about whom Paterson reads in Book III manages to perform both as a man and as a woman, for instance. Troubles beset both performances: the male version is externally endangered, while the female has to deal with problems of modesty:

A spectator on Morris Mountain, when [Harry] Leslie had gone out with a cookstove strapped to his back—tugged at one of the guy-ropes, either out of malice or idleness, so that he almost fell off. Having carried the stove to the center of the rope he kindled a fire in it, cooked an omelet and ate it. It rained that night so that the later performance had to be postponed.

But on Monday he did the Washerwoman's Frolic, in female attire, staggering drunkenly across the chasm, going backward, hopping on one foot and at the rope's center lay down on his side. He retired after that having "busted" his tights—to the cottage above for repairs.

(*P,* p. 103)

This association—the troubled reciprocity between male and female parts of the individual on the tightrope—leads Paterson directly into the ideal reciprocity represented in the hauntingly lyrical "Beautiful Thing" section of the poem, in which the Thing/woman is unnamed, while Paterson takes on both "male" characteristics (action, thought) and "female" (gentleness, healing). Similarly, Paterson in Book IV becomes a woman (Phyllis), who in turn has a rendezvous with an apparently male Paterson in New York City.

In these narrative inventions Williams accepts conventional associations of gender roles (masculinity as a mental and ordering force, femininity as physical and diversifying, associated with the earth). Submerged in these metaphors of poetic-realization-as-sublimated-eroticism is an argument like that Harold Bloom derives from his reading of Freud.[60] According to that model, the poet's struggle for poetic identity in the face of his predecessors is an oedipal encounter, in which a boy struggles (for autonomy, for poetic identity) against a dominant father-figure. The need for self-assertion (within this male model of creativity) requires that the boy identify himself with that model of (male) creativity and imitate his father's self-assertion. But that self-definition also forces the boy (poet) to suppress certain latent aspects of his character (feminine characteristics); those repressed aspects of the self return to the male poet personified as a (female) muse or love object (subjective, emotional, associated with nature, etc.). A union with her would yield the man/poet access to those subjective aspects of the self that his initial self-definition-through-male-identification had denied him. The Whitman-Williams connection fits this pattern in part, though the example of the narcissistic Whitman as Father somewhat troubles the waters, because Whitman's own use of the conventional "male" model of creative self-assertion is so overtly yawping and insistent as to seem slightly ironic or self-qualifying. Whitman celebrates his Self so extravagantly that he assumes a (traditionally "female") generosity or nurturing expansiveness; his poem claims to be the voice of the nation speaking itself. Whitman claims an ideal androgyny with his two "selves" (the giant Self is also "democracy, *ma femme*"), and for his "sons" the model he provides for identification with a dominant male creator-figure is neither exclusively male nor dominant. (Whitman is sexually polyvalent throughout *Leaves of Grass:* pursuer and pursued, male and female, active and passive, autoerotic, heterosexual, homosexual, and androgynous.)

Thus the example of Whitman can trouble those poets who need to use him in the Freudian pattern of individuation, because Whitman seems to short-circuit the Bloom/Freudian oedipal metaphor. He does not displace the subjective and emotional "female" parts of his psyche; he overtly credits those "Muse" qualities to his largest Self as part of his *primary* assertion of a poetic identity, not admitting a primary distance between "male" and "female" creative impulses. When Williams tries to establish a Bloomian/Freudian bond with such an "androgynous" father, he finds himself repeating Whitman's odd doubleness. Though Williams' relation to Whitman is partially "filial," it does not exactly fit the "male" model of creative self-assertion the oedipal pattern of poetic individuation describes. (The problem of the female writer in this Freudian schema remains mysterious, to Freud and to Bloom and to critics suspicious of such arbitrary assignments of intellectual characteristics to the sexes.) At times Williams does speculate about the relation between "male" thought and "female" physicality in his own life and work,[61] and Williams does question his Whitman-father on just those terms: he wonders at Whitman's equation between his public ("male") Self and his private ("female") self. But Williams does not fundamentally deny the "androgynous" definition of Whitmanian creativity. Rather, he asserts that such a union had also made his own work possible, and he continues to long for that first connection Whitman had made easily. Art is not exclusively a "male" process of self-integration for Williams—he admits no displacement in his primary "poetic identity"—but art begins with a "freedom" like that Whitman took as his internal marriage, in compensation after what Whitman had claimed was a thwarted love-affair. Art is a reciprocity between male and female aspects of the self, a reciprocity in which both male self-assertion and female generosity are forces within the poet's first assertion of a poetic identity. Paterson the son takes on characteristics of both father (giant) and mother (mountain, flower, seed). "Divorce" of poet and Muse in the Bloom-Freud model would make a poet a poor poet; in *Paterson* "divorce" would preclude any sustaining poetic identity at all.

The paradox of poetic identity in Whitman becomes in Williams the paradox of self-fulfilling prophecy: he writes a magnificent poem about the thwarted modern possibilities for poetry. The thematic hope for marriage or androgyny *within* the poem is an ambition *to realize* the poem: it *is* the poem *Paterson*. And *Paterson* works in structure as in theme; Williams tries to make his structures in the poem both "male" (patterned and ordered) *and* "female" (improvisational and diverse), as we'll soon see.

Objectivity and Structure

I have seldom seen such disorder and brokenness—such a mass of unrelated parts of things lying about. That's it! I concluded to myself. An unrecognizable order! Actually—the new! And so good-natured and calm. So definitely the thing! And so compact. Excellent. And with such patina of use. Everything definitely "painty." Even the table, that way, pushed off from the center of the room.[62]

In this visionary moment from his story "Comedy Entombed" (1930), Williams lets his doctor-protagonist observe a simple but pivotal scene during a hectic day. The doctor's recognition is not so much a fixed achievement as a transitory, almost accidental, glimpse of an incarnated ideal, a recognition of "composition" in an apparently random world: in short, an order in itself and also a metaphor for the kind of unity Williams wants in his work. The immediate problem for Williams is, of course, the question of form in this radically contingent world. If the new "order" (perceptual or poetic) is "unrecognizable," is it in fact an order or a form at all? If so, is Williams capitulating to the mimetic fallacy, merely repeating on a smaller scale the confusion he perceives in the world? Or conversely: if the new order is to remain externally "unrecognizable," of what use is it as a cohesive, communicable order? Is Williams resorting to oxymoron here, with his idea of an "unrecognizable" order, in order to avoid the more difficult task of organizing his materials into functioning formal structures? Is he substituting mimesis for poiesis?

The point in the Williams story is that the "new order" the doctor sees is "unrecognizable" as a preexisting form; it exists only as a function of its composed materials. Similarly, "objectivism" in the poem's language came to mean for Williams, as Bernard Duffey explains, "a declaration of the poem's self-sufficiency." "Perfect drawing," Williams claims in his essay on Marianne Moore, "attains to a separate existence which might, if it please, be called mystical, but is in fact no more than the practicability of design."[63] These metaphors of structural "order," reappearing constantly in Williams' prose, describe a process of artistic assembly and construction, of "painting," "design," "bricklaying," "bridging," "discipline," and (in its largest manifestation) "measure," a relative process of structural arrangement within the lines and sections of a poem. This process—in the example of Marianne Moore's poems—is the modern response to the problematic freedom of Whitman's form:

Who shall separate the good Whitman from the bad, the dreadful New England maunderers from the others, put air under and around the living and leave the dead to fall dead? Who? None but poems, such as Miss Moore's, their cleanliness, lack of cement, clarity, gentleness. . . . . Miss Moore undertakes in her work to separate the poetry from the subject entirely—like all the moderns.[64]

Through these metaphors Williams proposes a coherence different from the order that either traditional formalism or blind pioneering would yield. In *Paterson* I Williams describes the falls of the Passaic River as both static and moving, like the imagination it figures; when we read *Paterson* we ought to notice both the structured effect of organized sections *and* the inventive process or improvisational movement within the separate sections. The purified, objective use of words opens new sources of energy for the writer in the American landscape, but unlike the static and aggregative effect of Whitman's lists, the effects of Williams' structures should be a sense of objectively perceived things in their ontological completeness *and* a sense of the linguistic process that can publicly denote and thus liberate those static forms in verbal action. Though no poem is exclusively "objectivist," Williams tells an undergraduate audience at Dartmouth,

objectivism has to do with the whole poem—the structure of the poem as a metrical invention—a complete objective significance uniquely in itself above any partial image which it may contain.[65]

Williams wants to create both coherence and improvisational diversity within the same structures, and though he claims elsewhere that "unity is the shallowest, the cheapest deception of all composition,"[66] he does argue nevertheless for a "relative" composition, as he emphasizes the "structure, the basis, the actual making of the poem," in a new concept of poetic "unity."[67] These complementary ambitions require an alternating attention to freedom and to retrospective shaping; Williams describes the process, a bit crudely, in his essay "How to Write" (1936; written apparently in response to Gertrude Stein's *How to Write,* of 1931). In the primary, "demotic" stage of work, the writer lets the imagination run unimpeded by blueprints, by preconceived ideas, or by the writer's conscious intervention:

Write, write anything: it is in all probability worthless anyhow, it is never hard to destroy written characters. But it is absolutely essential to the writing of anything worth while that the mind be fluid and release itself to the task.

Forget all rules, forget all restrictions, as to taste, as to what ought to be said, write for the pleasure of it—whether slowly or fast—every form of resistance to a complete release should be abandoned.

After this first release—a microcosmic application of Whitman's first "freedom"—the other identity of the writer takes over, as he or she assumes the responsibility to determine critically whether the new discovery is of novel worth:

But once the writing is on the paper it becomes an object. It is no longer a fluid speaking through a symbolism of ritualistic forms but definite words on a piece of paper. It has now left the region of the formative past and come up to the present. . . . The written object comes under the laws of all created things involving a choice and once the choice has been made there must be an exercise of the will to back it.[68]

In this exercise of the "forebrain," the writer's historical and critical antennae feel the way as the writer examines the work (the "object") for evidence of the "new and the extraordinary." In a Joycean mood Williams calls these two stages "the she and the he of it," but the two modes are inseparable on psychological terms: what the writer discovers during this "male" process of editing is the formal appropriateness of those forms the "female" imagination had already generated. That is, Williams does not distinguish between "female" material and "male" form, but between the generation of form and the recognition of form. In brief, this doubled process is "the birth of a new language," and within a single piece of writing the process recapitulates—as ontogeny does philogeny—the history of American poetry, as Williams conceives it: first the breakthrough stage of Whitman, then the stage of formal consolidation by the modern generation. These progressive stages of abandonment and of editing, though they sound self-evident to us decades later, account for those simultaneous effects that characterize Williams' work at its best: both the excitement of improvisation and the formal satisfaction of gratified expectations, the "exhaltation at the concreteness of the procedure" that in Kenneth Burke's account is a reader's experience of literary form.[69]

Recognizing Williams' doubled process of composition ought to help us, as we read *Paterson,* to distinguish the purely improvisational elements from the structural. The point is not that Williams edits his poems—any responsible writer edits his manuscripts, unless like Jack Kerouac he is trying to write a pure transcript of experience—but that two activities happen simultaneously in a Williams poem. On an immediate level, the poem is "improvised," developing its direction by the poet's pure and enthusiastic submission to the materials. In the separate sections, this principle of minute cohesion works by a technique of "punning" or of overlapping significance that leads associatively from one section to another. (Those elements that the stories of Mrs. Cumming, Sam Patch, Dr. P's. walk, and the *Geographic* picture have implicitly in common, in Book I, the theme of the "first wife," make their presentation continuous and referential, for instance.) This effect on the details and on the movement of the poem—an effect that associates this first stage of composition with Romantic theories of "organic" form—accounts for the sense of improvisation, dream, association, or "process" in Williams' work, as many other critics have accurately described.[70] But also, on the level of structure, Williams provides an external frame for his improvisations; he lays "bricks" to establish a form that is shapely as well as immediate. He writes to James Laughlin in 1943:

If Stevens speaks of *Parts of a World,* this is definitely Parts of a Greater World—a looser, wider world where "order" is a servant not a master. Order is what is discovered after the fact, not a little piss pot for us all to urinate into—and call ourselves satisfied.[71]

Williams is working here with a new concept of organic unity: not only does the poem grow into its form, but the form itself continues to grow. (After he had published the first four books of *Paterson,* for instance, apparently completing the circuit he had prescribed for the poem, Williams published Book V—and began Book VI.) This combination of organic and mechanical structures for the new poem, incidentally, accounts for the many images of artificial or arrested flowers we've already observed in Williams' work: the geometrical flower of "To a Solitary Disciple," the metallic-petaled flower of "The Rose," the glass vegetation of "Between Walls." In *Paterson* the figure of the geometric flower reappears as the "green rose" and the "complex, ovate" flower of the "first wife" in Book I, as the "unwithering" flower of Book II, as the "deflowered, reflowered" flame-flower of Book III (when Paterson replaces his spoiled world with a "replica" in wax), as the pressed "bouquet" of remembered women scattered "in the meshes of Her hair" in Book IV (and the Yale mss.), and as the cloth and tapestry flowers of Book V.

   I think the immediate, improvised nature of the separate sections of *Paterson* is self-evident; we recognize this first model of "ordering," from within the materials themselves, primarily through Williams' colloquial tone and idiomatic pace. The larger orders of *Paterson* are a bit harder to recognize, for they are patterns generalized from these improvised materials. In its original organization (before Book V), Williams arranged *Paterson* in several such larger patterns. First, the poem represented the life of a single individual: Paterson, Dr. P., "only one man—like a city." In Book I, shortly after his "birth" in the "Preface" ("a nine-months' wonder, the city/ the man, an identity"), Paterson encounters as if for the first time the "elemental character" of his city-self, Paterson, New Jersey; in Book II, he walks among young lovers in the city's park, where he speculates about sexuality and politics and concludes with a love-letter and a love-lyric ("On this most voluptuous night of the year"); in Book III an adult Paterson searches through library chronicles to find some energizing language or local myth, but failing in that attempt he goes outside and recognizes the "riddle" of his quest in the sound of the river ("the being taut, balanced between eternities"); in Book IV Peterson travels to New York City, becomes a woman somehow and gets involved with his bisexual "female" self Phyllis, washes out to sea, and then returns to the New Jersey shore. By Book V, Paterson is an old man in his reveries, "learning with age to sleep my life away." Thus the poem travels through Paterson's conception ("Preface"), youth and adolescence (Books I and II), early adulthood (Book III), prime (Book IV), and old age (Book V). In his "Author's Note" Williams summarizes this structure, the life of a single man, in terms that associate the poem's structure with the process of verbal self-discovery that is the poem's central theme. Despite the poem's "improvisatory" methods, Williams had planned this larger structure from the start:

Paterson is a long poem in four parts—that a man in himself is a city, beginning, seeking, achieving and concluding his life in ways which the various aspects of a city may embody—if imaginatively conceived—any city, all the details of which may be made to voice his most intimate convictions. Part One introduces the elemental character of the place. The Second Part comprises the modern replicas. Three will seek a language to make them vocal, and Four, the river below the falls, will be reminiscent of episodes—all that any one man may achieve in a lifetime.

Besides the shape of a man's life, several secondary thematic structures also organize *Paterson*. The Passaic River systematically appears throughout the poem, as the books follow the river from place to place—as if the shape of the poem were a verbal map of the river's physical path. "I took the river as it followed its course to the sea," Williams recalls later. "All I had to do was follow it and I had a poem."[72] We've already seen several appearances of the image of the river, as in Book I, where it introduces the theme of the search for a new language. (In his early notes to *Paterson*, at Yale, Williams proposes that in the path of the river past the

Passaic Falls, along the "flank" of the giant-city, and toward the sea, the poem and the river outline Paterson the giant—so that the path of the river represents both the shape of the giant's body and metaphorically the shape of the life and art of Paterson the person.) Book I works the relation in one direction, from giant to private man ("the myth/ that holds up the rock" sustains Dr. P. in his search for an adequate language), and Book III works the relation in reverse, as Paterson recognizes in himself the potential for largesse, language, and desire:

> Spent from wandering the useless
> streets these months, faces folded against
> him like clover at nightfall, something
> has brought him back to his own
>
> > > > mind
>
> > > in which a falls unseen
> > tumbles and rights itself
> > and refalls—and does not cease, falling
> > and refalling with a roar, a reverberation
> > not of the falls but of its rumor
>
> > > > unabated
>
> > > Beautiful thing,
> > my dove
>
> > > > > (_P_, p. 96)

Besides Paterson's life-long quest, registered in the roaring progress of the river, the poem details also the course of one year in the seasons ("spring, summer, fall and the sea," as Williams describes Books I–IV) and in the months (in its twelve sections: associating Book IV especially with the influence of Whitman, Williams in the Yale mss. calls the winter months the "conservator and progenitor" of life).[73] The regular appearance of the four elements similarly makes the poem's patterns both progressive and cyclical (water at the Falls chiefly in Book I, earth in the Park in Book II, fire in the library in Book III, and air—radiance and height—in _Paterson_ IV, though all four elements appear irregularly throughout the poem).[74] A man's life, a river, a single body, four seasons, four elements, even the four directions of the compass (as the river rounds the city and returns in Book IV with the swimmer's turn inland): these patterns seem clear enough to account for that external ordering that Williams describes in "How to Write" as the second phase of composition. Though they organize the poem from within, however, these structures are not purely generated by the improvised materials; as his notes toward the poem suggest, Williams' plans for these "external" arrangements do precede the "improvisations" of the separate sections.[75] Eventually we can read the prefatory paragraph of descriptive images for *Paterson* as a statement not only of the poem's intentions, but also of possible images of the poem's largest collected forms. Williams plays that list between terms of collection and terms of dispersal:

> : a local pride; spring, summer, fall and the sea; a confession; a basket; a column; a reply to Greek and Latin with the bare hands; a gathering up; a celebration;
>
>   in distinctive terms; by multiplication a reduction to one; daring; a fall; the clouds resolved into a sandy sluice; an enforced pause;
>
>   hard put to it; an identification and a plan for action to supplant a plan for action; a taking up of slack; a dispersal and a metamorphosis.

(P, p. 2)

As we've noticed, Whitman's form is partly "organic" according to traditional Romantic theory; the poem "grows" like a plant, according to the exigencies of the mind's process of self-completion in the poem. "Song of Myself" grows as the Self it defines grows outward, regulated by its own laws in that process Emerson calls the "infinite enlargement of the heart with a power of growth to a new infinity on every side." (That is, Whitman's form recalls the concept of self Emerson proposes in his essay "Circles"; Emerson's essay itself recalls Hermes' and St. Bonaventure's spatial description of God as a circle, the perimeter of which is everywhere and the center of which is nowhere.) Williams' experiments in the form of *Paterson*, however, come from a different concept of the relation between the large Self and the private self; his *Paterson* combines this organic formal process with a modernist, objective, self-consciously mechanical form. Both generative and structural,

Paterson's patterns embody first the movement implicit in the Romantic notion of organic form (like the self-completion of a plant's growth or the motion of a dancer) [76] and also the machinelike stability of a modernist construct. *Paterson* "grows" by an accretion of experience, as does Whitman's Self, but Dr. P. also passes through recognizable stages of life and of time, through lyrical private interludes, and through prose "memories" of his history.

Paterson V does take the city into another dimension, into themes of time, memory, and imagination, after the other books of the poem have represented the four physical dimensions. In Book V Williams seems apparently to shift perspective. No longer as specific in description, as abrupt in style, nor as anguished in tone as *Paterson* I–IV, *Paterson* V relies on the drifting reveries of the tripartite line to carry the themes of the preceding books into Paterson's ruminative old age.

Paterson IV ends with the protagonist breaking through the bushes, identifying himself with the land, with America. He will finally die but it can't be categorically stated that death ends *anything*. When you're through with sex, with ambition, what can an old man create? Art, of course, a piece of art that will go beyond him into the lives of young people, the people who haven't had time to create. The old man meets the young people and moves on. [77]

But the earlier books of the poem had followed concerns appropriate to the stages of an individual's life (infancy and historical origins; individuation and sexuality; work and adult identity; coherence and consolidation). The apparent change in Book V, therefore, bespeaks the section's root consistency with the poem's preceding sections.

> In old age
>   the mind
>   casts off
>   rebelliously
>   an eagle
> from its crag
>   (*P,* p. 207)

The style of Book V is more ruminative, simpler and more allegorical; oddly, Williams still seems to be competing with Eliot, who throughout the *Four Quartets* (1935–42) had been meditating on the relations among history, place, and local identity.[78] *Paterson* V, like the *Quartets* and *The Tempest,* is both a testimony to and a departure from former modes of art. Unlike Eliot, however, Williams does not seek to retrieve the past nor to locate the present in a circling pattern of transcendence, and unlike Shakespeare's Prospero Williams does not abjure his art but continues the effort to work his magic on the diversities of his world. (The young female figures of *Paterson* V are not like Shakespeare's Miranda, for they are neither docile nor pliant—and the materials of the world they figure are not so ductile.) Book V reintroduces the "first wife" figure, both as a function of the metaphor of androgyny (the poem discusses Sappho and "translates" a Sapphic poem to a woman on the street) and as a continuation of the "marriage" motif (the "Beautiful Thing" who had haunted *Paterson* III reappears as the Virgin Mediatrix, as The Feminine that unites a list of Paterson's former lovers, as the Lady in the Unicorn tapestries, and as an unamed woman with a cloth flower pinned to her coat). By moving *Paterson* V in this direction, Williams can carry through a new argument and can also link Book V with the earlier parts of the poem ("have you read anything that I have written?" Paterson asks the anonymous woman, "It is all for you"; p. 220). That cloth flower, too, reminds us of the flowers and seeds of the first four books of the poem, especially of the seed of linguistic hope that Paterson earlier had hoped to plant. The seed that was endangered in Book I, thwarted in Book II, washed away in Book III, and replanted by the swimmer in Book IV germinates as art in Book V, both in the woman's cloth flower and in the tapestry flowers that surround the mythical Unicorn, with whom Paterson in Book V identifies himself. Attracted by the Virgin's purity, the Unicorn submits to his capture, and thus the imaginary creature lives penned in a place; the imagination can capture the invisible. And further, the imagination can liberate the visible. Objectified in an artwork, a form, the imagination lifts physical things (flowers) out of time and locates them in a new atemporal "field" or "place" (the artwork):

So through art alone, male and female, a field of
flowers, a tapestry, spring flowers unequaled
in loveliness.

> Through this hole
> at the bottom of the cavern
> of death, the imagination
> escapes intact.

- he bears a collar round his neck
   hid in the bristling hair.

                                           (*P*, p. 212)

Earlier books of the poem had detailed the industrial history of
Paterson as a textile-producing city, its mills powered by the Passaic Falls. These images of cloth flowers and flowered tapestries in
Paterson V surprisingly associate that history with the multitudi-
nous flowers of the earlier books, once more claiming both Romantic and modernist formal energies for the synthetic power of
art. Immediately following this image of the Unicorn among tapestry flowers comes another letter from Allen Ginsberg, who in a
tone of Whitmanian exuberance relates these images of flowers to
the theme of the continuity of Paterson's quest from one generation to another.

I do have a whitmanic mania & nostalgia for cities and detail & panorama and isolation in jungle and pole, like the images you pick up. When
I've seen enough I'll be back to splash in the Passaic again only with a
body so naked and happy City Hall will have to call out the Riot Squad.
. . . Paterson is only a big sad poppa who needs compas-
sion.   .   In any case Beauty is where I hang my hat. And reality.
And America.
     . . . I mean to say Paterson is not a task like Milton going down to
hell, it's a flower to the mind too   etc   etc. . . .

                        Adios.
                        A.G.

IF YOU DON'T HAVE ANY TIME FOR ANYTHING ELSE
PLEASE READ THE ENCLOSED
SUNFLOWER SUTRA

                                           (*P*, p. 213)

Its themes are consonant with those of the preceding books, and even in its radical discontinuity of style *Paterson* V in effect asserts the coherence of the first four books and the continuity of the entire poem's quest.

This technique of formal connectedness in Williams' work—the completion of Whitman's vitalistic beginnings with a modern shape, a machinelike efficiency, and a "relative" structure—has finally to do with Williams' developing objective language for *Paterson* as a whole. Whitman's expansive circles had brought us wider and wider, to a Self that "pauses waiting," but Williams' progressive form brings us more specifically "to man,/ to Paterson." Eventually, the "giant" identity Whitman had asserted as primary is shown implicit in the individual's life. Accordingly, Williams' structures in his poem combine the formal inclusiveness of the "giant" (in *Paterson*'s largest orders) with the improvisatory, experiential freedom of the separate citizen. The doubled figure of Dr. P.—both a distanced observer on the scene and a democratic participant in it—is Williams' final response to the idealizing democratic figure of Whitman, in his modes as giant and citizen. The particularly Whitmanian emphasis of *Paterson,* and the implications of that doubled Whitmanian perspective in Williams' poem, are the concerns of our final chapters.

PART III

The Two Whitmans Joined

SIX

Whitman in Paterson

Walt Whitman appears twice in Williams' *Paterson,* framing the whole poem: first in Book I as the slumbering giant who personifies the formless potential of the place, and again as the swimmer whose return and whose reorientation inland close the original four-part poem. In both appearances, Whitman personifies the characteristics of that "tradition" that Williams describes in his prose allusions to Whitman's work.

Whitman first appears tacitly, in the opening section of *Paterson,* "The Delineation of the Giants," in which the figure of a geological giant (Paterson pictured as a vista with rocks and water) underlies the city (also Paterson). This "elemental character" of Paterson as place seems physically and geographically to recall Whitman's first appearance in the grass in "Song of Myself," his giant self that follows, and his dissolution back into landscape, at the end of that poem. In *Paterson* the Whitmanian giant[1] is powerful and supine, "bequeathed" to the earth ("scattered broadcast") and therefore implicit in the history and geography of the place:

> Paterson lies in the valley under the Passaic Falls
> its spent waters forming the outline of his back. He
> lies on his right side, head near the thunder
> of the waters filling his dreams! Eternally asleep,
> his dreams walk about the city where he persists
> incognito. Butterflies settle on his stone ear.
> Immortal he neither moves nor rouses and is seldom

seen, though he breathes and the subtleties of his machinations
drawing their substance from the noise of the pouring river
animate a thousand automatons.

(*P*, p. 6)

Williams makes the giant Paterson, both terrain and city, resemble
Whitman in three ways: both are "cities" (as Whitman had imagined himself and his life's work in *Leaves of Grass*); both are giants
who "incarnate" their landscapes; both are figuratively "asleep" to
the life of the modern place and so both "dream" their people (as
in Whitman's "The Sleepers"). The giant Paterson sleeps in the
urban terrain as the spirit of Whitman "sleeps" in the modern
imagination, because his work remains unfinished. ("It was and
was meant to be only a beginning which we were enjoined to
carry on to new inventions," Williams insists in 1947, shortly after
he published this section of *Paterson*.)[2]

Between the world wars, as he had watched the literary imagination of America flee toward Paris, London, and Rapallo, Williams had seen the message of Whitman go dormant ("because the
secret of it was the same as the secret of a bud that will unfold
later into a leaf or a flower").[3] At the start of *Paterson,* therefore,
he pictures a nativist hero-poet whose body *is* his place; limited
and incognito, but dreaming the continued vitality of the modern
task, Whitman lies submerged in the image of Paterson the giant
near his female counterpart, Garret Mountain. Like Williams'
Daniel Boone, who surveyed the landscape "voluptuously," and
like Whitman, who because of a thwarted romance sublimated his
erotic sense until it extended to the textures of the landscape, Paterson the giant sleeps beside the fecund, "female," rural American
countryside. And as Whitman had returned American poets "to
the elements of the art" through his compensatory freedom, Williams in the poem *Paterson* works for a "marriage" of those two
"giant" figures. Like a bride, the mountain appears adrift in flowers:

And there, against him, stretches the low mountain.
The Park's her head, carved, above the Falls, by the quiet
river; Colored crystals the secret of those rocks;

farms and ponds, laurel and the temperate wild cactus,
yellow flowered   .   .   facing him, his
arm supporting her, by the *Valley of the Rocks,* asleep.
Pearls at her ankles, her monstrous hair
spangled with apple-blossoms is scattered about into
the back country, waking their dreams—where the deer run
and the wood-duck nests protecting his gallant plumage.
                                                    (*P*, p. 8)

Between the two giants, however, the Passaic River runs, separating male city and female landscape. In this first direct appearance of the river (aside from the metaphorical description of the
Passaic watershed in the "Preface") the sound of the water is a
preverbal mystery, an Ur-language Paterson must try to "un-
ravel."[4] Like Whitman as he "translates" the sounds and signs of
the world as they accrue to him ("I am afoot with my vision,"
"Now I will do nothing but listen"), Williams' Whitman-like giant
passively hears the noise of the local river of language as it approaches and passes a catastrophic fall of mythic, geological, and
social dimensions:

Jostled as are the waters approaching
the brink, his thoughts
interlace, repel and cut under,
rise rock-thwarted and turn aside
but forever strain forward—or strike
an eddy and whirl, marked by a
leaf or curdy spume, seeming
to forget   .
Retake later the advance and
are replaced by succeeding hordes
pushing forward—they coalesce now
glass-smooth with their swiftness,
quiet or seem to quiet as at the close
they leap to the conclusion and
fall, fall in air! as if
floating, relieved of their weight,
split apart, ribbons; dazed, drunk
with the catastrophe of the descent
floating unsupported

> to hit the rocks: to a thunder,
> as if lightning had struck
>
> (*P*, pp. 7–8)

Puzzled by this verbally chaotic phenomenon, Paterson begins his quest; in Williams' estimation, the modern writers will assume Whitman's task of "translation" where he had left it after his incomplete "beginnings." Throughout the poem Williams makes Paterson listen to the "code" of the falls, as he tries to translate into a "common language" the message the falling waters pour down the falls at the giant's head. Paterson's geography metaphorically contains elements of both a "pater" and a "son". The "father" is a personified verbal power ("Earth, the chatterer, father of all speech"), and the "son" is his translator, the modern poet:

> The water pouring still
> from the edge of the rocks, filling
> his ears with its sound, hard to interpret.
> A wonder!
>
> (*P*, p. 17)

This tacitly Whitmanian beginning of *Paterson,* with its definition of theme and purpose, points the direction Dr. P. (the individual Paterson) will take throughout Williams' long poem. As the river passes along the giant's flank, over the falls, and toward the sea, *Paterson* the poem should demonstrate, Williams claims, that a man "in himself is a city." Alternately the giant and Doctor P. the physician, Paterson in his various selves collects the poem with the shape of his experience. Obviously, the different systems of images that depict Paterson throughout the poem relate to each other slidingly. (If Paterson is both a man and a city, for example, then a map of the city is metaphorically a pattern of the man's life; thus as Paterson walks through the city, he self-consciously explores his own experience.) At crucial moments in the poem, these systems do join into single inclusive images—for instance, at the end of Book IV of *Paterson* (that is, at the end of the poem as Williams originally planned and published it). In Book IV the Passaic River reaches the sea "below the Falls," the individual Dr. P. "concludes his life," and the city of Paterson sprawls toward New

York; Williams describes the action of this section as a sequence of symbolic "episodes—all that any one man may achieve in a lifetime." At this point of collection, Williams overtly rouses a Whitman-figure, to synthesize several themes of the poem and to continue the motion of the poem by turning toward a new generation.

The last section of the original four-part poem concludes as the Passaic River spills into the Atlantic Ocean, but implicit in that dispersal is a promise of return. Literally, the water-cycle carries the river past the city to the sea, from which it rises again as rain and returns inland. *Paterson* the poem traces this movement stylistically in Book IV, section ii, when shortly before its end the poem enters a distracted and disconnected section, the formal equivalent of the broadcast scattering of the river's waters in the ocean. Paterson recalls a murder in his city's history and the execution of the murderer (a social "murder"), and he generalizes those bloody occasions into a single image of a modern "sea of blood" around him. This welter of modern and historical violence seems to vex his quest for an answer to his puzzling existence. Strangely, the sea offers to Paterson a seductive temptation toward the calm of merger and nonresistance.

> Drink of it, be drunk!
> Thalassa
> immaculata: our home, our nostalgic
> mother in whom the dead, enwombed again
> cry out to us to return   .
> the blood dark sea!
> nicked by the light alone, diamonded
> by the light   .   from which the sun
> alone lifts undamped his wings
> of fire!
>
> .   .   not our home! It is NOT
> our home.
>
> (*P*, p. 202)

Earlier in the poem the sea had been a "mother," the goal of the river's journey through particularity, but in Book IV, section ii, the sea appears as an image of seductive danger. Paterson fears the sea of "objectively indifferent men," Williams notes in the manuscripts to the poem (Buffalo mss.), and in the final version Williams dramatizes the sea's dangerous indifference by including among the final scenes of *Paterson* both a murder and the carnival-like execution of the murderer. In the context of this spectacle of indifference, Whitman's spiritually democratic ideal seems impossible. The social spectacle is sensational, violent, and popular; in keeping with the metaphor, the "sea" is also violent and seductive. The sea is "not our home," the sea is the destination of the chaotic verbal river of Book I, the sea is the blood-streaked lair of a vicious and self-destructive shark, and the sea is the past itself, "in whom the dead, enwombed again/ cry out to us to return." Williams recognizes the traditional history of American violence, the seductiveness of that violence both as spectacle and as tradition, and yet he resists those attractions and insists on a new orientation. "It is NOT/ our home." Finally, the sea is metaphorically the destructive, purifying energy that the generative impulses of love and of imagination paradoxically require.[5]

The river's rush to the sea in *Paterson* is therefore a metaphor of the process of risky historical change. Despite the dangers, Paterson (and his life's work) must undergo a metamorphosis in the sea, to effect a "sea change" and thus to make possible both a new cultural orientation and a new language.

```
              —you cannot believe
        that it can begin again, again, here
        again    .    here
        Waken from a dream, this dream of
        the whole poem     .       sea-bound,
                           rises, a sea of blood

        —the sea that sucks in all rivers,
                              dazzled, led
        by the salmon and the shad     .
                      .   .   .
        But lullaby, they say, the time sea is
        no more than sleep is   .      afloat
        with weeds, bearing seeds     .
```

Ah!

float wrack, float words, snaring the
seeds   .

(*P,* p. 200)

This diffuse, rhythmically wavering section, in which the murder-
ous "lullaby" of the generalizing sea tempts Paterson, concludes
with the recovery of those "seeds" that drift out to sea in the rush
of the river and then are washed back toward land. The seeds are
local ("here"), restorative ("again"), and cyclical ("again here"), in
a paradoxical tradition of specific germination: the "universal" sea
returns the "specific" seeds. In the section's repeated assertion that
"the sea is not our home," the fate of those "seeds" recalls the
endangered "multiple seeds,/ packed tight with detail," in the
"Preface" to *Paterson.* Like the juniper cones and like the "first
beauty, complex, ovate" that in Book I were endangered by the
threat of "divorce" and hence of separation from the "ground" of
fruitfulness, the local "seeds" of Book IV are endangered by forces
of violence and abstraction and indifference, "the sea that sucks in
all rivers." At that moment in Book IV when its extinction seems
most certain, however, the "seed" changes, from a vegetable "seed"
to a "seed of love" that can survive—indeed, that needs—the
metamorphosis[6] that the sea effects:

You will come to it, the blood dark sea
of praise. You must come to it. Seed
of Venus, you will return   to
a girl standing upon a tilted shell, rose
pink   .

(*P,* p. 202)

Though the sea is emphatically not our home, from that perilous sea-tumult rises the image of a love that can offer hope and
regeneration to the land. Like Venus rising from the seafoam, a
figure emerges from the confluence of the Passaic River and the
Atlantic Ocean: a man rises from the water that resists him with
its undertow. At first a dog on shore senses the man's approach,
as if a familiar master were returning after a tedious absence:

> A large, compact bitch gets up, black,
> from where she has been lying
> under the bank, yawns and stretches with
> a half suppressed half whine, half cry .
> She looks to sea, cocking her ears and,
> restless, walks to the water's edge where
> she sits down, half in the water   .

Like Odysseus washed ashore in the last country he visits before his return to Ithaca, the figure swims ashore and falls exhausted on the beach, where some girls—Nausicaa and her friends, in the *Odyssey*—are playing ball. The dog greets him:

> When he came out, lifting his knees
> through the waves she went to him frisking
> her rump awkwardly   .
> Wiping his face with his hand he turned
> to look back to the waves, then
> knocking at his ears, walked up
> to stretch out flat on his back in
> the hot sand   .   there were some
> girls, far down the beach, playing ball.

Regaining his strength after a sleep (like Odysseus, like Whitman, like Paterson the giant, like the hotel clerk of Book IV who finds a beautiful woman asleep in his bed), the man rises, dresses, and heads inland with his dog. (Williams later explained that the swimmer is walking toward Camden, where Walt Whitman spent the last 20 years of his life.) As he leaves, Williams' swimmer turns inland, dropping a single seed as he goes:

> —must have slept. Got up again, rubbed
> the dry sand off and walking a
> few steps got into a pair of faded
> overalls, slid his shirt on overhand (the
> sleeves were still rolled up) shoes,
> hat where she had been watching them under
> the bank and turned again
> to the water's steady roar, as of a distant
> waterfall   .   Climbing the

> bank, after a few tries, he picked
> some beach plums from a low bush and
> sampled one of them, spitting the seed out,
> then headed inland, followed by the dog
> *(P,* p. 203)

This swift understated section, the last fully developed interlude in the poem as Williams originally planned it, recapitulates in a concentrated narrative many of the Whitmanian themes from the opening sections of the poem. Williams is candid when he recalls how he conceived the section:

I had to think hard as to how I was going to end the poem. It wouldn't do to have a grand and soul-satisfying conclusion because I didn't see any in my subject. It didn't belong to the subject. It would have been easy to make a great smash-up with the beautiful sunset at sea, or a flight of pidgeons, love's end and the welter of man's fate. Instead, . . . we come to the sea at last. Odysseus swims in as a man must always do, he doesn't drown, he is able but, accompanied by his dog, strikes inland again (toward Camden) to begin again.[7]

The ocean, the seed, the dog, the man's swim, his sleep, his reorientation on a walk—even the detail of a man's knocking water from his ears to clarify his hearing: in the earlier sections of the poem, all these images had associated Paterson's quest for a comprehensive identity with his search for a new language to comprehend it. (The scene also changes the images of the first long poem "The Wanderer" from a melting with the Passaic River to establish a "paradise," to a more realistic swim and a more organic establishment of a new "hope.") Like the new language Paterson seeks, in fact, the image of the beachplum-seed the swimmer spits onto the shore suggests both a return to local conditions and a new vitality for those "seeds" the sea had threatened. Implicit in the image is a sense of the poet's power, for both the man (the poet who "spits out" the new word) and the seed (the poem) counter the unfruitful divorce of words from physical reality. Because of the poet's mediating effect on the language, the new "interpenetration" may help those fellow citizens (like Mrs. Cumming and the "automatons" of Book I) who, because of the current "failure to untangle the language," are "carried helplessly toward the sea (of blood) which by their failure of speech awaits them." The poet can begin this cultural revitalization, Williams anticipates, and in a letter written in 1950, during the Korean War and during the composition of this section of *Paterson,* he explains this image of deliverance in terms that link that social power of the word with the fate of the single seed the swimmer spits on the shore. Williams feels

a cold east wind today, that seems to blow from the other side of the world—seems at the same time to be blowing all poetry out of life. A man wonders why he bothers to continue to write. And yet it is precisely then that to write is most imperative for us. That, if I can do it, will be the end of *Paterson,* Book IV. The ocean of savage lusts in which the wounded shark gnashes at his own tail is not our home.

It is the seed that floats to shore, one word, one tiny, even microscopic word, is that which can alone save us.[8]

The quest of *Paterson* is to plant that one seed, or one word, that can generate an effective and physical and accurate language, to assure a fecundity of the verbal spirit in American "soil." The notes to *Paterson* IV in the Yale collection, in fact, even more closely associate the swimmer's dropped seed, the "word" that was the giant's potential power, and the specificity that emerges from the sea. To link these themes, Williams uses an image that changes the Whitmanian Paterson from a giant to a swimmer. The encoded Passaic runs to the sea, and the "sea is vocal,"

> varied as
> a speech that has been born to
> that giant, the first word; that we
> must imitate. One single word from
> which to build up a language   .
> One enormous word in which Leviathan
> swims like a minnow.
>
> (Yale mss.)

Thus, followed by a dog—dogs are a recurrent image of intuitive life throughout *Paterson,* linking urban and rural worlds[9]— the swimmer of *Paterson* IV spits out the one seed, turns, and walks inland. This characteristic turn of the swimmer associates him with Daniel Boone, with Columbus and Poe, and with those other pioneers in Williams' mythology who encounter the American landscape voluptuously, turning inland to local experience and to the immanent forms of the new. Above all the image of the swimmer summons Williams' image of Walt Whitman, whose giant form from Book I of the poem awakens here, revitalized after a "sea change." Whitman had turned inward—or inland, in the topographical metaphor—"toward the unknown future." [10] The modern poets, subsequently, need to effect a "sea change" in the poetic line, Williams claims, a modern change that both continues and modifies Whitman's formal discoveries. Williams directly associates the swimmer with Whitman when in his autobiography he summarizes the last section of *Paterson* IV:

> In the end the man rises from the sea where the river appears to have lost its identity and accompanied by his faithful bitch, obviously a Chesapeake Bay retriever, turns inland toward Camden where Walt Whitman, much traduced, lived the latter years of his life and died. He always said that his poems, which had broken the dominance of the iambic pentameter in English prosody, had only begun his theme. I agree. It is up to us, in the new dialect, to continue it by a new construction upon the syllables. [11]

Williams sees Whiman, as Whitman had imagined himself, as the reader of a mysterious text the natural world spells out to him, and in a late essay on *Leaves of Grass* Williams pictures Whitman encountering that secret "language" on the beach:

> There is a very moving picture of Whitman facing the breakers coming in on the New Jersey shore, when he heard the onomotopoeic waves talk to him direct in a Shakespearean language which might have been Lear himself talking to the storm. But it was not what it seemed; it was a new language, an unnamed language which Whitman could not identify or control. . . . But the waves on the Jersey shore still came tumbling in, quieting him as their secret escaped him, isolating him and leaving him lonesome—but possessed by the great mystery which won the world to his side. [12]

This vignette of the lonely poet of democracy indicates how much the Whitman who is the presiding genius of place in *Paterson* I revives in the swimmer who brings hope to Book IV of the poem;

he is a composite of what Williams considers useful and permanently progressive in the Whitmanian tradition. The giant (whom water had threatened) becomes the individual man (who swims); the individual then turns inland, to the nation that is his largest self.

This continuation of the Whitmanian ambition to find reciprocities between public and private experiences is not a direct application of Whitman's poetic strategies, in part because Whitman tried too hard to assert his simple equation of Self and self. In poems like "Out of the Cradle Endlessly Rocking" and "As I Ebb'd with the Ocean of Life," Whitman had been too susceptible to the temptations of the seductively generalizing sea; in those poems he too eagerly anticipates those fluid unions, longing for a universality-through-mortality in the maternal sea. Williams is alert to the death-wish implicit in Whitman's melting and merging, however; he hears in those amniotic reversions a life-denying tone, a "nostalgia for the mud." Accordingly, Williams shows instead a Whitman-figure emerging healthily from the sea; at the end of *Paterson* IV he revitalizes a Whitman of positive influence, after his "sea change." In the original ending to the poem (*Paterson* IV), Williams pays tribute to the Whitman who made a start in an American idiom and whose spirit revives in the attempt to break through, to lead inland or inward, to shape a new new dialect ("again here"). In fact, Williams had planned to end the poem on an even stronger image of a Whitman for moderns. The notes to the final section of the poem, now in the Beinecke library at Yale, foresee an image of Whitman looking back out to sea. Like the poet of *Paterson* I, this Whitman-figure answers with realized "words" the wild crashings of water on rock.

> the greatest moment in the history
> of the american poem was when
> Walt Whitman stood looking to sea
>
> from the sheving sands
>   and the waves
>
> called to him and
> he answered, drilling his voice to
> their advance

> drifting the words above
> the returning clatter of stone.
> with courage, labor, and abandon
> the word, the word, the word.[13]

As if to confirm that this historical example is applicable for modern stylistic needs, in later drafts Williams also preceded this image with an unidentified quotation from Whitman's "By Blue Ontario's Shore":

> We level that lift, to pass and continue beyond.
> Ages, precedents, poems, have long been accumulating undirected
>   materials,
> America brings builders, and brings its own styles.
> (Williams' transcription, *LOG,* p. 342)

In the final version of the poem Williams stresses even more strongly the need to reject the sea's seductiveness, which had tempted Whitman and which had thus compromised his precision. Instead of concluding the poem with a Whitman who is overtly summoned and sent against the modern welter, *Paterson* I–IV ends with a tacit, reawakened "Whitman" re-turning positively and vigorously toward Camden. The figure who swims to shore, spits out the plum seed, and heads inland is both Whitman (the progenitor) and those who follow in Whitman's tracks: both tradition and new poet, pater and son, giant and private person.[14] Williams' notes to *Paterson* V, in fact, stress even more strongly how future generations will complete the swimmer's promise. In the "River of Heaven" section (in which he translates the Passaic to a higher dimension than the physical), Williams had sent a group of people back to that beach: "we went there, later, to gather the sea plums" (Yale mss.). (Williams saved the line and used it later, in "Asphodel," *PB,* p. 156.)

Thus the paternal Whitman-figure advances himself, indirectly, into the future. Indeed, the poem is full of images of parenthood of various kinds. Throughout the poem, for instance, Dr. P. receives letters from a younger poet in Paterson, who clearly means to follow in the direction Dr. P. (Williams) had defined. The writer—Allen Ginsberg—sends letters signed "A.P." (either "Al-

len Paterson" or, as Williams later claims, "A Poet").[15] Several of
those letters make a point of crediting the young writer with a
"Whitmanic" poetic "mania." Similarly, in Book IV Marie Curie
both discovers the power of radium and has a baby. Those two
achievements seem equally generative, as Williams associates the
discovery of a new element and the birth of a child with the invention of a new language, like the effects of the swimmer's "seed."
When Dr. P. attends a lecture on uranium (on an occasion that
leads him to associate the splitting of the atom with the splitting-
open of the poetic line), he attends with his own son: that image
of familial continuity associates the theme of "love, that smashes
the atom" with the theme of poetic discovery through objectivism.
After the combination of all these images of parenthood and fer-
tility, Williams ends his poem in the original (four-part) version
with an image that combines the best of Walt Whitman's influence
in a new and regenerative movement. The poem evokes its own
father and, in turn, by his seed generates the "son," the inheritor
of the tradition. The closing scenes of *Paterson* thus reenact Whitman's gesture toward the open road, at the end of "Song of Myself."

At the end of *Paterson* IV, Whitman the sleeping giant of the
first part of the poem has "awakened from a dream, this dream/ of
the whole poem," roused from his sleep by the force of the modern world's drift toward violence, divorce, and linguistic decay. In
his new form he walks privately again toward the "Beautiful Thing"
that lodges inland (or inward) in the American spirit. Thus the
appearance of Whitman at the end of *Paterson* IV rounds off the
cycles the "Preface" to the poem had begun; the ending also points
toward a unity of conception in *Paterson,* a structural coherence in
its largest parts, which critics who recognize the poem's "improvisational" structure sometimes overlook. The poem closes on a
somersault that signifies both the regeneration of the father in the
son (the return of Whitman and the swimmer) and also the turning of a baby about to be born. The poem that began with a
promise of evolution toward "man,/ to Paterson" ends with a birth
that is a beginning and also an end to a poem of recurrent beginnings:

This is the blast
the eternal close
the spiral
the final somersault
the end.
(*P.* p. 204)

As he summons the giant sleeping figure of Walt Whitman to re-awaken and to turn inland again—to the open road (the large structures) *and* to the local place (the internal structuring of the American poem)—William Carlos Williams salutes and qualifies Whitman's achievements, acknowledging the continuity of his own modern quest with the difficult origins that his image of Whitman represents.

SEVEN

Doctor Paterson

The Dual Perspective

"Rigor of beauty is the quest. But how will you find beauty
when it is locked in the mind past all remonstrance?"

(*P,* p. 3)

Faced with this blockage, Williams begins Paterson's attempt to
move from the beauty locked within toward the potential beauty
that mutely surrounds him. As we've seen, *Paterson* is Williams'
largest Whitmanian effort to bridge the internal world ("our own
complexities") with the outer world, which also needs this mediation. The quest is private, Dr. P.'s encounters with his own life,
but his quest is also social, the attempt to link, through the model
of a binding language, the private experience of the American individual with the objects and other people of his problematic environment. Throughout the poem the other inhabitants of the city
(the lovers in the Park, the "colored girls," Mrs. Cumming, Miss
Cress, Sam Patch) lack a language to "redeem" them from the
stasis and the cultural dishonesty in which they find themselves.
Recognizing the social need, Williams' Paterson undertakes both
to minister to his city objectively, as a doctor would do, and to
assume a personal responsibility for the establishment of the
new language:

> I must
> find my meaning and lay it, white,
> beside the sliding water: myself—
> comb out the language—or succumb
>   (*P,* p. 145)

Like several of the protagonists in Williams' stories, Doctor P. is a dedicated physician: a general practitioner and pediatrician who makes house calls in all parts of town, a diagnostician who examines patients in his office, and a surgeon who figuratively "operates" on the local language in order to cure a verbal and physical malady afflicting his society and its individuals.[16] One of the startling experiences in reading the manuscripts to *Paterson* at Yale and SUNY/Buffalo is to discover Williams' notes for the poem scrawled on prescription blanks from his medical clinic. That historical coincidence is telling, for Williams wants *Paterson* to be metaphorically both a descriptive diagnosis and a prescriptive treatment of the disorders of modern American culture. In his *Autobiography* Williams corrects those critics who marvel at his ability to pursue two professions; writing and medicine, Williams claims, "amount for me to nearly the same thing."[17]

Gertrude Stein, also, had studied medicine, acknowledging that "the practice of medicine concerns the whole man no matter what the stylistic variants may be." But Stein dropped out of medical school when the abstraction of anatomical facts began to yield to the practical business of clinical medical practice. Williams' involvement with the "whole man" is implicitly less scholarly, more Hippocratic. Remembering the "fulsome bits of flesh" who were his patients, Williams recalls:

They were perfect, they seem to have been born perfect, to need nothing else. They were there, living beside me, and I lived beside them, associated with them. Their very presence denied the need of "study," that is study by degrees to elucidate them. They were, living, the theme that all my life I have labored to elucidate, and when I could not elucidate them I have tried to put them down, to lay them upon paper to record them: for to do that is, after all, a sort of elucidation.

What the writer elucidates in this "medical" approach to the verbal theme is a living secret presence:

This immediacy, the thing, as I went on writing, living as I could, thinking a secret life I wanted to tell openly—if only I could—how it lives, secretly about us as much now as ever . . . . And my "medicine" was the thing which gained me entrance to these secret gardens of the self. It lay there, another world, in the self. I was permitted by my medical badge to follow the poor, defeated body into those gulfs and grottos. And the astonishing thing is that at such times and in such places—foul as they may be with the stinking ischio, rectal abcesses of our comings and goings—just there, the thing, in all its greatest beauty, may for a moment be freed to fly for a moment guiltily about the room.[18]

The apparition of that luminous, ephemeral "thing" invigorates like a nap—or more specifically, like the refreshing sleep-and-awakening of the swimmer of *Paterson* IV. "I lost myself," Dr. Williams recalls, "in the very properties of their minds: for a moment . . . nothing of myself affected me; it was as though I were reawakening from a sleep." Similarly, in *Paterson* III Dr. P.'s work as a physician takes him into a slum basement, where he meets the battered young woman who seems to him a "Beautiful Thing," an image of the purity and innate splendor of his local world. The *Autobiography*'s description of Williams' encountering his patients and recognizing a beautiful, ephemeral "thing" clearly underlies this moving section of *Paterson:*

> Persephone
> gone to hell, that hell could not keep with
> the advancing season of pity.
>
> —for I was overcome
> by amazement and could do nothing but admire
> and lean to care for you in your quietness—
>
> who looked at me, smiling, and we remained
> thus looking, each at the other   .   in silence   .
>
> (*P*, p. 125)

We might also compare these "secret gardens of the self" that Paterson thus encounters with the "indestructible gardens of pleasure" that Marianne Moore's objective poetic language formally opens for Williams as a reader. In their clarity and in their "swiftness of movement," Moore's spare poems offer an "illumination," a "swiftness impaling beauty":

It is a rapidity too swift for touch, a seraphic quality, one might have said yesterday. There is, however, no breast that warms the bars of heaven: it is at most a swiftness that passes without repugnance from thing to thing.[19]

Like the doctor's moment of encounter with a special patient, such an "objective" poem can give the "impression of a passing through." The *Autobiography* describes the moment alone with the "Thing" in the flesh:

It is an identifiable thing, and its characteristic, its chief character is that it is sure, all of a piece and, as I have said, instant and perfect: it comes, it is there, and it vanishes. But I have seen it, clearly. I have seen it. I know it because there it is. I have been possessed by it.[20]

In his descent toward this Persephone, Paterson resembles Boone and Whitman, Williams' heroes who turn and descend toward the hidden life of America. Under the "mud plashed windows among the scabrous/ dirt of the holy sheets," Paterson meets the "Beautiful Thing" objectified in another person:

> I can't be half gentle enough,
> half tender enough
> toward you, toward you,
> inarticulate, not half loving enough
>
> BRIGHTen
> the cor
> ner
> where   you   are!
>
> —a flame,
> black plush, a dark flame.
>
> (*P*, p. 128)

These lines, which echo an old revival song,[21] split the word "corner" into syllables, revealing the "cor" or heart in the linguistic components, like a "radiant gist." The word "you," addressed to the woman, aligns spatially with "cor," for she is the heart of the dark light; in their corner-effect the lines converge on the single verb "are" of the ongoing present. In these lines Williams works the images of physical fire and imaginative light from Book III into a vision of objective illumination, personified in the "Beautiful Thing," in lines that have as their piercing edge the ongoing verb "are." At the pivot of that angle is the Thing expressed as a verb: being-in-time, seen luminously, which is Williams' lure and his theme.

The phrase "Beautiful Thing," in fact, recalls exclamations by other discoverers in Williams' mythology, men like Einstein (" 'sweet land/at last!' ") and Christopher Columbus of *In The American Grain,* as that explorer sets foot for the first time on American soil: "During that time I walked among the trees . . . [I saw] . . . the most beautiful thing which I have ever seen."[22] Like America in her grittiness and potential splendor, the woman in the white dress is the "beautiful Thing" observed empirically but sympathetically; like Einstein and Columbus and Boone and the others who encounter the local on its own terms, Dr. P. here is the spiritual and physical healer—and potential lover—of that woman. Because his view of the locality includes other persons as well as things, Williams wants to give voice to the elusive beauty of America as it appears among American persons, as well as among the inanimate objects of his landscape, the red wheelbarrows, broken glass, and improbable flowers. To encounter that vagrant beauty, however, Dr. P. needs to perceive a unity of composition or a vitality that runs deeper than the individuality of the beings he meets. To this end, Williams objectifies other people in his poems, making them momentarily embody that "Thing" that is beautiful, American, elusive, and impersonally true. We never learn the name of the young woman who is the "Beautiful Thing" personified, for instance, because her personal identity is unimportant to Williams the poet and to Paterson the doctor, who respond to her representative identity. Dr. P.'s model is Shakespeare's Lear, both king and suffering man, who meets Edgar/Tom o'Bedlam on the heath. Lear's projective sympathy at that moment forces him into an oddly objective tenderness. In the suffering of this Other, Lear tries first to recognize his own grief ("What, have his daughters brought him to this pass?"). Failing in that projection, Lear has to encounter Tom as a completely distinct creature, with whom he shares a common human condition. "Thou wert better in a grave than to answer with thy uncovered body this extremity of the skies," Lear exclaims. ". . . Thou art *the thing itself;* unaccommodated man is no more but such a poor, bare forked animal as thou art" (italics added).[23] Such a tone of affectionate objectivity—tending toward an even greater intimacy because of the range and depth of vision it allows—also makes Pound in Canto 80 speculate that Homer had been a medic among the Greeks during the Trojan War. Pound tacitly associates this lesson of objectivity that Homer learns in war with the "affair of the southern Nancy" that had energized Whitman. Typically, Williams' method arrives at the same conclusion as Pound's, but through a more locally recognizable situation, the encounter of an ordinary doctor with a patient.

Thus Williams' doctor both objectively surveys the facts of human life and simultaneously participates, through his human sympathy, in the emotions of the moment. Carl Jung similarly describes the position of the "Doctor," in archetypal terms. According to Jung, the "Doctor" or healer is a "primal image,"

the figure of a doctor and teacher of mankind, the arch-type of the wise man, the helpful and redeeming man. This image has been engraved in the unconscious from time immemorial; there it sleeps until the unpropitiousness of the age awakens it, till the time when a great error leads the people away from the right road.[24]

Jung extends his respect for the Doctor also to the Poet, who similarly responds to the "unpropitiousness of the age" and who satisfies with dreamlike visions the needs of the culture. Like a doctor, the poet enjoys a participatory union with the people *because of* the distance from them provided by poetry's diagnostic, objective, oneiric perspective. The poet is the "collective man":

The psychic need of the people is fulfilled in the work of the poet, and therefore the work means more to the poet in action and truth than his personal destiny, whether he may be conscious of it or no. He is essentially the instrument. . . . The great work is like a dream which, all obvious qualities notwithstanding, does not interpret itself, and is therefore, unequivocal. . . . it presents a picture, the way nature lets a plant grow, and it is up to us to draw conclusions from it.[25]

Essentially an "instrument," Jung's ideal Poet does not simply displace personal neurotic energies into art (as Freud would claim); art is not self-ish. Rather, the poet "dreams" the work, and that dream has social force. The poet at work is "in the highest degree *objective,* impersonal." This Jungian figure of the Poet clearly parallels Williams' Paterson, who in his form as a Whitmanian giant "dreams" his town and its population, who in his form as the individual Dr. P. is "jostled" by his incarnated "thoughts" on the bus, and who in his form as the poem *Paterson* tries to fill the needs of his people for a new articulation.

> The language, the language
> fails them
> They do not know the words
> or have not
> the courage to use them
> —girls from
> families that have decayed and
> taken to the hills: no words.
> They may look at the torrent in
> their minds
> and it is foreign to them.   .
> (*P.* pp. 11–12)

Jung's theory of the reader's role in the realization of a socially formative poem is also close to the theories behind Williams' technique of juxtaposition throughout *Paterson;* we might, in fact, see Jung's essay "Psychology and Poetry" as one of the most important theoretical influences behind Williams' poem. Both Jung's article and Williams' essay "The Simplicity of Disorder" appeared in *transition* magazine in 1930 (in an issue that also featured a section from James Joyce's *Finnegans Wake,* the dream-montage style of which also influenced Williams' work). Williams must have read Jung's essay, for he summarizes Jung's argument in his own essay "Caviar and Bread Again," written later that year. Using Jung's conclusions as a stick with which to beat Freud, Williams in that essay defends the psychic autonomy of the writer against the Freudian tendency to characterize art as a displacement or a resolution of some neurotic energy in the artist's psyche. The poet explores not the shallow waters of personality, Williams maintains, but the depths of the "unpropitiousness" of the age:

> as reported in the last number of *transition,* an abler man than Freud, Dr. C. G. Jung, has finally revealed the true state of affairs to be profoundly in favor of the poet. It is he, the poet, whose function it is, when the race has gone astray, to lead it—to destruction, perhaps, but in any case, to lead it.
>
> This he will do not by mere blather but by a magnificent organization of those materials his age has placed before him for his employment.
>
> At the same time he usually invents a technique.[26]

The work of the artist, Jung explains, "grows beyond him." Such expansion and contraction are possible for the Doctor/Poet because the art-work shares in a collective primal energy: by delving inward, the doctor and the poet arrive at a wellspring of energy or of vision from which all draw their psychic life. The two processes are similar and complementary: the doctor recognizes private energy in others, the poet recognizes a widening otherness in the private self. For "every creative man is a duality or a synthesis of paradoxical qualities. On the one hand he is human and personal, on the other hand, an impersonal creative process." The writer undergoes a "descent" or a crossing between private and public territories; art is the vehicle by which we can follow that descent and can sympathetically arrive at the "impersonal" depth from which the writer's impulse originated.

> In order to understand its meaning, we must allow ourselves to be formed just as [the "dream"] formed the poet. And then we will also understand what his primal experience was: he has touched that salubrious and redeeming psychic depth. . . . Delving once more into the primal state of the "participation mystique" is the secret of artistic creation, and the effect of art, for at this stage of experience it is no longer the individual, but the people who experiences something; nor is any longer the welfare of the individual at stake, but the life of the people itself. For this reason the great work of art is objective and impersonal, albeit touching the deepest things in us.[27]

As in Dewey's argument about the historically fixative power of artworks in a culture, in Jung's theory what is most intimately personal becomes an objective and generative power, through the objectification art affords. This notion of the socially diagnostic and healing powers of the Doctor/Poet informs much of Williams' own work. In his *Autobiography* he characterizes the belief in Jungian terms when he writes about his encounters with his patients:

My business, aside from the mere physical diagnosis, is to make a different sort of diagnosis concerning them as individuals, quite apart from anything for which they seek my advice. That fascinates me. . . . To do this is what makes a writer worth heeding: that somehow or other, whatever the source may be, he has gone to the base of the matter to lay it bare before us in terms which, try as we may, we cannot in the end escape. There is no choice then but to accept him and make him a hero.[28]

The doctor's connection between an essentially "locked" inner world and the hard external facts is the same jump the imagination must make in its effort to marry the mind with the world of circumstances. Thus Williams renegotiates the terms of Milton's dilemma—Whitman's paradox—by inventing a synthetic third category between "I" and "you": the "doctor," who participates in the energies of both the private and the public selves. Like the poet's, the "doctor's" work reconciles the abstract (male, urban, giant, Einstein) with the particular (female, landscape, diversity, St. Francis). Williams wins this integrity through the objectification of subjective experience (poetry aspiring to scientific efficiency), while maintaining a generous empathy (the flowers may be "geometric" but they're still flowers); Williams and Dr. Paterson are skeptical of both extremes, objective "science" and subjective "slither." Williams, who at times classifies science as an "emotion," is suspicious of "pure" science's impulse toward abstraction beyond time and—more dangerously—beyond the limitations of a personal incarnation of truth. Unlike art, which changes the composition of the "truth" in different generations and in different places, both science and philosophy are dangerously impersonal in their rage for order. Paterson is objective as a scientist and poet, but he is a physician, treating the "whole man."[29] And conversely, Williams is wary of extreme Romantic diversity and individuation. When Paterson imagines a flood, in Book III, he is dismayed by the detritus of separate things. Like Lear repeating "Never, never, never, never, never," the stunned Paterson can only enumerate: a Poundian mélange of allusions, a geological list of minerals in an artesian well.

> —of this, make it of *this*, this
> this, this, this, this   •
>
> (*P.* p. 141)

To reunite these disparate pieces Paterson hopes for a synthesis, a "digestion," a marriage, or an "interpenetration, both ways." To know the external world, Paterson is an objective scientific observer, who can glimpse the thing itself. To know the interior world, Paterson is an individuated democratic citizen with his own internal experiences. To satisfy both roles at once, he is a general practitioner who makes house calls.

> Inside the bus one sees
> his thoughts sitting and standing. . .
>   .   .   .
> Who are these people (how complex
> the mathematic) among whom I see myself
> in the regularly ordered plateglass of
> his thoughts, glimmering before shoes and bicycles?
> They walk incommunicado, the
> equation is beyond solution, yet
> its sense is clear
>
> (*P,* p. 9)

Once we acknowledge the dual perspective Williams provides for his hero Paterson, we should recognize also that Williams' much-touted fealty to the common man in the local surroundings is largely a fiction. Williams is insistently loyal, rather, to an essential energy often evident among the poor, the vulnerable, the sick. But such respect for the energy that sparks people, setting them moving and giving them form, does not necessarily suggest a sympathetic respect for the individual. As in the long section in the Park in Book II of *Paterson,* Williams often betrays a disgust at, or a condescension toward, the "great beast" of people—Williams adopts Alexander Hamilton's phrase—and toward the individuals in that mass. Though socially responsive, his linguistic-and-aesthetic objectivity depends on a psychic objectivity; like the doctor, the writer is an observer of life as well as a participant in it. Like Whitman, Williams objectifies himself in his poem in order to earn a vantage from which to criticize and to wonder simultaneously. As Whitman has it, the poet is "both in and out of the game and watching and wondering at it." In Williams' long poem the effect is the more remarkable, for Paterson can shift suddenly from first-person meditation to third-person commentary, without disrupting the pace. Williams' Paterson can be even more impersonal than Whitman's abstracted and universalizing personality and can also be quirky, personally involved, and emotionally subtle in ways Whitman does not often allow himself. One of my favorite examples of this imperceptible shifting between objective and subjective perspectives is the sequence of the grasshoppers, early in Book II of *Paterson*. It's worth quoting at some length, I think, to illustrate how the "objectification" of the imagination's vision makes for interesting shifts between distanced observation and a more personal associative "revelation" of internal experience; the effect is like that of Williams' mechanical, geometrical or arrested flowers. In this "indirect-free style," Williams moves without demarcation between the objective and the personal, as if within the world of the poem the two modes were fluid. When Paterson walks through the Park in Book II, his steps stir a cloud of locusts from the grass. As they fly off, they provoke in Dr. P. the memory of another grasshopper, an ancient Mexican figure carved in red basalt. Like Wordsworth, Paterson is frankly associative, but he associatively remembers an objective, sharable artifact; his theme is neither the autonomous thing nor the Romantic/subjective history of the thing, but the survival of the experience (grasshopper) through time, by means of art. The artwork objectifies an experience (in Dewey's term) and so becomes a "thing" itself. Thus Paterson responds simultaneously to the immediate fleeing grasshoppers and to the stable remembered experience of the red grasshopper. Both mental images merge, and Paterson draws a memorable aphoristic conclusion:

When! from before his feet, half tripping,
picking a way, there starts   •
                  a flight of empurpled wings!
—invisibly created (their
jackets dust-grey) from the dust kindled
to sudden ardor!

                  They fly away, churring! until
their strength spent they plunge
to the coarse cover again and disappear
—but leave, livening the mind, a flashing
of wings and a churring song   •

AND a grasshopper of red basalt, boot-long,
tumbles from the core of his mind,
a rubble-bank disintegrating beneath a
tropic downpour

Chapultepec! grasshopper hill!
              •   •   •

These wings do not unfold for flight—
no need!
the weight (to the hand) finding
a counter-weight or counter buoyancy
by the mind's wings   •
              •   •   •

his mind a red stone carved to be
endless flight   .
Love that is a stone endlessly in flight,
so long as stone shall last bearing
the chisel's stroke   •

                            (*P*, pp. 47–49)

From the inception of *Paterson*, Williams anticipated that this mixture of objectivity and subjectivity should be both a thematic and a structural requirement for the poem. As early as 1928, Williams notes to himself that he should "so remotely influence the plot objectively using incidents as blocks in *his* thoughts, to *be* his thoughts, interacting, and so get 'action' and cause by objective pieces—so construction" (Yale mss.). Paterson's personal associations present him as an individual, but Williams organizes those mental events in a "construction" that tends toward an "objective" idea or generalization. In a section from chapter 58 of his *Auto-biography* (repeated as part of the "Author's Note" to *Paterson*) Williams further details his ambitions for the long poem. These purposes are significant for what they suggest about Williams' concepts of largeness and intimacy in the man-city-poem, as Williams discovers that the desire for a comprehensive structure leads him directly to recognize the need for local detail:

> The first idea centering upon the poem *Paterson,* came alive early: to find an image large enough to embody the whole knowable world about me. The longer I lived in my place, among the details of my life, I realized that these isolated observations and experiences needed pulling together to gain "profundity". . . . I wanted, if I was to write in a larger way than of the birds and flowers, to write about the people close to me: to know in detail, minutely what I was talking about—to the whites of their eyes, to their very smells.
>
> That is the poet's business. Not to talk in vague categories but to write particularly, as a physician works, upon a patient, upon the thing before him, in the particular to discover the universal.

In a political mode, this tension between unity and diversity is a democracy's tension between the group and its individual constituents. In a narrative mode, the same tension results in Paterson's shifting between his perspective of pure objectivity and his sympathetic perspective as an individual, in order "to write particularly, as a physician works, upon a patient, upon the thing before him."

The Modern Democrat and the Modern Poem

Thus Paterson is both a city and a citizen, his work as a doctor mediating between the two roles; Williams' attitude toward "the people" of the country he wants verbally to represent is complex. Though *Paterson* is not a "democratic" poem like "Song of Myself," at times Williams does side with "the people"—for instance, against leaders who claim to wield power autonomously (as an "idea") instead of democratically and representatively (arising from the diverse constituents of a democracy). In Book I of *Paterson* a voice "P," apparently quoting Ezra Pound and espousing a Poundian historical overview,[30] challenges the "I": "Your interest is in the bloody loam but what I'm after is the finished product" (*P,* p. 37). In the published version of the poem, the "I" answers this challenge with a series of equally aphoristic historical conclusions: "Leadership passes into empire; empire begets insolence; insolence brings ruin." These conclusions explain the poem's contempt for overly strong or aristocratic leaders; their leadership tends toward an expansive power that is "imperialistic" in its tendency to extend into other territories. Such an attitude, Williams insists in his essay "The American Background" and in *Paterson,* is the cause of much of modern America's political and spiritual difficulty. Williams is particularly vehement against those "Puritans" who exploit the natural wealth of America while aspiring toward social or aesthetic forms alien to the American surroundings. Throughout the poem, for instance, Alexander Hamilton's appropriative schemes for Paterson as an industrial center constantly provoke Williams' contempt. The structural economic problem has persisted through the city's history; at his first inauguration George Washington wore a shirt made of material woven in Hamilton's mills in Paterson. Hamilton's influence is particularly insidious, for his Society for the Establishment of Useful Manufacture—SUM—historically dominates Paterson's economic systems, having as its primary collateral a monopoly on the industrial use of the Passaic Falls. When in the poem the Falls become an image of linguistic power and possibilities, therefore, the Society becomes, by implication, an image of both linguistic and political "empire." Williams' notebook sketches, the original versions of the conversation between "P" and "I", stress even more strongly Williams' dispute with a Poundian theory of cultural and literary oligarchy:

I. Leadership passes into empire: empire begets insolence: insolence brings ruin.

P. Read your papers. Look. "This may be the century of the common man." It certainly is of the common cliché—but I prefer to look for the uncommon man, the man of genius and ability. Such men are in themselves more interesting, more rewarding, and in the end the country has greater need of them.

   I. Who needs what? If you reject the primary, you reject that which
      springs from it and leaves there, also, its end.

  P. Which is primary?

   I. History.

  P. Made by whom?

   I. Survivors from the disasters brought on by the leaders.

(Yale mss.)

The term "empire" is Williams' historical shorthand for the attitude of those leaders, like Alexander Hamilton or Caesar, who do
not respect the cultural integrity of the local territories they gov-
ern.[31] Even Whitman's democratic urge had led him toward an
"imperialistic" attitude embodied in a vast Self, through a confla-
tion of Emersonian self-reliance and Manifest Destiny. Williams in
Paterson does aspire to a similar inclusiveness, but not at the cost
of abandoning a separate, responsible self. Just as the Many generate the One in the "Author's Note" to the poem, so early in
Paterson Williams works the equation painfully in the other direction, from abstract unity back to particulars:

> But never, in despair and anxiety,
> forget to drive wit in, in till it discover
> his thoughts, decorous and simple,
> and never forget that though his thoughts
> are decorous and simple, the despair
> and anxiety: the grace and detail of
> a dynamo—
>
> So in his high decorum he is wise.
>
> A delirium of solutions, forthwith, forces
> him into back streets, to begin again:
> up hollow stairs among acrid smells
> to obscene rendezvous.

(*P*, pp. 27–28)

Williams' advocacy of the "primary" material leads him to a compassion for, if not to a total sympathy with, the "great beast" of
the people, and he is intent to observe historical processes at work

among the democratic population, not among its leaders or among its consolidated institutions like SUM. Williams' political argument is a subset of his linguistic argument, for in both cases the One is an authentic generality only as it emerges from massed particulars: "no ideas but in things." As the city, Paterson is a suprahistorical giant, like Joyce's Tim Finnegan or one of Pound's heroes, but throughout the poem Dr. P. also walks his dog in the park, cleans his ear with a hairpin, scrapes the label from a mayonnaise jar. Such a personal inclusiveness is a tone Pound discovered only under difficult circumstances; the *Pisan Cantos* (1948) represent Pound's lyrical, troubled acceptance of the intimacy his political commitments had made him ignore.

Williams is often skeptical of such structure, especially if the aesthetic distance it requires should seem to suggest a separation from or an indifference toward the people he imaginatively or physically encounters. As he writes in Book I of *Paterson*, "If I as an artist have separated myself from the scene, it would be a defeat. But I have not. I have made myself part of the scene." Williams' disagreement with Pound centers on this issue of the writer's distance from the immediate materials, and the disagreement takes the form, throughout *Paterson*, of strenuously repeated, at times shrill, observations of the gap between cosmopolitan and local attitudes toward art.

> Sniffing the trees,
> just another dog
> among a lot of dogs. What
> else is there? And to do?
> The rest have run out—
> after the rabbits.
>
> (*P*, p. 3)

Other dogs, like Pound and Eliot, have gone off toward "other peripheries," but the plucky Williams dog stays to sniff the local trees, investigating the "primary scene." By running off after "rabbits," Williams claims, Pound had rejected the American potential, and that rejection led Pound to a linguistic and political acceptance of an "imperialist" attitude toward the "primary" native idiom. By staying and "digging" in the local loam, by contrast, Williams' "dog" stays eligible for local experience. Although that choice proves to have its difficulties in a repressive culture (Book II, i, ends with the sign: "NO DOGS ALLOWED AT LARGE IN THIS PARK"), it does sustain the hope for a new fruitfulness (having escaped her confinement, Paterson's dog "is going to have puppies," p. 54): thus that vitality, in the figure of the dog, can accompany the swimmer who heads inland at the end of Book IV. Williams admits he envies the possibilities available to the expatriots, as he compares their lives and their projects to his own. Comparing himself to the frozen body of Sam Patch's bear (the equivalent of the swimmer's dog), to Mrs. Cumming, and to others who fail to negotiate the bridging attempt over the Falls, Paterson makes himself a figure of frozen hope, holding a potential "springtime" in suspended animation:

> Moveless
> he envies the men that ran
> and could run off
> toward the peripheries—
> to other centers, direct—
> for clarity (if
> they found it)
>   loveliness and
> authority in the world—
>
> a sort of springtime
> toward which their minds aspired
> but which he saw,
> within himself—ice bound
>
> and leaped, "the body, not until
> the following spring, frozen in
> an ice cake"
>
> (*P,* p. 36)

That *Paterson* is a "democratic" or nativist poem in content ought to be clear. Some critics, in fact, confusing Williams' surface colloquialisms with his poem's deepest concerns, have claimed (after Tocqueville) that once again the leveling principles of democracy, mistakenly applied, have generated a bland poetic, a language of the lowest common denominator. William Empson, for instance, is stern with Williams, claiming that in *Paterson* Williams has

renounced all the pleasures of the English language, so that he is completely American; and he says only the dullest things, so that he has won the terrible fight to become completely democratic as well.[32]

Williams had anticipated such criticism and had answered it in advance. In his 1931 essay on Marianne Moore, for instance, he speaks to the issue of democratic banality *versus* oligarchic elegance in art. "There cannot be two arts of poetry," he writes.

There is weight and there is disencumberedness. There can be no schism, except that which has always existed between art and its approaches. There cannot be a proletarian art—even among savages. There is a proletarian taste. To have achieved an organization even of that is to have escaped it.[33]

Williams does not want to write to a "proletarian" taste, nor, as Empson claims, to fix a cultural form in language on the basis of democratic ideals. Williams' attitude toward America and American culture is too complex to be so dismissed, as is, I believe, his remarkable achievement in the American language, as he works the idiom against its tendency toward abstraction and flaccidity. (In this sense the effect of his diction resembles the rhythmic effects of Robert Frost's poems, which play the poetic metric against conventional rhythms of speech.) Williams' attitude is not that of a missionary nor of a convert who accepts unquestioningly the tenets or conditions of a new program. (In Book II of *Paterson* he parodies, in fact, such self-serving naiveté in the speeches of Klaus Ehrens the evangelist. Listening to Ehrens in the park, Dr. P. associates him with Hamilton and imagines a reply to both in a parodic patriotic anthem: "America the golden!/ with trick and money/ damned . . .// . . . We love thee bitter/ land.") Williams' attitude is, rather, the concerned involvement of a citizen who, declaring his loyalties, claims the responsibilities and rights of citizenship: to evaluate and to criticize the circumstancing society, to abhor brutal tendencies and injustices, to propose alternative cultural forms.

If Williams were the master only of the glimpse or of things as they are in their formal completion, as some critics of his work seem to presume, then he might be accused of a static aesthetic— and finally of a conservative poetic. An aesthetic escape into particularity suggests a willingness to ignore general conditions or to accept the status of the *status quo.* Some readers hear in Whitman, for instance, such a static acceptance of political realities, especially in his poems before the Civil War. When he reworks Emerson's image of the (passive) "transparent eyeball," Whitman observes his America, listening and watching, as if he is describing abstractly determined forces. It's no coincidence that most of Whitman's catalogues are nouns, nor that this combination of passivity and static enumeration leads Whitman to postulate an ordering abstraction, a giant Self at the center of his kosmos. Like Emerson and Carlyle, Whitman anthropomorphizes that abstraction into an heroic figure, who exhibits dangerous "imperialistic" tendencies. As we've seen before, however, Williams' focus is motion: "To imitate nature involves the verb."[34] His "glimpse" of minute things and details is not so passive as Whitman's parallel enumeration of things; the brevity and objective juxtaposition of things in Williams' work suggests, rather, an argument about active perception, imagination, and emergent language in a democracy. The Williams "glimpse" is also, of course, a celebration of the particular, nonpolitical "thing," but for a political purpose. The objectivity of language is to reflect a realistic—not ecstatic—encounter with "things"; in language Williams wants to register the self's "new" experience of the familiar, nonpolitical thing.[35] In Williams' politics of perception, that "new" experience should be the basis for a new "measure." From old materials, Williams is inventing a "New World," furnishing it with "things," and organizing a new "measure" by which to evaluate their worth. Thus in a positive mode Williams is rewriting Pound's complaints against "Usury":

> Without invention nothing is well spaced,
> unless the mind change, unless
> the stars are new measured, according
> to their relative positions, the

line will not change, the necessity
will not matriculate: unless there is
a new mind there cannot be a new
line, the old will go on
repeating itself with recurring
deadliness: without invention
nothing lies under the witch-hazel

(*P,* p. 50)

Sometimes the things of the world hold their beauty only in potential, because the political and economic conditions of entrepreneurial capitalism have exploited or stultified the energies of the natural world. In such conditions, language must try to bridge between the internal beauty "locked in the mind" and the squalid objective "thing." At times, Williams' depiction of the minute sordidness of American "things" is part of his argument about the exploitation of the natural world in a corrupt democracy. Williams accepts contemporary local conditions as primary material but not as a cultural terminus. Fetishistic belief in such stasis, he argues, is the result of the inflexibility of minds like those in the "university," where an unquestioning acceptance of earlier forms of thought and of art have ossified the living impulses of the culture. Though he is a rhetorician and a lyricist, Williams is not an idealist, and his efforts to adopt an American (distinguished from an English) idiom spring from a desire not to impose a cross-culturally equalizing "democracy" of diction among English-based languages. Because the conditions of life in Britain and America differ substantially, Williams argues, no such international equivalence should obtain in poetry. Though he accepts the American idiom as the medium for his work, Williams does not fight the "terrible fight to become completely democratic," nor does he project that ideal for poetry. To wage that fight would suggest either that an operative political structure already intellectually informs the poetic structure, or that the poet is writing toward that ideal reciprocity. Either way, Williams is careful. On the one hand, he finds no practical democracy in contemporary America to sustain a mimetic language or form ("the language fails them," is "divorced from their minds"). On the other hand, simply to propose an ideal of political democracy is not his purpose; *Paterson's* theme of democratic representativeness is an extension of his linguistic argument into political metaphors. Like Whitman, Williams *is* inventing a country to claim as his audience—though Whitman does so by postulating a positive ideal, while Williams works often by showing how his contemporary culture falls short of such an ideal form. In snippets of "overheard" speech and in "historical" documents, throughout *Paterson* Williams records instances of economic oppression, of arbitrary social discriminations, of vicious labor disputes and obstinate resistance to reform, of the collusion of Protestantism and capitalism, of the struggle between "authority" and "beauty." In these examples Williams demonstrates that democracy in America is clearly inadequate as it has developed in historical and modern forms. He chooses indigenous American speech as the vehicle of his reconstruction, not like Whitman to praise the *status quo* in order to project a future, but to make us self-conscious of our problematic social structures. "Deformed verse was suited to deformed morality," Symonds wrote of Hipponax; Williams quotes this comment in *Paterson,* somewhat ironically, in order to demonstrate that his concern with an appropriate poetic language is also a social and moral concern, the wish to register such conditions clearly and specifically—and hence to make us perceive in America the "near Paradise it might be with Plenty staring us in the face on all sides."[36] The detailed pattern of divergences from a norm indirectly but vividly defines that norm.

In his essay "The Work of Gertrude Stein," Williams explains both his ambivalence about "democratic" art and his impulse to use the American language as a specialized weapon to counter corrupt American social conditions. Significantly, Williams in that essay faces again the problem Empson raises, acknowledging the predicament of the artist in a democracy (especially in a problematic, linguistically corrupted democracy). Williams concludes that just as art is not to mirror life in the *content* of a work, so the artist of the new in a democracy should avoid the mimetic tendency in the *form* of a work, too. Despite Whitman's example, Williams is not concerned to develop a mimetically "democratic" structure for the new poem. Paradoxically, such arbitrary (and politically naive) constructions result in a formlessness like that Williams recognizes in the most representatively "American" efforts by Whitman and Stein, where it ultimately undermines the self-reliance that theoretically ought to be the formal and political basis for an authentically democratic art. A legitimate poetic of democracy, in the modern circumstances, need not be "democratic" in form, in content, or in ambition. Rejecting the possibility of a general and finally flaccid "democratic" structure, Williams calls for an invention or construction upon the local, personal, and idiosyncratic elements from which the democratic ideal is puzzled together. His dictum "no ideas but in things" is Williams' response not only to abstract poeticizers who sickly over the physical world with unearned sentiment, but also to idealistic iconoclasts whose "completely democratic" forms ultimately deny the integrity of individual experience.

How in a democracy, such as the United States, can writing which has to compete with excellence elsewhere and in other times remain in the field and be at once objective (true to fact) intellectually searching, subtle and instinct with powerful additions to our lives? It is impossible, without invention of some sort, for the very reason that observation about us engenders the very opposite of what we seek: triviality, crassness and intellectual bankruptcy.[37]

The hero of the democratic epic, in a specific place and idiom, appears as the unheroic democratic bourgeois individual. Whitman's joyous paradox, asserting the equivalence of Self and self as a centering energy, is no practical solution; it leads toward formlessness. Conversely, in Gertrude Stein's work Williams recognizes the related problem of uncentered diversity. Whitman had organized diversity arbitrarily, but Stein does not organize enough; the two represent the two dangers of "democratic" art.

Williams' example of the treacherous nature of diversifying democratic mimesis is Stein's "Melanctha," a novella based on Stein's medical experiences, as many of Williams' stories are based on his. In "Melanctha" the writing seems, according to Williams, "like the United States viewed from an airplane—the same senseless repetition, the endless multiplication of toneless words." The problem arises from the materials of the American scene, intractable and toneless, with which the American artist has to work. Facing this diversity, Stein chose to represent it formally; thus she wanders into the fallacy of imitative form. Stein herself had similarly defined the problem in the philosophical-rhetorical terms she had learned from William James: democratic mimesis takes the form of relentless "description" of particulars, in art as in science.

When I was working with William James I completely learned one thing, that science is continuously busy with the complete description of something, with ultimately the complete description of anything with ultimately the complete description of everything. If this can really be done the complete description of everything then what else is there to do. We may well say nothing, but and this is the thing that makes everything continue to be anything, that after all what does happen is that as relatively few people spend all their time describing anything and they stop and so in the meantime as everything goes on somebody else can always commence and go on. And so description is really unending.

Apparently the description of the process of description is difficult to end, too—until Stein tries to circumvent the problem by imagining a formal "complete description" both moving and static, in time and out of it: "as it is a possible thing one can stop continuing to describe this everything. That is where philosophy comes in, it begins when one stops continuing describing everything."[38] For "philosophy" here read Williams' verbal "idea," a re-creation of the internal structure of the imagination's description to itself of the world.

Stein's temptation, according to Williams, is illustrated in her predicament of the endlessness of "description" as a mental activity: the problem is one of too much "freedom." Surprisingly, Williams is accusing Gertrude Stein (of all people) of being too literal-minded. As he works to correct Whitman, Williams also projects himself into Stein's predicament, moving—as she herself eventually did—toward a more immediate statement of the terms of the dilemma—and thence toward a possible resolution, through "organization" of "democratic" materials "scientifically" or "philosophically," within the writing itself:

To be democratic, local (in the sense of being attached with integrity to actual experience) Stein, or any other artist, must for subtlety ascend to a plane of almost abstract design to keep alive. To writing, then, as an art in itself. Yet what actually impinges on the senses must be rendered as it appears, by use of which, only, and under which, untouched, the significance has to be disclosed . . . . The thing, the United States, the unmitigated stupidity, the drab tediousness of the democracy, the overwhelming number of the offensively ignorant, the dull nerve—is there in the artist's mind and cannot be escaped by taking a ship . . . . The purpose of art, so far as it has any, is not at least to copy that, but lies in the resolution of difficulties to its own comprehensive organization of materials. And by so doing, in this case, rather than by copying, it takes its place as most human.[39]

Just as Paterson is a practicing physician in the "diseased" city where he lives, so Williams' political position is sympathetic to the general tenets of democracy but skeptical of the diffusing, universalizing forces of American democracy in politics and in poetics. But this skepticism reflects an awareness of the democracy's unacknowledged need for a new ordering, a new political "measure." His essay "The Somnambulists" (1929) measures the distance Williams has quickly come since his first enthusiastic advocacy of Whitmanian exuberance in his "place":

There is, in a democracy, a limit beyond which thought is not expected to leap. All men being presumed equal, it then becomes an offense if this dead limit be exceeded. But within the opacity which encloses them the American people are bright, active, and efficient. . . . Fear to vary from the average, fear to feel, to see, to know, to experience—save under the opacity of a mist of equality, a mist of common mediocrity is our character.[40]

Ultimately Gertrude Stein had avoided the difficulty by a stringent adherence to a verbalism that Williams associates with his own Objectivism: a rose is a rose is a "rose." (In 1928 Stein's friend René Magritte had ironically insisted on the representational objectivity of painting by writing under a realist sketch of a briar pipe: "Ceci n'est pas une pipe." What we see, that is, is not a pipe but an image of a pipe: neither purely literal nor abstract, but abstracted (in Dewey's term), made an "essence." Similarly, by organization and composition and self-conscious invention of form, by operating on the language that is now divorced both from internal *and* from external experience, Williams hopes to achieve a new integration. For Williams the imagination's flower, objectively constructed for others to consider, is the third "rose." As a counter to "democratic" encumbrances, Williams proposes a superstructure of "almost abstract design" and an objectivity of language in order to achieve the new ordering that the disheveled local conditions obviously need.

Such an abstract idea may sound foreign to us at first, accustomed as we are to the popular notion of Williams as the poet of the momentary affectionate fix of the minor physical detail. *Paterson,* however, details Williams' anti-idealist insistence on remaking our perceptions of the world and on fixing with an organic-geometric form those phenomena we thus see anew. In the world of the poem, divorce is a sign of the times, linguistically as well as sexually and economically, as we've already seen. Divorce of male and female implies a divorce of mind from world, of "giant" language from private experience: Whitman's general problem. But the democracy is also threatened by a broadcast corruption of language (Stein's problem of mimetic diversity through individuation). As dangerous in its way as divorce is in its, the crudeness of public sexuality in modern America is the coefficient of Stein's problem:

> Semi-naked, facing her, a sunshade
> over his eyes,
> he talks with her
>
> —the jalopy half hid
> behind them in the trees—
> I bought a new bathing suit, just
>
> pants and a brassier   :
> the breasts and
> the pudenda covered—beneath
>
> the sun in frank vulgarity.
> Minds beaten thin
> by waste—among

> the working classes SOME sort
> of breakdown
> has occurred.
>
> (*P*, p. 51)

Acknowledging the "breakdown," Williams both describes the degeneration and admits that, though the "flagrant" loiterers he sees in the park personify the problem, the individuals caught in this corruption are not personally to blame; he concludes they are "not undignified," that "their pitiful thoughts do meet/ in the flesh." Immediately before this section, Book II had expanded in that Poundian section about the need for "invention," which had also been Williams' antidote to the maladies affecting the work of Whitman and of Stein. The proleptic or prophetic organization of a new poetic, that is, can provide a model for a new social organization as well, a new system in which the individual (word or citizen) can claim proper autonomy and yet can allow the group (poem or social structure) to remain cohesive. *Paterson* is not specific about these proposals: it is a poem more of complaint and prophecy than of hope and clear projection. "It cannot be *said* what we are going to do"—but Williams can anticipate the shape of the new social program metonymically, by clarifying his ambition for the new "measure" in verse.

> without invention the line
> will never again take on its ancient
> divisions when the word, a supple word,
> lived in it, crumbled now to chalk.
>
> (*P*, p. 50)

These ancient divisions, which the "line" has lost in modern parlance, are not a nostalgic precedent for Williams, but a relative standard he hopes to define in the new invention. That invention will have its own "divisions," like the "interstices" of Marianne Moore's poems,[41] which focus the background light of vitality. And that reticulated "line" is punningly both the poetic line and the line of generation that the poem (pater-son) celebrates. The lovers in the park in Book II of *Paterson,* though their union is linguistically sterile and flagrant, manifest the power of the "line" of generation that the social "breakdown" can debase but cannot extinguish. In this park sequence, too, *Paterson* first records a dance of almost primitive intensity and Brueghel-like vigor. Despite the inadequacy of the language of scholar or dancer to register its gusto, life continues, physical, opaque, and lusty. As he does as a doctor, here Williams again celebrates that energy most intensely in the unselfconscious actions of his "simple" people. One old woman, an immigrant (who carries ancient cultural traditions into the New World but who lacks a new language to articulate them), dances in the afternoon air. The poem, too, "dances" at this point, in half-lines and dactyls, as Williams sets the old woman's exclamations by themselves into the air of the page:

> The rest are eating and drinking.
>
>   The big guy
> in the black hat is too full to move   .
>
>   but Mary
> is up!
>   Come on! Wassa ma'? You got
> broken leg?
>   It is this air!
>   the air of the Midi
> and the old cultures intoxicates them:
> present!
>   —lifts one arm holding the cymbals
> of her thoughts, cocks her old head
> and dances! raising her skirts:
>   La la la la!
> What a bunch of bums! Afraid somebody see
> you?   .
>   Blah!
>   *Excrementi!*
>   —she spits.
> Look a'me, Grandma! Everybody too damn
> lazy.
>
>   (*P,* p. 57)

This joyous but verbally crippled dance recalls several other dances throughout the poem (in some sense the entire poem is a "dance," as Book V declares) and also prefigures the conclusion to Book V:

> We know nothing and can know nothing   .
>   but
> the dance, to dance to a measure
> contrapuntally,
>   Satyrically, the tragic foot.
>
>   (*P*, p. 239)

Despite the poem's claims about divorce, crass sexuality, and social breakdown, in his depiction of Mary's dance Williams shows the same gentleness and wily admiration for the sprightly and the human, especially among the poor, which he claims to enjoy as the first fruits of his medical practice. "This," Paterson interjects, "is the old, the very old, old upon old,/ the undying." The oldest cycles of art—the dance, the reshaping of desire, the vigorous energy belying her inadequate language—all revolve through Mary's dance in the park. Here, as in his appreciation of Toulouse-Lautrec's choice to live in a brothel, Williams' attitude is both sympathetic and pleased, an "instinctive affection."[42]

Nevertheless, despite Mary's example, not all the people in the park—or in the poem—have adequate ways to articulate the vital energies they share. Though Williams' arguments about language may seem to move in a "democratic" direction, they do so by stringently challenging the democracy of the contemporary United States, which chokes the lives of those who live in the "swill-holes" of American cities. Williams' objective sympathies lie with his ignorant fellow-citizens who are caught in the social breakdown— most often, without recognizing their condition or its causes. The three girls who stroll flagrantly through the park have "vagrant" voices, "their laughter wild, flagellant, dissociated/ from the fixed scene" (p. 17). Mrs. Cumming, who drowns more or less accidentally in the river, had been "married with empty words" (p. 83). The crowd in the park in Book II is "amnesic," "scattered" by linguistic divorce or gathered by exploitative, dumb sexuality. The crowd strains to catch "the movement of one voice," but it hears a voice that speciously calls to them: "pleasure" (p. 60). Even more particularly, the victims of the fire of Book III of *Paterson* die in inarticulate silence, like Paterson's silent desire for the "Beautiful Thing."

> (we die in silence, we
> enjoy shamefacedly—in silence, hiding
> our joy even from each other
>   keeping
> a secret joy in the flame which we dare
> not acknowledge)
>
> > (*P*, p. 121)

Williams has sympathy with those who suffer and even die "incommunicado," and to them he extends his bridging language, as Joel Conarroe explains:

It is to save these [people], to find the words by which their premature deaths might have been prevented, that is, by which they might be *alive,* that the poet, attempting to unlock the mind, seeks the redeeming language.[43]

Williams is equally direct: "The brunt of the four books is a search," he writes, "for the redeeming language by which a man's premature death . . . might have been prevented."[44] Sections of Book IV also generalize the problem into an economic argument, as Paterson recalls the image of Marie Curie's discovery of the luminous potential of pitchblende, quotes Columbus' praise of the "Beautiful Thing" in America, and associates radium, pregnancy, and exploration with the power to generate capital for the common weal, " 'the radiant gist' against all that/ scants our lives."[45] Money should generate credit, as uranium generates energy and as the body generates connective desire. To block any of these processes is to invite danger: "cancer," "premature death," "breakdown" in the polis, sexual coarseness, "divorce."

So Williams' concern for a new construction in the poem, a new connective and generative language, is also a social concern, largely conceived. In *Paterson* and other poems Williams claims his imaginative form is also a new social form, the paradigm of a modern common bond between two constituent parts of the self, to serve as a model for a bond between individuals (self and Self, writer and reader)—and so to be a prototype for other social and linguistic bonds. By portraying the culture's divergence from an ideal condition, *Paterson* will assert the "Paradise it might be" in America.[46] This prophetic, experiential social argument—beginning within the actual facts of the situation—relates to Williams' insistence on reversing the terms of Whitman's equation: beginning with the smaller self (as in "Danse Russe"), Williams "goes down" in order to inform the larger assertion with the "facts."

Such a construction on the common language demands both an analyst's distanced knowledge of the causes of the situation and also a participant's immediate experience of the emotions and conditions of democratic individuals. Paterson the doctor, both giant city and separate person, is Williams' integral figure who assumes both perspectives. Sharing the immediacy of the "local" scene but looking for words with "style," an "almost abstract design" to release us from the imprisonment of habituated perceptions, Williams works to strike both tones simultaneously. Though he faults Whitman for often slipping into an aggressively universalizing rhetoric, Williams does follow Whitman's pioneering example, walking the tightrope between outside and in: between on the one hand a complete submission to the external object (as in the work of other moderns and post moderns, like the *nouveau roman* of Alain Robbe-Grillet and the "descriptive-definition-literary art work" of Francis Ponge) [47] and on the other hand a neo-Romantic veneration of the private imagination (as for instance in Hart Crane's *The Bridge*). The temptation of the first mode is the danger of mechanistic scientism, the modernist trap. The temptation of the second mode—personalism—is the danger of extreme "Romantic" diversity through the private self, the trap that endangered Milton and Wordsworth and Stein.

I do not mean to press the case too strongly here; every good poet maintains a psychic distance from the immediate materials, as an aesthetic control, but the difference between Williams' modern doubleness and Wordsworth's Romantic doubleness, for example, amounts to a difference in perspective. When Wordsworth reconsiders his experience at Tintern Abbey, he builds into the rhetorical situation of his poem the distance of time and of personal change. He is not the same man who stood with his sister at the scene five years earlier; the subject of his poem, like that of Coleridge's "Frost at Midnight," is memory, the measure of psychic distance through time. And Wordsworth's formula for poetry—strong emotion recollected in tranquillity—presumes a technical "distance" reinforcing that temporal distance:

However exalted a notion we would wish to cherish of the character of a Poet, it is obvious, that while he describes and imitates passions, his employment is in some degree mechanical, compared with the freedom and power of real and substantial action and suffering.[48]

Williams' distance, by contrast, flattens time; he does not remember his materials (except in Book V) but represents himself in the middle of things ("Who are these people?"), simultaneously feeling and thinking about the passion and diversity of his world.

Frequently in *Paterson* Williams unites his two perspectives, and the results are stunningly clear, like certain Cézanne paintings that represent objects from both lateral and disappearing perspectives simultaneously.[49] Or to take an analogy from a verbal art: in this synthesis of distance and compassion, Williams' achievement resembles that of Anton Chekhov—another modern doctor—whose stories and plays combine a distanced comic perspective with an emotionally sympathetic understanding of his characters as they seem to themselves. But unlike Whitman's expansive first-person mode and unlike Chekhov's dramatic third person, Williams' doubled perspective synthesizes the personal American lyric with the forwarding motion of narration. The most memorable sections of Williams' "modern epic," it seems to me, are those lyric-dramatic interludes in which he states *and* enacts the problems Paterson faces as a doctor (and thence as a poet), and in which he articulates the tensions between American expansiveness and personal identity, between a language of generality and a language of sensation:

> Why even speak of 'I,' he dreams, which
> interests me almost not at all?
>
> The theme
> is as it may prove: asleep, unrecognized—
> all of a piece, alone

in a wind that does not move the others—
in that way: a way to spend
a Sunday afternoon while the green bush shakes.

.   .   a mass of detail
to interrelate on a new ground, difficultly;
an assonance, a homologue
                         triple piled
pulling the disparate together to clarify
and compress

                                        (*P,* pp. 19–20)

This redemptive "objective" flower—here and in a dozen other poems we've read—represents Williams' most consistent attempt to resolve the Whitmanian paradox—or the Miltonic conundrum. The Romantics' responses to the structural problem of Milton's Satan had been gestures either of deliberately Satanic rebelliousness (as in Blake's prophecies) or of theogenic personalization (as in Wordsworth's epic of the developing poetic-egotistical sublime individual self). Those Romantic poets who tried to synthesize both directions sometimes became artistically paralyzed, distrustful of their own poetic power (like Coleridge in "Kubla Khan"). The Whitman problem, as we've seen, has similarly seemed to demand a modern response either to Whitman's giant "message" (Pound, Crane) or to his stylistic representativeness (implicitly, in Neruda and others). The peculiar difference of Whitman as a model here is that, unlike Milton, Whitman overtly embraces the "Satanic" or egotistic implications of his expansive form; he tries to admit the danger to the poetic structure that his "democratically" structured Self presents. When William Carlos Williams works to apply the Whitmanian "message" to the "new world," he finds the Whitmanian equation both desirable and unworkable, potentially formless; like Coleridge, Williams has to face the possibility of self-canceling synthesis. For Williams the solution seems to be to address the problem directly: he writes a long poem *about* the incompatibility of giant ambitions and private experience, and he proposes a synthesis on the basis of a metonymic self-consciousness registered in the self-reflexiveness of the artistic medium itself. For Coleridge the philosophical problem preceded the poetic-structural problem; Williams proposes to neutralize the philosophical question metonymically, by working on the structural problem first, so to make a model of integration for other modes. "It cannot be *said* what we are to do. It can only be proved by our creation."

Throughout *Paterson* Williams discovers how to associate several of his primary commitments: he discovers there are necessary associations among "objectivity" as a poetic form, democracy as a political norm, and immanence as a philosophical mode. Whitman had mistaken the terms, presuming that metaphor—transcendence—is the characteristic trope of democracy:

> I celebrate myself, and sing myself,
> And what I assume you shall assume,
> For every atom belonging to me as good belongs to you.
>   (*LOG,* p. 28)

This Whitmanian paradox of identity (public = private, private = public) is the crux of Whitman's reliance on metaphor: his parataxes are equations. Williams carefully uses Whitman's terms but works to arrive at the position Whitman had naively assumed; it is no longer so joyously obvious that we share anything *but* "atoms." Thus Williams tries to break down Whitman's paradox into its component presumptions. To put the case in thematic terms: if the size of Whitman's Self troubles the proportions of the single poem, Williams works to resolve that tension by starting with the individual citizen (Whitman's weaker side) and by finding the largest collective implications of the "giant" within the range of the individual's experience. (Especially in his synthetic perspective as a doctor, Patterson unites the two Whitmanian perspectives in a new way.) Or to put the case in stylistic terms: Williams finds that Whitman's paradoxical equation of Self and self has dissolved in the modern circumstances, so that Whitman's technique of listing things comes to seem static and merely enumerative. Thus Williams works to make an "objective" subjectivity—a form shaped by Whitman's juxtapositions but directed, involving verbs—so that Whitman's first paradoxical presumption can become again an active, informing identity.

Whitman had asserted a perfect metaphor, an equation of Self and self. For Williams, however, the characteristic trope (of "objective" poetry, of troubled democracy, of immanence) is metonymy. Williams' ideal of metonymy is a formal poetic ambition ("no ideas but in things"), a political ideal (democratic individuation within a federated whole, *e pluribus unum*), and a philosophical commitment (each thing is itself so completely, so "objectively" presented, that it comes to represent a category of discrete things). In Williams' poem metonymy as a trope generates images (marriage, tightrope-walking, androgyny), tone (the giant becomes personal, the person achieves largesse), and structure (both composed and improvised).

> Which is to say, though it be poorly
> said, there is a first wife
> and a first beauty, complex, ovate—
> the woody sepals standing back under
> the stress to hold it there, innate
>
> a flower within a flower whose history
> (within the mind) crouching
> among the ferny rocks, laughs at the names
> by which they think to trap it.
>
> (*P*, p. 22)

Beginning with a slumbering giant and originally ending with an awakened swimmer who turns inland and who plants a seed of verbal hope, the poem *Paterson* thus relies on Dr. P's combination of perspectives to carry the Whitmanian quest of a democratic epic of the double self into the local, diffracted, and alienating North America of the twentiety century. Williams eagerly acknowledges that he inherits this ambition from Whitman. He claims further, though, that modern contingencies require a new formal model, a "relative" or mechanical or scientific structure to organize Whitman's subjective observations. In *Paterson* Williams works to prove that this combination of Romantic ambition and modern technique can yield new poetic forms to articulate the new America, as definitively and vividly as Walt Whitman had articulated his nineteenth-century place.

Notes

PART I
A Whitman for Moderns

1. See R. W. B. Lewis' account of the "fable of the critics," in which nineteenth-century theorists are seen increasingly to call for an indigenous American literature. *The American Adam: Innocence, Tragedy and Tradition in the Nineteenth Century* (Chicago: University of Chicago Press, 1975), pp. 77–90. For readers of Whitman, of course, Emerson is the most important prophet of the new "Poet." See also Roy Harvey Pearce's discussion of the anticipatory criticism, in *The Continuity of American Poetry* (Princeton: Princeton University Press, 1961), 6 ff, and all of Jerome Loving's *Emerson, Whitman, and the American Muse* (Chapel Hill: University of North Carolina Press, 1982).

2. "I hold that a long poem does not exist," Poe writes in an essay published in 1850. "I maintain that the phrase 'a long poem' is simply a flat contradiction in terms." Presuming a poem must be a lyric in order to produce a rhythmic and concentrated effect of Beauty, Poe concludes that *Paradise Lost* is finally a "series of minor poems" linked by stretches of didactic prose, and that the *Iliad* must have been intended originally as a "series of lyrics," not as a coherent epic or cycle. "The Poetic Principle," *The Poetical Works of Edgar Allan Poe* (London: Ward, Lock, 1880), pp. 185–87.

3. See James Breslin, "Whitman and the Early Development of William Carlos Williams," *PMLA* (December 1967), 82:613–21, and "William Carlos Williams and the Whitman Tradition," in *Literary Criticism and Historical Understanding: Selected Papers from the English Institute,* ed. Philip Damon (New York: Columbia University Press, 1967), pp. 151–80.

4. See Gay Wilson Allen, "Walt Whitman: The Search for a 'Democratic Structure,'" *Walt Whitman,* ed. Francis Murphy (Baltimore: Penguin, 1970), pp. 404ff. Many other critics have commented on the politically democratic underpinnings of Whitman's style and structures. See, for instance, George Santayana's "The Poetry of Barbarism," and Edward Dowden's "The Poetry of Democracy: Walt Whitman," both in *A Century of Whitman Criticism,* ed. E. H. Miller (Bloomington, Indiana: Indiana University Press, 1967). Also Hugh Fausset's *Walt Whitman: Poet of Democracy* (New Haven: Yale University Press, 1942), and J. Middleton Murry's lovely essay "Walt Whitman: The Prophet of Democracy," in

'Leaves of Grass' 100 Years After, ed. Milton Hindus (Stanford: Stanford University Press, 1955), pp. 120–48.

5. See F. O. Matthiessen's discussion of the "idealist strain" in Whitman's concept of language, in *American Renaissance* (New York: Oxford University Press, 1941), pp. 520ff. Matthiessen's discussion of Whitman's debt to Emerson is enlightening, as is Richard Adams' "Whitman: A Brief Revaluation," *Tulane Studies in English* (1955), 5:135ff. All quotations here from Whitman's poems and prose will be taken from *Leaves of Grass: Comprehensive Readers' Edition,* ed. Harold Blodgett and Sculley Bradley (New York: Norton, 1965), abbreviated in the text as *LOG.*

6. See Whitman, *Walt Whitman: Complete Poetry and Selected Prose and Letters,* ed. Emory Holloway (London: Nonesuch, 1938), pp. 949–50. In his notebooks, as well as in his poems, Whitman elaborates this image of the poem as a single composite body:

my poems when complete should be a unity, in the same sense that the earth is, or that the human body (senses, soul, head, trunk, feet, blood, viscera, man-root, eyes, hair) or that a perfect musical composition is.

Whitman, *Complete Writings,* ed. R. M. Bucke et al. (New York: Putnam's/Knickerbocker, 1902), 9:3. We should remember these organic images of the poem's "human" form when we come to the implications of the structure of William Carlos Williams' man/city/poem *Paterson.*

7. See Todd Lieber, *Endless Experiments* (Columbus, O.: Ohio State University Press, 1973), p. 26.

8. William Carlos Williams, *Paterson* [I–VI] (New York: New Directions, 1963), p. 140. References to *Paterson,* from the complete 1963 edition, abbreviated as *P,* will be given in the text.

9. Williams, *I Wanted to Write a Poem,* ed. Edith Heal (Boston: Beacon Press, 1958), p. 8.

10. Williams, *Autobiography* (New York: Random House, 1951), p. 53.

11. Williams, *I Wanted,* p. 5.

12. Ezra Pound, *Selected Letters,* ed. D. D. Paige (New York: New Directions, 1950), pp. 168, 322.

13. Williams, *I Wanted,* p. 8.

14. Vivienne Koch, *William Carlos Williams* (Norfolk, Conn.: New Directions, 1950), pp. 33–34. Other critics have written extensively on the relations between Pound and Williams. In my opinion, some of the most helpful discussions are Pearce's in *The Continuity of American Poetry* and Hugh Kenner's ideogramic survey of a literary vortex, in *The Pound Era* (Berkeley: University of California, 1974). Emily Wallace's "Pound and Williams at the University of Pennsylvania" is an interesting piece of literary history; *Pennsylvania Review* (1967), 1:41–52. For discussion of the economic motifs in the *Cantos* and *Paterson,* see E. F. Racey, "Pound and Williams: The Poet as Redeemer," *Bucknell Review* (March 1963), 2:21–31; Guy Davenport's "Nuclear Venus: Dr. Williams' Attack on Usura," *Perspective* (Autumn 1953), 6:183–90; and Benjamin Sankey's *A Companion to William Carlos Williams' "Paterson"* (Berkeley: University of California, 1971), pp. 97ff.

15. Pound, "What I Feel about Walt Whitman," printed in Herbert Bergman's "Ezra Pound and Walt Whitman," *American Literature* (March 1955), 27:59.

16. Pound, *The Spirit of Romance* (New York: New Directions, 1968), p. 168.

17. Pound, "What I Feel," p. 60.

18. Pound, *Personae* (New York: New Directions, 1926), p. 89.

19. Late in his life Whitman, too, tries to associate his structural principle of active juxtaposition with new scientific theories and with the organization of a democracy: "I consider 'Leaves of Grass' and its theory experimental," he writes in 1899 at age 70, "as, in the deepest sense I consider our American republic itself to be, with its theory." This "scientific" metaphor leads him to restate his central theme as the representation of an "objective universe" through the "ultimate vivification" of readers. "A Backward Glance O'er Travel'd Roads," *LOG,* pp. 562, 565.

20. Pound uses the principles of the "ideogramic method" as early as 1913, in *The Serious Artist,* some six years before he publishes his account of Ernest Fenollosa's work with the Chinese language. T. E. Hulme, whose philosophical speculations about poetic language encouraged the first wave of Imagists, had also written about the possibility of a "mosaic" form for Anglo-American poetry, before Pound met the Chinese characters.

21. Pound, *Cantos* (New York: New Directions, 1971), p. 526. See Kenner's *Pound Era,* pp. 486–88, and Pearce's "Pound, Whitman, and the American Epic," in *Ezra Pound,* ed. Walter Sutton (Englewood Cliffs: Prentice Hall, 1963), p. 171. In this brief discussion of Pound's later notions of Whitman, I am indebted to the lucid treatment of the same topic by Kenner and Pearce. For other critical discussions of Pound's use of Whitman, see Charles Willard, "Ezra Pound's Debt to Walt Whitman," *MLN* (1957), 72:19–26, and "Ezra Pound and the Whitman 'Message,' " *Revue de Litterature Comparée* (1957), 21:94–98; also Herbert Bergman's "Ezra Pound and Walt Whitman," pp. 56–61, and John Kinnaird's "Paradox of an American Identity," *Partisan Review* (1958), 25:580–605. Roy Harvey Pearce makes a causal connection between Williams' avoidance of Pound's influence and the emerging influence of Whitman on Williams at this time. Williams and Crane, says Pearce, "struggled to break free, to establish not only their own identities but those of their modern readers. . . . The record of that struggle is in 'The Bridge' (1930) and *Paterson* (1946–51), in which Whitman's hero—the simple separate person, yet democratic, en masse—tries to come of age"; *Continuity,* p. 101.

22. Oddly, Pound's developing image of Whitman—his use of Whitman as a metaphor—corresponds to Whitman's own development: from the first—inexplicable—lurch of energy and of discovery, through the robustness of "Song of Myself" and of early editions of *Leaves of Grass,* through the disillusionment of the Civil War poems, to the more sublimated and saddened late poems of spiritualized democracy.

Biographers of Whitman conclude, incidentally, that the story of the New Orleans woman—and of the children—was Whitman's invention, offered probably to conceal his homosexual inclinations. See, for instance, Justin Kaplan, *Walt Whitman: A Life* (New York: Simon and Schuster, 1980), pp. 47–49, 142ff; also, less directly, Gay Wilson Allen, *The Solitary Singer* (New York: Macmillan, 1955), pp. 97–99.

23. Williams, *Collected Earlier Poems* (New York: New Directions, 1966), pp. 3,5, hereafter *CEP.* The *Collected Later Poems* (New York: New Directions, 1963) will be cited as *CLP,* and *Pictures from Brueghel* (New York: New Directions, 1962) as *PB.*

24. Breslin suggests a Freudian repression of Whitmanian tendencies in Williams' character until about 1914; see "Whitman and the Early Development of William Carlos Williams," pp. 619–21. In another important essay on Whitman and Williams, Breslin enlarges the discussion of Whitman's influence to include many of the shorter lyrics throughout Williams' life and the Whitmanian aesthetic that underlies them. In that later essay Breslin repeats his premise that in Whitman's work Williams recognized a "quest" for a poetic to

"testify to the ardor and intimacy of his contact with the physical world." Breslin also causally relates the emergence of Whitman at this point in Williams' development with the "challenge" from Eliot:

By contradicting Whitman's myth of plentitude with the myth of sterility, Eliot prompted Williams to identify his own informing myth—the discovery of plenty lodged, as it must be in the modern world, in barrenness.

See "William Carlos Williams and the Whitman Tradition," pp. 158–80. Other critics have remarked on the Whitmanian exuberance and ardent devotion to the physical scene in Williams' work. See Philip L. Gerber's "So Much Depends: The Williams Foreground," *Profile of William Carlos Williams,* ed. Jerome Mazzaro (Columbus: Charles E. Merrill, 1971), pp. 5–25 (an anthology which will be abbreviated as *Profile* in future references); Walter Sutton, "Dr. Williams' *Paterson* and the Quest for Form," *Studies in 'Paterson,'* ed. John Engels (Columbus: Chas. E. Merrill, 1971), pp. 43–61 (an anthology hereafter given as *Studies*); and Parker Tyler's "The Poet of *Paterson* I," *Briarcliff Quarterly* (October 1946), 3:168–75.

25. Frontispiece to Williams' *Al Que Quiere!* (Boston: Four Seas, 1917).

26. Williams, *Autobiography,* p. 138.

27. Meyer Schapiro, "Introduction to Modern Art in America: The Armory Show," *Modern Art* (New York: Braziller, 1978), pp. 135–38. See also Bonnie Costello's excellent discussion of the influence of the visual arts on Williams, in "William Carlos Williams in a World of Painters," *New Boston Review* (July 1979), 4:11–14. For a fuller discussion of Williams' use of the tenets of Cubism, see Bram Djikstra's *Hieroglyphics of a New Speech* (Princeton: Princeton University Press, 1969).

28. Williams, "An Essay on 'Leaves of Grass,' " *"Leaves of Grass" 100 Years After,* p. 24. In his *Autobiography* Williams somewhat disingenuously denies this "sour grapes" attitude, at least in reference to the title of his 1921 volume. "But all I meant, " he writes, "was that sour grapes are just the same shape as sweet ones: ha, ha, ha, ha!" (*Autobiography,* p. 158).

29. See Louis Simpson, *Three On the Tower* (New York: Norton, 1971), pp. 253–56.

30. Pound, *Letters,* p. 160.

31. Williams, "The Work of Gertrude Stein," *A Novelette and Other Prose* (Toulon: Cabasson, 1932), p. 108.

32. Williams, *Autobiography,* p. 392.

33. Williams, "Spring and All," *Imaginations* (New York: New Directions, 1970), p. 89.

34. Ibid., pp. 112–13.

35. Ibid., p. 89.

36. It's worth noting, in this context, how much Williams' development from Imagism to Objectivism and onward (while he retains residual techniques from earlier movements) parallels the development of several of his closest contemporaries. The example of Pound is discussed elsewhere in this essay (see especially Part II, note 40). This use of the image of the arrested or artistically formalized flower recalls also the work of Joyce, for instance (especially in the "flower" imagery of Leopold Bloom's life; later Molly "the flower of the mountain" becomes ALP, the tree and mountain).

In an example closer to home, this interest in the flower as a metaphor for the ability of art to stop and to formalize experience recalls also the work of Williams' friend from their college days, Hilda Doolittle (H.D.). As she moved beyond her early Imagist phase, H.D. focused on the possibilities of classical form as a structural model for the stability she desired in modern poems; that commitment resembles Williams' movement (in a different vocabulary) toward Objectivism. H.D.'s volume *Red Roses for Bronze,* the title and title poem of which clearly reflect this interest in assimilating formal (metallic) modernist fixity into organic matter (roses), was published in 1931, the same year as Williams planned his *Collected Poems 1921–1931* with the Objectivist Press. Like Williams, H.D. frequently returned to this issue—and to the image of the "fixed" aesthetic flower to express it. There are many examples in H.D.'s work; see her famous poems "Sea Rose" and "Orchard" (1916), the "tapestry-flower" image of poems like "Fair the Thread," and the "golden apples" section (#5) of *The Flowering of the Rod* (1946). See *Red Roses for Bronze* (Boston: Houghton Mifflin, 1931), pp. 1–8, and *Selected Poems* (New York: Grove, 1957), pp. 15, 18, 67, 105.

37. See the notes to *Paterson* in the Beinecke library, Yale University, New Haven, Connecticut, folders numbered ZA 185–191 and also uncatalogued letters and mss. Hereinafter given as "Yale mss."

38. See Mencken, *The American Language* (New York: Knopf, 1949, rpt. 1919), pp. 69ff, in which Mencken emphasizes the importance of *Leaves of Grass* as a "language experiment." Relating Whitman's linguistic arguments to Whitman's historical context, Mencken associates Whitman's expansion of vocabulary and of the self with the expansionist politics of Jacksonian America; Whitman's slang, neologisms, and "federated" lists are clearly formal literary responses to the political and social conditions of his day. Williams discusses Mencken's work in his *Autobiography,* p. 147.

39. Williams, "Walt Whitman's 'Leaves of Grass': A Comment and Analysis," unpublished ms. in Yale mss., p. 4.

40. Ibid., p. 5.

41. Joel Conarroe, "A Local Pride: The Poetry of 'Paterson,'" *PMLA* (May 1969), 84:548.

42. D.H. Lawrence, *Studies in Classic American Literature* (Baltimore: Penguin, 1971), p. 181.

43. Lawrence, "Poetry of the Present," *Complete Poems* (London: Heinemann, 1967), p. 183.

44. See "E.T." [Jessie Chambers], *D.H. Lawrence: A Personal Record* (London: Cape, 1935), p. 122.

45. D.H. Lawrence, *Collected Letters* (New York: Viking, 1962), p. 221.

46. Lawrence, *Poems,* p. 307. See also Sandra Gilbert's discussion of Whitman's influence on Lawrence's poems, in *Acts of Attention: The Poems of D. H. Lawrence* (Ithaca: Cornell University Press, 1972), pp. 79–84.

47. Hart Crane, *The Bridge* (New York: Liveright, 1970), pp. 44, 47.

48. Hart Crane, *Letters: 1916–1932,* ed. Brom Weber (Berkeley: California, 1965), p. 308.

49. Crane, *Bridge,* p. 46.

50. Diane Middlebrook, *Walt Whitman and Wallace Stevens* (Ithaca, Cornell University Press, 1970).

51. Sometimes the "giant" seems almost a literal figure for Stevens' poems, at other times exclusively a conceptual metaphor. In both cases the tensions are complementary: between spirit conceived as a collective identity and largesse as a personal attribute. Watch, for instance, how Stevens' poem "Gigantomania" concludes, as the individual soldiers on a march consolidate into a single corporate identity. This incorporation involves an increased sense of the individual importance of the single soldiers:

> Each man himself became a giant,
> Tipped out with largesse, bearing the heavy,
> And the high, receiving out of others,

As from an inhuman elevation,
And origin, an inhuman person,
A mask, a spirit, an accoutrement.
For soldiers, the new moon stretches twenty feet.

Stevens, *Collected Poems* (New York: Knopf, 1967), p. 298.

52. Ibid., p. 19.

53. Eventually Stevens works these images to a consideration of Williams' methods, too—though his criticism of Williams amounts, I think, to a misunderstanding of the relation of the self to the world in Williams' early work. In his "Preface" to Williams' *Collected Poems 1921–1931* by the Objectivist Press, Stevens concludes that Williams is "by nature, more of a realist than is commonly true of a poet"—faint praise, perhaps, from Stevens the maker of self-contained verbal fictions. Stevens concludes by observing that Williams complements his "realism" with "sentimentality":

Something of the unreal is necessary to fecundate the real; something of the sentimental is necessary to fecundate the anti-poetic. . . . generally speaking, one might run through these pages and point out how often the essential poetry is the conjunction of the unreal and the real, the sentimental and the anti-poetic, the constant interaction of two opposites. This seems to define Williams and his poetry.

Clearly, crude realism and sentimentality are a paired antinomy; though neither is an attractive mode, Stevens claims to find of primary interest Williams' combination of two undesirable modes. One suspects Stevens of criticism-by-obvious-tact here, in the terms he chooses to characterize the components of Williams' synthesis. Both realism and sentimentality are in any case modes of a false sublimity; each falsifies the relation of self and world, in Stevens' view. Part IV of Stevens' "Esthétique du Mal" opens with the same tensions between a specious unity consisting of discrete particulars and a dynamic unity of subordinated particulars:

Livre de Toutes Sortes de Fleurs D'Après Nature.
All sorts of flowers. That's the sentimentalist.
When B. sat down at the piano and made
A transparence in which we heard music, made music
In which we heard transparent sounds, did he play
All sorts of notes? Or did he play only one
In an ecstasy of its associates,
Variations in the tones of a single sound,
The last, or sounds so single they seemed one?

The "sentimentalist" attends only to random particulars—to single flowers regarded in the diversity of perception, without an ordering or transcendent vision; the sentimentalist paraphrases the sight of the flower in French, according to his private, effete understanding. Immediately, then, Stevens offers the first of two explanations for the music he has heard. The first explanation is a form of naive empiricism: the piano music is a sequence of notes ("All sorts of notes," like "All sorts of flowers"). That is, aesthetic sentimentality is a false and subjective sublimity, unable to represent the flowers clearly (simply "all sorts"), though it claims to value diversity and singularity—and more damagingly, such sentimentality leaves the listener unable to hear the sequence of notes in a piece of music. But oddly, the sentimental position—the ordering of perceptions through simple private valuation—also resembles the "realist" position—the enjoyment of simple physical diversity, unordered. Both sentimentality and realism falsify the real "transparency." Stevens' preferred mode, his second explanation of the nature of the music, avoids both the sentimental and the realist dangers ("only one [note]/ In an ecstasy of its associates"). This alternative of "transparency" seems preferable to the sentimental-realist alternative because of the para-doxical liberation of the materials (the "ecstasy") it organizes.

After this distinction, the second stanza of Part IV of "Esthétique du Mal" presents an overt image of Williams and of his purposes, described according to the terms of the dis-tinction. As Paul Mariani has mentioned, Stevens occasionally referred to Williams as "Car-los," or "Carlos the wild Spaniard." In Part IV of the poem, Williams—the "Spaniard of the Rose"—represents the combined dangers of the sentimental-realist mode: he willfully imposes an exclusively personal, mental ordering on the diverse physical world he claims to enjoy for itself. At first this ordering seems to "rescue" the rose by identifying the external world completely with an internal human understanding:

> And then that Spaniard of the rose, itself
> Hot-hooded and dark-blooded, rescued the rose
> From nature, each time he saw it, making it,
> As he saw it, exist in his own especial eye.
> Can we conceive of him as rescuing less,
> As muffing the mistress for her several maids,
> As foregoing the nakedest passion for barefoot
> Philandering?

Even the images here are Williams', especially from *Paterson:* the rose that lacks tran-scendence except through the poet's verbal reordering, the erotic metaphors of the physical world as a "first wife" whose mysterious attractiveness somehow implies the attractiveness of other women, the problematic relation between the external world and internal experi-ence. But Stevens characterizes the Spaniard's method as a completely subjective ordering, "in his own especial eye." Here Williams' method is made to seem both sentimental *and* realist, suggesting in fact a Miltonic inclination toward "evil" because of the subjective order the observer imposes on his world, an order with the self at the center. The "genius of misfortune" is "not a sentimentalist" according to the pure definition of sentimentality, but he does combine the dangers both of sentimentality and of realism:

> He is
> That evil, the evil in the self, from which
> In desperate hallow, rugged gesture, fault
> Falls out on everything: the genius of
> The mind, which is our being, wrong and wrong,
> The genius of the body, which is our world,
> Spent in the false engagements of the mind.

Thus though at first he seems to "rescue" the rose, the Spaniard's handling of the particulars of the world ultimately corrupts the physicality of existence by endlessly subject-ing it to abstract, sentimental, and solipsistic projections, "wrong and wrong." The prob-lem, once again, is that of Milton's Satan: what seemed tempting and sensual and attractive in the first image of the Spaniard comes to seem treacherous because of the domination of the Spaniard's Self in the "rescue" of the rose. Stevens handles his tacit criticism of Williams in the same terms he uses to worry his question about Whitman: whether the gigantism of Whitman's ideal does not contradict the integrity of particulars. The Whitmanian giant is problematic for its largesse of personal enthusiasm; the Williams-like Spaniard is equally problematic because of the false sublimity of his ultimately solipsistic enthusiasm.

54. Aside from these apparent references to Williams, Stevens' work reflects at least two

subtle patterns of Stevens' use of Williams. I suspect the first important influence of Williams on Stevens occurs during Stevens' middle period, when he is concerned to allow the "anti-poetic" its own integral power to articulate itself. (As the military metaphors of "Gigantomania" suggest, this issue tends to coincide, for Stevens, with the World Wars.) In "An Ordinary Evening in New Haven," the perception ("the eye's plain version") is quite distinct ("a thing apart,/ The vulgate of experience"), as if the worlds of physical reality and of the imagination were distinct realms in which we live discrete experiences. (See the discussion of this dualist tendency in Stevens, in Samuel Morse's *Wallace Stevens: Life as Poetry* [New York: Pegasus, 1970], pp. 196–200.) At this point Stevens seems interested in Williams' work, even sympathetic to Williams' social concerns from his fiction throughout the 1930s.

Gradually Stevens comes more to insist on the postulated fiction of the imagination, which could make "another world" and could at the same time manifest the "sensual nature" of reality. In this sense Stevens' development toward the autonomous image is not so different from Williams' movement toward a belief in the "objectification" of the "imagination's flight." Thus the later Williams' work seems an analogue for Stevens' work, as Stevens acknowledges, in poems like "The Man With the Blue Guitar" and "No Ideas about the Thing but the Thing Itself," the title and opening concepts of which Stevens clearly adopted from Williams.

Conversely, Williams cites Stevens as a contemporary user of "objective language" but disagrees with Stevens about the practical applicability of what Stevens had called the "anti-poetic" facts of the modern world. In fact, for years afterwards Williams seems sensitive to the tone of condescension in Stevens' preface to the 1934 volume. Williams later dismisses Stevens' distinction between prose and verse styles—between the "poetic" and the "anti-poetic"—as "plain crap" (*Letters,* 265).

55. Allen Ginsberg, "A Supermarket in California," *'Howl' and Other Poems* (San Francisco: City Lights, 1956), p. 23. Louis Simpson, *Selected Poems* (New York: Harcourt Brace and World, 1965), p. 121.

56. Williams, "America, Whitman, and the Art of Poetry," *The Poetry Journal* (November 1917), 8:27.

57. 29. Compare this attitude of Williams with Whitman's own virulent anti-British sentiments (e.g., *Notes, Complete Writings,* 9:35). In his later years Whitman—like Williams—tempers his antagonism enough at least to approach the image of Shakespeare and to suggest an ideal of cosmopolitan internationalism for American letters. He reaches this perspective, however, only through a hard-minded nationalism, by claiming to allow the "feudal" traditions of Europe to be "enfolded" or to "flow into" the New World's dominant mainstream. In the "twilight of the dawn" of the New World's ascendancy, Whitman claims, American poets might even learn from the aesthetic models of "that past and those poets we spring from." For this adult apprenticeship, "Shakespere [sic] has served, and serves, may-be, the best of any." "Poetry today in America—Shakespere—The Future," *Complete Prose Works* (New York: Mitchell, Kennerley, 1914), p. 294. See also Williams' comparison of Whitman and Shakespeare, on similar terms, in "An Essay on 'Leaves of Grass' " (1955), pp. 29–30.

58. Williams, "Example of a boy beginning his education," *The Embodiment of Knowledge,* ed. Ron Loewinsohn (New York: New Directions, 1974), p. 9.

59. Williams, *In the American Grain* (Norfolk, Conn.: New Directions, 1925), p. 136. Walter Scott Peterson convincingly demonstrates that the informing themes of *Paterson* are already implied in *In the American Grain,* written some twenty years earlier. (See Peterson's *An Approach to "Paterson,"* [New Haven: Yale University Press, 1967], pp. 40–41.) Joseph

E. Slate also links both Williams and Hart Crane with the tradition of Whitmanian fidelity to American themes and places, especially through Crane's *The Bridge* (in which Whitman appears as a guide and as a bridge-builder) and through Williams' *In the American Grain*. Slate points out that Whitman appears directly only once in Williams' book, in Williams' praise for Whitman's "descent" into American particulars. From this apparent reticence about Whitman—and from the praise of Poe in the same book—Slate concludes that Williams is deliberately avoiding Whitman at this point, especially Whitman's visionary and subjective historical method. Slate does, however, find evidence of Whitman's influence on Williams' treatment of Christopher Columbus as an image of the American visionary threatened by a hostile environment. Slate, "William Carlos Williams, Hart Crane, and the 'Virtue of History,' " *Texas Studies in Language and Literature* (Winter 1965), 6:496–511.

60. Parker Tyler, for instance, maintains that Williams dislikes Whitman's "passive" desire for universality. See "The Poet of 'Paterson' I," p. 170.

61. See Frederick Jackson Turner, *The Significance of the Frontier in American History* (New York: Ungar, 1973 [rpt.]), pp. 58–59.

62. Williams, *Grain*, p. 226.

63. Williams, "Spring and All," p. 111.

64. Williams, "The Refinement," *Embodiment*, p. 116.

65. Williams, *Letters*, p. 142.

66. Joel Conarroe, *William Carlos Williams' 'Paterson'* (Philadelphia: University of Pennsylvania Press, 1970), p. 16.

67. Williams, "Summary: The Logic of Modern Letters," *Embodiment*, p. 143.

68. Williams, *Letters*, pp. 287, 135–36.

69. Walter Sutton, "A Visit with William Carlos Williams," *Minnesota Review* (Spring 1961), 1:312.

70. Williams, "Letter to an Australian Editor," *Briarcliff Quarterly* (October 1946), 1:207.

71. Williams, "The Modern Primer," *Embodiment*, p. 19.

72. Williams, *Letters*, p. 202.

73. Williams, "America, Whitman, and the Art of Poetry," p. 31.

74. Walter Sutton, "Doctor Williams' 'Paterson' and the Quest for Form," p. 60. See Williams' "Essay on 'Leaves of Grass,' " p. 31.

75. Leslie Fiedler, "Images of Walt Whitman," *'Leaves of Grass' 100 Years After*, p. 59.

76. Franz Fanon, *The Wretched of the Earth*, trans. Constance Farrington (New York: Grove, 1968), p. 226. For an example of Williams' admiration for René Char, see "To a Dog Injured in the Street," *PB*, pp. 86–88.

77. José Martí, "El Poeta Walt Whitman," *Obras completas*, (Havana: Lux, 1946), p. 1135. For an excellent translation of the full essay, see "The Poet Walt Whitman," in *Walt Whitman Abroad*, ed. Gay Wilson Allen (Syracuse: Syracuse University Press, 1955), p. 205. For a full discussion of Whitman's influence in Spanish America, see Fernando Alegría, *Walt Whitman en Hispanoamerica* (Mexico: Studium, 1964).

78. Rubén Darío, "Medallones, no. III, Walt Whitman," *Azul* (Buenos Aires: Losada, 1969), p. 107. My translation; this poem and others relevant Darío pieces are available in English in *Homage to Walt Whitman*, ed. and translated. by Didier Tisdel Jaén (University, Alabama: Alabama State University Press, 1969), p. 24.

79. See for instance Octavio Paz's *The Bow and the Lyre* (New York: Norton, 1973), p. 79.

80. My translation. A good translation of the entire poem is available in *Rubén Darío: Selected Poems*, trans. Lysander Kemp (Austin: University of Texas Press, 1973), p. 70.

81. Pablo Neruda, "El hombre invisible," *Odas elementales*, (Buenos Aires: Losada, 1980),

pp. 8–9. Translation mine; in the original the entire poem, the first of the Odes, appears in italics. Neruda's "Oda a Walt Whitman" appears as the final poem in *Nuevas odas elementales,* (Buenos Aires: Losada, 1963), pp. 172–76.

82. Pablo Neruda, quoted in *Twenty Poems of Pablo Neruda,* ed. Robert Bly and James Wright (Madison, Wisconsin: Sixties Press, 1967), p. 103.

83. Federico García Lorca, "Oda a Walt Whitman," in *Poeta en Nueva York* (Buenos Aires: Losada, 1962 [7th ed.]), pp. 72–76. Translation mine, from pages 72, 74, and 76. For a full translation, see "Ode to Walt Whitman," in *Poet in New York,* trans. Ben Bellitt (New York: Grove, 1955), pp. 119–27. Neruda's "Ode to Walt Whitman," *Twenty Poems,* pp. 146–55. Williams himself places Lorca in a "national" tradition, in "Federico García Lorca," *Selected Essays* (New York: New Directions, 1969), pp. 219–29. In *The Poet in the World* Denise Levertov associates Williams with Lorca and with the Spanish "duende." (New York: New Directions, 1975), pp. 254–66.

84. See Allen's *Walt Whitman Abroad,* pp. 220–23, and Jaén's *Homage to Walt Whitman,* p. 75.

85. See Paz, "Whitman: Poet of America," *The Bow and the Lyre,* p. 274, where Paz also associates Whitman with the myth of "Saxon America."

86. Jorge Luis Borges, "Autobiographical Essay," *The Aleph and Other Stories* (New York: Dutton, 1970), pp. 203–60.

87. Borges, "Walt Whitman: Man and Myth," *Critical Inquiry* (June 1975), 1: 707–18.

88. See Allen, *Walt Whitman Abroad,* pp. 187–89, 190–93. For a comparative version of Whitman's reception in England, see Harold Blodgett's *Walt Whitman in England* (Ithaca: Cornell University Press, 1934).

89. Allen, pp. 274ff. About Turgenyev, see V. S. Pritchett, *The Gentle Barbarian* (New York: Random House, 1977), pp. 228–36. The imposition of Marxist vocabularies and presumptions onto Whitman's poems has made for some interesting distortions. In most translations, the word for "Camerado" is "tovarishch," the word English translates as the Russian "comrade," for instance—an association that seems to enlarge the applicability of the Whitman message. By contrast, Soviet interpretations of the erotic motifs of Whitman's poems are more restrictive. Until a recent translation (1981), all nouns and pronouns referring to Whitman's sexual partners and lovers were translated by words with feminine genders and endings, for instance. Soviet criticism has been equally resistant to biographical suggestions that Whitman's sexuality was not completely orthodox. In his study of Whitman, the definitive biography in the Soviet Union, Maurice Mendelson stoutly defends Whitman's heterosexuality. See *The Life and Work of Walt Whitman: A Soviet View* (Moscow: Progress, 1976).

90. Vladimir Mayakovsky, "Brouklinskiya Most," *Polnoe Sobranie Sochinenii* (Moscow: Zydo. Lit, 1958), p. 85. Translation mine; a good, readable translation of the full poem is available in *The Bedbug and Other Stories,* trans. Patricia Blake (New York: Meridian, 1961), p. 122. For a good survey of the response of contemporary Russian writers to Whitman, see Mendelson's *Life* and Wiktor Woroszyski's *The Life of Mayakovsky* (New York: Orion, 1980), 104–5.

91. For an excellent survey of Whitman's reception and influence in France, see Betsy Erkkila, *Walt Whitman Among the French: Poet and Myth* (Princeton: Princeton University Press, 1981). Erkkila scrupulously follows the influence in both directions: first the effects of French positivism and Romanticism on Whitman, and then the subsequent influence of Whitman's work on French Symbolist and post-Symbolist poetic theory.

92. Hugh MacDiarmid, *Lucky Poet* (Berkeley: University of California Press, 1972), p.

327. See also MacDiarmid's discussion of Whitman and the American tradition, e.g., pp. 187–89, 269.

93. Other critics writing on Williams have often found traces of a directly or indirectly Emersonian aesthetic in Williams' poems. Vivienne Koch was probably the first to make the case, and, as a general summary, her observations are the most helpful. (Koch, *Williams*, p. 31.) See also William Heyen, "The Poet's Leap into Reality," *Profile*, p. 28, and also Yvor Winter's pejorative account of the Emersonian/Williams style, for which Winters invented the phrase "the fallacy of imitative form." *Primitivism and Decadence: A Study of American Experimental Poetry* (New York: Arrow, 1937), pp. 41–48.

94. Williams, *Autobiography*, p. 138.

95. Wittgenstein eventually uses the same image, that of language as a city containing within itself the integral stages of its philogenic development, to explain the disorganized growth and developing self-consciousness of language. *Philosophical Investigations* (New York: Macmillan, 1958 [3d ed.]), Number 18.

96. See note 6, above.

97. Gaston Bachelard, *The Poetics of Space* (New York: Orion, 1964), p. 193.

98. Sister Bernetta Quinn, a perceptive critic of Williams' work, explains that the prose sections of the poem are a "study in sources," an attempt to come to terms with the "bloody loam" or "roots" of the local origins of the city. See *The Metamorphic Tradition in Modern Poetry* (New Brunswick, N.J.: Rutgers University Press, 1955), 94ff.

99. In this sense, Breslin calls *Paterson* a "pre-epic" to distinguish its themes from those of finality and "sterility" in *The Waste Land*. See "Williams and the Whitman Tradition," pp. 179–80, and note 24, above.

100. Quinn, p. 123.

101. Williams, *Letters*, pp. 225–26.

102. Williams, "America, Whitman, and the Art of Poetry," p. 27.

103. Williams, "An Approach to the Poem," *English Institute Essays: 1947* (New York: AMS Press, 1965 [reprint]), pp. 53–4. In a 1917 letter to Williams, Pound had indulged in some amateur Freudianizing on this point, concluding that Williams' attitudes toward English traditions and toward England were simple adolescent rebelliousness toward authoritarian father-figures; as Pound knew, Williams' father was of English descent. See Pound, *Letters*, p. 124.

104. John Dewey, *Art as Experience* (New York: Milton, Balch, 1934), p. 293. Stuart Sperry discusses the chemical use of "abstraction" in a similar context, in Keats' use of certain critical words—like Dewey's use of "essence" and Williams' use of "pith" and "essence." For Keats, who like Williams had studied medicine, "ether," "abstraction," "refinement" and "essence" were concepts of poetic craft that carried overtones of chemical distillation from a fluid solution. The poetic process, metaphorically, was a form of such chemical refinement, the removal of the central truth from a fluid material context. Stuart Sperry, *Keats the Poet* (Princeton: Princeton University Press, 1973), chapter 2, "The Chemistry of the Poetic Process," pp. 30–72.

105. Dewey, p. 326. See also Mike Weaver's discussion of the influences of Dewey and Whitehead on Williams' concepts of objective art, in *William Carlos Williams: The American Background* (Cambridge: The University Press, 1971), pp. 32, 50.

106. Williams, "Against the Weather," *Essays*, p. 198.

107. Williams, "The Fatal Blunder," *Quarterly Review of Literature* (1944), 2:12.

108. Arthur Schlesinger, Jr., *The Age of Jackson* (Boston: Little, Brown, 1945). Williams was especially interested in Schlesinger's chapters "Jacksonian Democracy as an Intellectual

Movement" and "Jacksonian Democracy and Literature," in which Schlesinger stresses the cultural ideals Whitman's prose propounds. See Williams' "Letter to an Australian Editor," p. 207.

109. Georg Lukács, "Introduction to a Monograph on Aesthetics," *The Hungarian Review* (Summer 1964), 5:62.

110. J. G. A. Pocock, "Time, History, and Technology in the Thought of Thomas Hobbes," *Politics, Language, and Time* (New York: Atheneum, 1971), p. 157.

111. See Tocqueville's discussion of the effects of democracy on the American language, in *Democracy in America*, trans. Henry Reeve (New Rochelle: Arlington House, 1966 [rpt.])., vol. 2, p. 75.

112. Williams, "The Importance of Place," *Embodiment*, p. 134. See also Conarroe's discussion of the importance of specific place names in *Paterson*, in his *'Paterson'*, p. 121.

113. Williams, "Chapter 469, Etc.," *Embodiment*, p. 54.

114. Compare this section of Williams' essay "The Embodiment of Knowledge" with Whitehead:

> Before any of the arguments begin they must be placed, for from place, a place, begins everything—is in fact a place. Synchronically occupied by everything and at the same time space itself—nothing but. Before science, philosophy, religion, ethics—before they can begin to function—is a region unsusceptible to argument. It is not the past, whose sole property is place. (*Embodiment*, p. 130)

In his notes for this paragraph Williams refers to this section of Whitehead's *Science and the Modern World*:

> The unity of the perceptual field therefore must be a unity of bodily experience. My theory involves the entire abandonment of the notion that simple location is the primary way in which things are involved in space-time. In a certain sense, everything is everywhere at all times. For every location involves an aspect of itself in every other location. Thus every spatio-temporal stand-point mirrors the world.

Williams had read Whitehead's book in 1927 (see the *Selected Letters*, pp. 79, 85). In *A Novelette* (written in 1929 and published in 1932) Williams first records the equation that he will repeat throughout the rest of his career, even into *Paterson* V: "So all things enter into the singleness of the moment and the moment partakes of the diversity of all things."

115. Williams, "Blunder," p. 126.

116. Williams, "Importance of Place," p. 132.

117. Denis Donoghue, "For a Redeeming Language," *William Carlos Williams*, ed. J. Hillis Miller (Englewood Cliffs: Prentice Hall, 1965), p. 125.

PART II
Reading Williams

1. Hyatt Waggonner even claims that for most of his career Williams "really knew very little about Whitman," and that only the pressure of preparing to address an academic audience in 1947 forced Williams to read Whitman attentively. Waggonner carefully concludes that through his active and materialist poems Williams "was in the Whitmanic tradition, very deeply so, even if he didn't, with a part of his mind, 'intend' to be." *American Poets from the Puritans to the Present* (New York: Dell, 1968), pp. 377–78. Waggonner emphasizes Williams' suspicion of Whitman's "freedom," though I suspect that skepticism makes a bit more sense in context. Williams needs to find a way to temper his acceptance of Whitman in order to make room for his own formal experiments; thus he makes Whit-

man's thematic freedom a virtue but his formal licence a flaw. Questions of intention in the poems aside, it is not strictly true that Williams "knows" only very little of Whitman. The pattern of his allusions to *Leaves of Grass* suggests, rather, that Williams attends to those poems that confirm his useful choice of "Song of Myself" as Whitman's best and most representative work. In the later poems of Whitman that Williams does cite or use (including "This Compost," "Out of the Cradle," "By Blue Ontario's Shore," and "Crossing Brooklyn Ferry,") Whitman seems to be reworking materials he had already handled well in "Song of Myself."

According to Waggonner, Williams did not in fact admit his debt to Whitman until Randall Jarrell "taught him that it was all right to have been impressed by Whitman once and to have continued to be like Whitman without knowing it" (p. 377). This argument has something of a chronological problem in it; Williams *was* publishing generous essays about Whitman as early as 1917 and was admitting his allegiance to a Whitmanian aesthetic throughout the '20s and '30s. Waggonner is hard on Williams for his "inconsistencies" about Whitman, claiming that Williams reversed himself from one reduction (Whitman starts formless and gets even looser) to another, in 1947 (the formalism of the later Whitman poems like "Lilacs" is a "defect"), and then back to the original misconception. Insofar as Williams claimed that the poems of *Leaves of Grass* after the 1855 version became programatically looser, he *is* misreading Whitman's development—though one ought also to say that Whitman's tightening of form, indeed his formal development in general, is neither consistent nor continuous. I don't mean to sound a defensive tone here; Williams does oversimplify, and he does use Whitman for his own propagandistic purposes at times. But it is not entirely contradictory to say (as Williams does in the 1947 speech for the English Institute) that the tight formalism of some of Whitman's later poems (like "Captain, My Captain," I suspect) is a "defect," although the claim does at first sound like a double-bind (when Whitman becomes looser he gets worse, but when he becomes more formal his poems are defective). The difference seems to lie in the manner in which Whitman's work is seen to become "formal." According to Williams, Whitman's first and greatest work is "Song of Myself," because of its astute formal combination of politics (Williams calls "democracy" the "meaning" of "Song of Myself") and poetic form. When Whitman makes his later poems formally tighter, he does so often to sharpen the personal emotion of the single moment, not to emphasize the political argument. Whitman simply comes to take himself—his personal self—too seriously; he confuses his self and his role as poet. "Whitman was romantic in a bad sense. . . . He composed 'freely,' he followed his untrammeled necessity. What he did not do was to study what he had done, to go over it, to select and reject, which is the making of an artist" (Williams, "Against the Weather" [1959], *Essays*, p. 218).

2. Williams, "America, Whitman, and the Art of Poetry," p. 30.

3. Williams, "Against the Weather" p. 218. *Letters:* see for instance p. 334.

4. Williams, "Approach," pp. 61, 68.

5. Williams, *Autobiography,* p. 61.

6. Williams, "An Essay on 'Leaves of Grass,' " p. 24; "Measure," *Spectrum* (Fall 1959), 3:153; see also Williams in conversation, in Walter Sutton's "Visit with William Carlos Williams," p. 312.

7. One of those essays, probably unfinished, is still unpublished. Now in the Yale collection, "Walt Whitman's 'Leaves of Grass': A Comment and Analysis" seems to be an informal early draft of the first two-thirds of "An Essay on 'Leaves of Grass,' " (1955) which it resembles in argument though not in style.

8. Williams, dustjacket to *Paterson* III (New York: New Directions, 1949).

9. Williams, "Measure," p. 153.

10. Williams, "Approach," pp. 67–8. See note 14 of Part I, above.

11. Ibid., p. 68.

12. Williams, "Comment," *Essays,* pp. 27, 28.

13. Much as he adulates Einstein without having read Einstein, Williams in the 1940s is fascinated with Proust's "relative" technique, having read Edmund Wilson's description of Proust's method. Wilson associates Proust not only with Bergsonian theories of time but also with popularized Einsteinian theories of relativity in physics and in philosophy as well—associations which to Williams seemed the promise of a "new" measure. When he alludes to Proust, Williams usually makes clear that he means Wilson's Proust; see "The Poem as a Field of Action," p. 287, and Edmund Wilson's *Axel's Castle* (New York: Scribner's, 1948), pp. 157ff.

14. Williams, *Letters,* p. 335. I am grateful to Professor Lisa Steinman of Reed College for pointing out to me, in conversation and in an insightful unpublished essay, this pattern of Williams' allusions to Einstein.

15. Ibid., p. 334.

16. Coincidentally, Williams in his later work also repeatedly invokes Sappho and her poems as models of the passionate poet and of stately poems of passion. Sappho's example seems appropriate historically because of the ancient novelty it suggests, thematically because of the passion of her poems, and formally because of her stately triple rhythms. Much of Williams' image of Sappho seems to derive from John Addington Symond's *Studies of the Greek Poets* (first published in 1920), which Williams read and even quotes in *Paterson* (p. 40). Williams "translates" a Sappho poem in *Paterson* V (p. 219) and discusses the appropriateness of her example (using Symond's version of her) in *I Wanted to Write a Poem* (p. 92).

17. Thus Williams writes to himself in his notes toward Book V (Yale mss.): "No prose. Throughout: form to embody whatever I have learned of form (with variants): a triple line (all the same line really) on three levels across the page. unchanging."

18. Paul Fussell, *Poetic Meter and Poetic Form* (New York: Random House, 1965), pp. 15–16, 148.

19. For Williams on American speech as the generator of "basic structure," see "The Poem as a Field of Action," *Essays,* pp. 290–91.

20. Donoghue, p. 128.

21. See, for instance, Williams, "Approach," p. 347. Sculley Bradley and Harold Blodgett take issue with Williams' notion of Whitman's lack of form, arguing convincingly, from evidence in the Whitman manuscripts, that Whitman revised extensively and "released his verses only after he had recast them again and again to find the form he wanted." The tension here is an interesting one: often the form Whitman wanted was one that would appear wholly spontaneous and impulsive—as if he had (as Williams mistakenly describes him) released his poems unselfconsciously. *Leaves of Grass,* "Introduction," p. xlvi.

22. Williams, "Preface," p. 349; also "Approach," p. 69.

23. Williams, "The Poem as a Field of Action," p. 290.

24. Williams, "Preface," p. 349.

25. Williams, "Approach," p. 60.

26. Charles Olson, "Maximus to Gloucester: Letter 27," *The Maximus Poems* (New York: Jargon, 1960). Even more than Whitman, Melville is Olson's messenger of American "space." See the comparison of the two in Olson's *Call Me Ishmael,* for instance: "Whitman appears, because of his notation of the features of American life and his conscious identifi-

cation of himself with the people, to be the more poet. But Melville had the will. . . ."
(London: Jonathan Cape, 1972), p. 18.

Among the writers who pursue the long poem in our day, Olson is probably the most influential theorist of this Whitmanian direction—though the line is snarled because of the influence of Williams—and of Williams' version of Whitman—on Olson's work. Adopting from Melville and from Whitman the American sense of geographical space, and adopting, too, Williams' experimental sense of the poem as a "field" where the verbal action shapes itself, Olson devises a theory of the poem that links its political responsibilities and its form with the breath and character of the speaker. As it enacts the history of a specific place, the poem is an open space, Olson writes. And "metric then is mapping." This notion of the poem as a mapped field of experience comes through Williams' example, both in specific poems and in critical pieces like "The Poem as a Field of Action" and the *Autobiography,* in which Williams formalizes his ideas developed in his approach toward Paterson.

The poet thinks with his poem, in that lies his thought, and that in itself is the profundity. . . . It called for a poetry such as I did not know, it was my duty to discover or make such a context on the "thought." To *make* a poem, fulfilling the requirements of the art, and yet new, in the sense that in the very lay of the syllables Paterson as Paterson would be discovered, perfect, perfect in the special sense of the poem.

Other writers after Williams and Olson elaborate and formalize this general theory (though not all who pursue similar purposes or use similar means are disciples of Olson, by any means). The results are some of the most memorable work of our day: Robert Duncan's *The Opening of the Field,* John Montague's Ulster epic *The Rough Field,* Edward Dorn's *Gunslinger,* and the endlessly innovative poems of A. R. Ammons, such as his handsomely mapped "Corsons Inlet." More than any single poem, Ammons' entire career thus far seems to embody this exploratory passion to "map" experience: in "small and easy" lyrics, in exhaustive lists, in poems written as notations, in longer poems that take the form of "spheres" or meditations or "tapes." Ammons resembles Neruda in his joyous, formally innovative imagination; although he resists categorization he remains centrally within the North American tradition, working like Neruda independent of the tradition but contributing to it vitally through his formal discoveries. That paradox is at the heart of the Emersonian/American "tradition."

Diverse as all these contemporary poets and poems are, they share some central concerns: the cohesive force of the speaking voice, the westering or homeward lope of the imagination, the poetry of the integral body, the spatial nature of the American or "field" aesthetic, with its open form and pliant meter. All these concerns, incidentally, were first shaped in American poetry by Whitman (and indirectly in prose by Emerson, Melville, and Thoreau, with the "home-cosmography" of *Walden.*) Later these themes were elaborated in Williams' long poems and in Pound's theories of the "periplum' or map of experience. In his own work Olson links the strands together vibrantly, as in his "Maximus" series:

> An American
>
> is a complex of occasions
>
> themselves a geometry
>
> of spatial nature.
>
> I have this sense,
>
> that I am one
>
> with my skin.

> Plus this—plus this:
>
> that forever the geography
>
> which leans in
>
> on me I compel
>
> backwards I compel Gloucester
>
> to yield, to
>
> change
>
>   Polis
>
> is this

Above this difficult territory of evolving forms, Whitman the formal innovator often hovers—as does Williams himself. Increasingly, too, Olson's work is becoming a model for the development of the long American poem, but I think it is important to recognize the tradition into which Olson consciously places himself, along a line extending backwards through Williams to Whitman, Melville, and Thoreau.

27. Susan Sontag, "On Style," *Against Interpretation* (New York: Dell, 1969), p. 25. For an excellent discussion of Whitman's influence on contemporary North American poets, see James Wright's "The Delicacy of Walt Whitman," in R.W.B. Lewis, ed., *The Presence of Walt Whitman: English Institute Essays,* (Columbia, 1962), pp. 164–90.

28. See Williams' review of West's novel, in 1933, "Sordid? Good God!," reprinted in *Twentieth Century Interpretations of "Miss Lonelihearts,"* ed. by Thomas Jackson (Englewood Cliffs: Prentice Hall, 1971), pp. 99–104.

29. In that plane of the Unicorn tapestries in Book V, the "web" of interstices becomes a plane of the imagination's world. See Louis Martz' essay "The Unicorn in 'Paterson,' " in Miller, ed. *William Carlos Williams,* pp. 62–75.

30. Williams, "Revelation," *Essays,* p. 268.

31. Williams, "Spring and All," pp. 115, 134–35, 120–21.

32. *Ibid.,* p. 112–13.

33. *Ibid.,* p. 150. I admire J. Hillis Miller's discussion of this theme in Williams' work, in *Poets of Reality* (Cambridge, Mass.: Belknap, 1965), although I disagree with Miller's general reading of *Paterson* as a poem without unifying thematic structures. Critics who find a sequential argument in the poem include Sankey, Conarroe, and Peterson. I suspect that this distinction—between those who find the poem unified and those who, for various theoretical or practical reasons, do not read the poem for unifed argument—is the largest distinction that needs to be made among critics of the poem. Within the second group some do claim that the "horizontal" or "improvised" unity of the poem is in fact the poem's supervising form. See also note 70, below.

34. Williams, "Marianne Moore," *Essays,* p. 128.

35. Williams, "Author's Introduction," p. 256. Williams may have been influenced, in this context, by Hulme's antivitalistic notion of the "machinelike" character of modern visual art. See also Breslin's discussion in *William Carlos Williams: An American Artist* (New York: Oxford University Press, 1970), pp. 40–41. For Valéry's essay, see his *Oeuvres,* ed. Jean Hytier (Paris: Gallimard, 1957), vol. 1, pp. 1337ff.

36. Williams, *Autobiography,* p. 240.

37. *Ibid.,* 380–81.

38. *Ibid.*, p. 318. See also the discussion of the analogy with painting, discussed above. Also John Malcolm Brinnin's *William Carlos Williams* (Minneapolis: Minnesota Pamphlet Series, 1963), and Jerome Mazzaro's *William Carlos Williams: The Later Poems* (Ithaca: Cornell University Press, 1973), pp. 40–77, and especially Bonnie Costello's discussion in "William Carlos Williams in a World of Painters," pp. 11–14.

39. Williams, *Autobiography*, pp. 364–65.

40. In this discussion we've been calling "Objectivist" Williams' attention to the texture of things—and of words—as they are registered in the verbal "object" of the poem. Williams' tendency here *is*, I think, "Objectivist" in its application to the poems themselves. In the light of our brief discussion of Pound, however, I think it's important also to remember that the tendency we are calling "Objectivist" does not relate solely to the theories of the New York school of Objectivists (Zukofsky, Oppen, and others), but is rather a sophisticated application of ideas that had percolated through Modernist circles for some time. We might as profitably associate Williams' obsessions with other literary movements in the United States, in England, and even on the Continent.

Williams is frequently called an American Imagist—especially in his short poems—and the association is apt, in light of the early Imagists' insistence on "hard light and clear edges," on the sufficiency of the "natural object," and on that "certain clarity and intensity" that Pound claims are the characteristics of the Imagist poem. In its attentions to the physical properties of good verse, to simultaneity, and to formal parallelism as a structural technique, Imagism offers a handy analogue to much of Williams' work—and at the same time serves as the transition, for Pound, from the medieval and Symbolist reveries of his early poems to the more sharp-edged and admonitory tone of Futurism. Louis Simpson, in an excellent discussion of Pound, Eliot, and Williams together, explains that the tenets of Objectivism are implicit in the "rules" of Imagism, if rightly understood. (Simpson, *Three On the Tower*, p. 286.)

The Futurist movement, for that matter, might also serve as an ingress or an analogy to Williams' work. The Imagist technique of simple parallelism suggests motion in the juxtaposed images of the argument; the Imagist technique thus points toward the more complex techniques the Futurists devised to represent simultaneity and motion through apposed images. Machines—especially automobiles and trains—were the modern cultural icon and structural ideal for many Continental and British Futurists, like Marinetti: several years after the first big splash of Futurism in London, in fact, T. E. Hulme pressed for the creation of an art that had a "structure like that of a machine." Williams certainly has sympathies with both the Futurists' contempt for revered cultural objects and with their respect for art structured like a mosaic or a machine. Pound himself eventually moved from his temporary fascination with the strident iconoclasm of the Futurists, to an involvement with Vorticism, a movement we might also see as a more complex and socialized application of essentially Imagist ideas. Instead of considering the Image as the presentation of an intellectual and emotional complex in an instant of time, Vorticism expanded the synchronic parallelism of the Image to include "planes in relation." Those "planes" of the Vorticists clearly represent one stage in the continuous development of Pound's career. In the Vortex (Pound gave the movement its particularly galvanizing metaphor) forces intersect in a place that is itself still: the image of the Vortex clearly relates in one direction to the parallelism and simultaneity of the earlier Imagists and Futurists, and in the other direction to Pound's later fascination with the binding power of the "ideogram" as a structural device.

Any of these metaphors might profitably be used to explain Williams' work, as they might also be used to point toward Pound's later techniques in the *Cantos*. For a point of comparison we could use any of Pound's metaphors—the Image, the machine, the Vortex, the ideogram—to discuss Williams' development. Though he insists on a fidelity to American themes and language, Williams is not as parochial as he and many of his commentators would have us believe. He was in contact, at least indirectly, with the movements through which Pound passed, for instance, in the course of Pound's more international career; nor does Williams make any secret of his continuous involvement with the New York literary and artistic scene, an hour from his home in Rutherford. Many of the phases through which Pound moved, and many of the momentary or lasting trends in American arts, appear in Williams' prose writings and, at least implicitly, in the poems. I think that in the long run the largest contribution of Paul Mariani's awesome biography of Williams (*William Carlos Williams: A New World Naked* [New York: McGraw Hill, 1981]) will prove to have been the successful task of locating Williams within the context of the contemporary intellectual movements mentioned above. (Bram Dijkstra and Mike Weaver, in their books on Williams, also work admirably to describe Williams' work in the context of several aesthetic movements.) Our response to this biographical work ought to be a new critical orientation toward Williams' deceptively simple-looking poems, and a greater respect for Williams' conceptual intelligence: surely the best results a biographer could ask for.

If we are calling Williams' attention to the verbal object of the poem a form of "Objectivism," therefore, we do so with the understanding that we might also call that aesthetic commitment a developed form of Imagism, or of Futurism, or of Vorticism—or even of the Ideogramic Method—in the same sense that Pound's own procession of movement shares, at root, a concern with the objectivity of the word, and an attention to the structure and the "purified" language of the Modern poem. See Louis Simpson's *Three on the Tower* for a clear discussion of the series and consistencies of Pound's various "isms." For a good discussion of the tenets of Objectivism in the work of other writers, see David McAleavey's "If to Know is Noble: The Poetry of George Oppen," (Ph.D. dissertation, Cornell University, Cornell University, 1975), especially the introduction and chapter 1.

41. T. S. Eliot, "Hamlet and His Problems," *Collected Essays* (New York: Harcourt, Brace, and World, 1960), pp. 124–25. "The only way of expressing emotion in the form of art is by finding an 'objective correlative'; in other words, a set of objects, a situation, a chain of events which shall be the formula of the particular emotion; such that when the external facts which must terminate in sensory experience, are given, the emotion is immediately evoked." Aside from obvious cultural and aesthetic differences between Eliot and Williams, we should notice here that the attitudes toward the self differ, though finally their commitments to techniques of objective correlation do not differ widely. Eliot is concerned with an ideal anonymity for the objective poet; Williams moves toward a similar objectivity, in order more accurately to "reveal" a truth by the mediation of things and of images. Eliot's Tiresias is much less involved in the life of his city than Williams' Dr. P. is in Paterson. See also Parker Tyler's comparison of Eliot's "objective correlative" and Williams' technique in *Paterson,* in "The Poet of 'Paterson One,' " p. 196.

42. See chapter 3 of Max Black's *Models and Metaphors* (Ithaca: Cornell University Press, 1962) for a pertinent discussion of metaphor as verbal "interaction," pp. 25–48. I think it's important in this context to remember that Williams does not harbor any special fondness for the machine *qua* machine. Book II of *Paterson* and Williams' own comments about the "contrast between the mythic beauty of the Falls and Mountain and the industrial hideousness" of the modern city should indicate his mistrust of the industrialization of an expansive, Whitmanian landscape. The image of Dürer's *Melancholy* in Book III of *Paterson* ("gears/ lying disrelated to the mathematics of the machine/ Useless" p. 119) is another image of the

dissolution and spiritual deathliness of the imagination when it is oppressed by past forms, the human spirit lost among the machine parts. In this pejorative sense, too, Eliot, who "spoke of April," is an "insane engineer," because of his advocacy of older forms of art and of former cultures:

> There is no recurrence.
> The past is dead. Women are
> legalists, they want to rescue
> a framework of laws, a skeleton of
> practices, a calcined reticulum
> of the past which, bees, they will
> fill with honey   .
>
> (*P*, 142)

What Williams demands for his theoretically machinelike poem is a new mechanical construction that defies mechanics, a relative and new machine, to channel the energies of the present moment. It will be relative, not like the sonnet or iambic line, which are merely agents of the automatic transferral of present energies into past shapes. See Williams quoted in conversation by John Thirlwall, in "William Carlos Williams' *Paterson:* The Search for a Personal Epic in Five Parts," *New Directions* (1961), 17: 236–37.

43. Denise Levertov, "An Admonition," *The Poet in the World*, p. 53.

44. Marianne Moore, "Marriage," *A Marianne Moore Reader* New York: Viking, 1965), p. 13. In 1935 the poem appeared in Moore's *Selected Poems,* where Williams read it while he was finishing work on *Adam and Eve and the City* (1936)—though he had probably read the poem, or some version of it, earlier. For a fine discussion of the "Capacity for Fact" in Moore's work, see the chapter by that title in Bonnie Costello's *Marianne Moore: Imaginary Possessions* (Cambridge: Harvard University Press, 1981), pp. 65–108. Costello's careful, brilliant study, which reads the poems individually and also places Moore in the context of Modernist concerns, is the best critical work available on Moore.

45. William Butler Yeats, "The Secret Rose," *Collected Poems* (New York: Viking, 1965), p. 13.

46. Williams even parodies such allusiveness, in Corydon's poem in Book IV, section i of *Paterson*. Though ostensibly describing the "elemental scene" of the view of the East River, Corydon echoes or blatantly cribs from Yeats, Eliot, Pound, Hart Crane, and others. The urban "Idyll" of this section elaborately parodies the pastoral tradition (including the *Idylls* of Theocritus and the *Eclogues* of Virgil), but like Joyce's "mythic method" in *Ulysses* Williams' parody leaves uncertain whether the tradition or the modern world is responsible for the apparent silliness of the comparison: is the tradition simply outmoded, or is its application to this world inappropriate? Or—like Leopold Bloom—does Corydon, almost despite herself, embody an unexpected dignity, an attitude that finally validates the unlikely classical comparison? Williams claimed later that, despite his worst intentions, while writing the section he came to like "the old gal." (*Letters*, p. 302.)

47. J. Hillis Miller, "Introduction," *Williams*, p. 11.

48. Williams, "Marianne Moore," p. 147.

49. Early drafts of these lines emphasize even more strongly the relation between the beauty locked in the individual mind and the things that surround it. " 'Beauty' is the quest," the poem originally began, "and how will you find beauty when it is locked in the mind? It is not in the things about us until transposed there by our employment. Make it free, then, by the art you have, to enter these starved and broken pieces." (Ms. in the Rare

Books and Manuscript Collection, State University of New York at Buffalo—a collection hereinafter given as "Buffalo mss.")

50. Williams, "Marianne Moore," pp. 126, 127.

51. Williams, "Prologue" to "Kora in Hell," *Essays,* p. 16.

52. For a helpful discussion of the "epic" tendency in Whitman, Pound, Crane, and Williams, see Pearce's *Continuity,* pp. 100ff. Joseph E. Slate, among others, compares the techniques of Williams and Crane, though he pays closer attention to the dialogues with history in *In the American Grain* than to *Paterson* (see Part I, note 58). Slate claims also to see in *Paterson* I references to Crane's work and to his apparent suicide by drowning. In the context of our discussion here, the most pertinent evidence is probably Williams' ambivalent euology for Crane, shortly after Crane's death in 1932. In an opinion that remains constant despite changes in his other attitudes toward Crane as a fellow American writer, Williams praises the "music" of Crane's "words" but concludes that in his oceanic subjectivity Crane had tended too strongly toward a prolix sentimentality:

> His agony, which was real and which raised him to distinction above danger from attack, throws a white glare over his best work—in the manner of the light in Van Gogh's painting. But the sheer objectivity of the pigment kept the latter anchored whereas Crane appears to me often to have neglected the equal objectivity of words in making up his composition. Edges, facets often escape him—to his undoing.

"Hart Crane (1899–1932)," *Contempo* (July 5, 1932), 2: 5.

53. Williams, *Autobiography,* p. 392; see also Peterson, p. 181.

54. The name "Faitoute" seems to be a French neologism meaning "Jack-of-all-trades."

55. See note 29 above. Also Peterson, pp. 23–36. John Malcolm Brinnin, in the context of an excellent discussion, also mentions what he calls the "tightrope-walking progress of an idea" as the mode of *Paterson*'s development, p. 14.

56. Williams, "Measure," p. 135.

57. "Everything in the poem," Lowell concludes, "is either masculine or feminine, everything strains toward marriage, but the marriage never comes off, except in the imagination, and there, attenuated, fragmentary, and uncertain." Lowell's qualification is important; the marriage of the universal and the local, of spirit and world, can happen in the imagination, and there only fleetingly, though "objectified" in the poem. In this sense the difficulty of the "marriage" theme is not so humanly problematic as Lowell suggests. Lowell, "Paterson II," *Nation* (June 19, 1949), 166: 693. See also Lowell's "William Carlos Williams," *Hudson Review* (1961–1962), 14: 530–36.

58. As Williams writes in his "Essay on Virginia": "ability in an essay is multiplicity, infinite fracture, the intercrossing of opposed forces establishing any number of opposed centers of stillness." Compare this interrelatedness with Williams' praise of Marianne Moore's poems for their "intersection of loci."

59. Pearce, *Continuity,* p. 112.

60. See for instance Harold Bloom's *The Anxiety of Influence* (New York: Oxford University Press, 1973), where the theory is first propounded; it does seem anticipated in Bloom's earlier work on the high Romantic poets. It is not coincidental that Bloom's Freudian schema takes the Milton-Romantic axis as its chief model, paralleled in the later American Romanticism by the axis between Emerson and later writers. The example of the Romantics—especially Coleridge and Wordsworth—as the primary model works especially, perhaps uniquely, well for the Bloom program, because of the Romantics' theories of aggressive subjectivity and of creative self-assertion (the repetition in the human mind of the "I

AM" of the Logos, and so forth). The theory brilliantly explains problems of influence among British and American Romantic poets; it is primarily a theory about British and American Romanticism, not a general theory of poetry, because it is postulated on a transmission of Romantic aesthetic values as a definition of poetry.

61. One might object, with reason, to Williams' limiting characterization, here and throughout his other work, of the "feminine" experience as essentially materialistic, mindless, and nonverbal. Nevertheless, his attitude is intended finally as a tribute to the "female" and erotic consciousness of surroundings that Williams claims, as a writer, to share with women. (Compare Simone de Beauvoir's argument about female eroticism and sense of place in *The Second Sex,* trans. H. M. Parshley [New York: Knopf, 1971, reprint], pp. 376–77, 529, for example.) Throughout his life Williams associates the energy and "proportion" of women with the materials of verse, balanced against the "technical" and formal preoccupations of men (see his "Letter to an Australian Editor," p. 222). He even criticized Pound for having cut himself off from the fecundating "female" principle of American place. America speaks as a woman throughout *Paterson* and *In the American Grain,* where Abraham Lincoln appears as an old woman with a full black beard: another androgyne. Considering Williams' admiration for the American "voice," and weighing this characterization of the "female" against his characterization of the "male" mind as overly ordered, sterile, and abstract, we might conclude that this characterization of the "feminine" is not entirely pejorative. As in his attitudes toward many of his female patients, Williams' attitude here *is* domineering and manipulative and opportunistic—and yet intended to be tender and respectful.

62. Williams, "Comedy Entombed," first collected in *Beer and Coldcuts,* reprinted in *Make Light of It* (New York: Random House, 1950), p. 322.

63. Bernard Duffey, "Williams' 'Paterson' and the Measure of Art," *Studies,* 61 and Kenneth Burke's more literal discussion of Williams' objectivism, in *A Grammar of Motives* (New York: Prentice Hall, 1945), pp. 486ff. Also Williams, "Marianne Moore," p. 125.

64. Williams, "Marianne Moore," p. 123. In several essays Williams unites both sets of images. In a piece entitled "Some Hints Toward the Enjoyment of Modern Verse," Williams combines the image of the machine with the idea of a poem as a grid imposed on a luminous background, as he describes the poet as an engineer designing a construction in which the words are bricks or metal and the spaces of the page an airy mortar. *Quarterly Review of Literature* (1952), 8:174.

65. Williams, quoted by Vivienne Koch, p. 77.

66. Williams, "An Essay on Virginia," *Imaginations,* p. 321.

67. Williams, "The Poem as a Field of Action," p. 291.

68. Williams, "How to Write," *New Directions in Prose and Poetry,* ed. James Laughlin (New London: New Directions, 1936), pp. 45, 47.

69. See Burke's description of literary form in *Counterstatement* (New York: Harcourt, Brace, 1931), p. 40.

70. See note 33, above. Todd Lieber and James Guimond, for instance, call the idea "invention," John Malcolm Brinnin calls it "discovery," and Walter Sutton describes the idea in action:

The poet is a maker, an inventor of form. He is active, engaged in the world of experience, and the proper form for the poem must be sought—painfully, laboriously—as the poet attempts to achieve an order of words compatible with the time, and language, flux in which he lives. This search is the major theme of "Paterson."

See Walter Sutton, "Quest," p. 46; also Lieber, p. 212, and Guimond, *The Art of William Carlos Williams* (Urbana: University of Illinois Press, 1968), p. 181. Many critics have written cogently on the question of "form" in *Paterson*. Randall Jarrell, for instance, is hard on Williams, calling his form "the organization of irrelevance (or Irrelevance of Organization)"; "Three Books," *Poetry and the Age* (New York: Vintage, 1959), p. 693. Joseph Bennett and John Malcolm Brinnin seem to belong in this camp of critics, who claim to see a deliberate "formlessness" in the poem (Bennett, "The Lyre and the Sledgehammer," *Hudson Review* [Summer 1952], 6:305; Brinnin, pp. 36ff), though Brinnin does agree with those critics who see the specter of formlessness as a theme of Williams' poem. Sister M. Bernetta Quinn describes the poem as Williams' "testament of perpetual change," Vivienne Koch insists on the "process" of the poem, and Richard Macksey explains the movement of the poem in terms of its "kinetic syntax" (Quinn, p. 112; Koch, p. 144; Macksey, "A Certainty of Music: Williams' Changes," *Williams*, ed. Miller, p. 146). Other critics, like Macksey as well, have explained the process of *Paterson* in terms of music, dance, and dream: all images which run through the poem. See also Gordon Grigsby's "The Modern Long Poem: Studies in Thematic Form" (Ph.D. dissertation, University of Wisconsin, 1960), pp. 67ff.

71. Williams, *Letters,* p. 214.

72. Williams, *I Wanted,* p. 73. George Zabriskie has mapped out the path of the poem onto the literal geography of the city Paterson, New Jersey. See "The Geography of Paterson," *Perspective* (Winter 1953), 6:201–16.

73. James Guimond, who also discusses this "seasonal" arrangement of the sections of the poem, interestingly relates this seasonal motif to the "Author's Note" and to the collection of "introductory" images at the beginning of the poem (p. 176). Whitman, too, divided "Song of Myself" into 52 sections, like the weeks of the year—as if to make the poem seem to recapitulate a year-cycle. That division of the unnumbered sections, however, did not appear in the poem until after the early editions, and was added apparently as an afterthought. (Around 1857 Whitman began to think of *Leaves of Grass* as a collection of potentially 365 poems; only in the late 1860s did he begin to think of the book as "groups" of poems organized like the organs of a single body.)

74. Both Guy Davenport and Joel Conarroe have observed the repetition of the four essential elements throughout *Paterson*. See Davenport, p. 189, and Conarroe's book, p. 85.

75. Evidence in the manuscripts to *Paterson* in the Yale collection suggests, in fact, that originally Williams had even more strongly organized the 12 original sections around a set of abstract "absolutes":

Paterson
1. absolute love
2.   "   poetry
3.   "   religion
4.   "   science (power)
5.   "   finance (in persons devoid of bunk)
6.   "   labor
7.   "   criminality
8.   "   law
9.   "   style
10.   "   learning
11.   "   music
12.   "   pity

These "absolute" structures were abandoned in later drafts of *Paterson,* though traces of all these themes remain—often in this order—in the final version of the poem.

76. See Frank Kermode's discussion of these Romantic themes as they are carried into the poetry of the early twentieth century, especially through Yeats, in *Romantic Image* (New York: Macmillan, 1957).

77. Williams, quoted in conversation by Walter Sutton in "A Visit," p. 322.

78. See, for instance, Eliot's concept of memory and place in "Little Gidding." In the argument of that poem, memory leads to "liberation"; loyalty to a place begins as "attachment to our own field of action," but ultimately frees us from such parochial concerns. See *Four Quartets* (New York: Harcourt, Brace, 1968), p. 36.

In his own concept of fealty to a "field of action," Williams continues to resist Eliot's apparent avoidance of a commitment to the specificity of a place, referring to Eliot's "fatal blunder" of thinking that place is finally insignificant except as material for memory, or as the springboard for a liberating transcendence. See note 107, Part I, above.

PART III
The Two Whitmans Joined

1. Richard Pascal, in an unpublished doctoral dissertation, also briefly notes the resemblance between Whitman's aggregated self and the topographically giant Paterson ("The Radiant Gist: Romantic Strains in 'Song of Myself' and 'Paterson,' " [Ithaca: Cornell University, 1971], p. 106). Pascal's treatment of the poems is most helpful when he relates the major themes of both poems to a high Romantic concern with the philosophy of perception.

2. Williams, "Approach," p. 67.

3. Ibid., p. 67.

4. All these qualities also strongly recall the sleeping hero of James Joyce's *Finnegans Wake,* exerpts of which had appeared throughout the 1930s and '40s in issues of magazines with Williams' work. A man who is also a city, who sleeps in his giant form beside a female counterpart (Joyce's ALP, like Williams' Garret Mountain), who mythically dreams the history of his race and of his place, and whose dreams define a new objective use of language, Finn clearly anticipates Williams' Paterson. See also *Paterson* III, i, in which the Passaic Falls (like the "falls" of Joyce's Adam/HCE/Humpty Dumpty) spells out a Joycean "riddle." This "marriage riddle" links the various metaphors of marriage throughout *Paterson* with the theme of language: the connections define a Joycean theme, the marriage of the mind and its world, in language. See Williams' essays on Joyce, especially the 1927 "Note on the Recent Work of James Joyce," *Essays,* pp. 75–80.

In Joyce's publications during the early 1920s, the first published sections of the *Wake* clearly seemed to follow from the late sections of *Ulysses;* the Anna Livia Plurabelle section was written early in the 1920s, apparently carrying Joyce with the momentum of the "Penelope" section of *Ulysses.* The continuity of Joyce's career is pertinent here because sometimes (as in the *Autobiography*) Williams claims that *Ulysses* was his Joycean model for *Paterson,* while at other times he seems to claim the *Wake* as his model; the 1927 essay on the "Recent Work of Joyce" seems to be as much about the "Penelope" section as about "ALP."

5. See Peterson, pp. 204–6.

6. Williams writes, for instance, of the need for a "sea change" in the poetic line, to make possible a new language, "a line loose as Whitman's but measured as his was not." *I Wanted,* p. 8.

7. Williams, "New from New Directions," news release, May 31, 1951, unpaginated.

8. Williams, *Letters,* pp. 291–2. The image of the potent seed is vital to Williams' notion

of the efficacy of art in the culture. The image relates, similarly, to the various images of flowers in the short poems and in *Paterson*. Using the same metaphor, Williams in the *Autobiography* comments on Pound's propaedeutic purposes in the *Cantos:* "the poem is a capsule where we wrap up our punishable secrets. And they confide in themselves the only 'life,' the ability to sprout at a more favorable time, to come true in their secret structures to the very minutest details of our thoughts, so that they get their specific virtue. We write for this, that the seed come true" (p. 342).

9. Ralph Nash, "The Use of Prose in *Paterson*," *Studies,* p. 20; see also Williams, *Letters,* p. 266, and Peterson, pp. 69, 166.

10. Williams, *Autobiography*, p. 61.

11. *Ibid.*, 392.

12. Williams, "An Essay on 'Leaves of Grass,' " p. 26.

13. In the Yale mss, Williams has numbered the final four lines for a different order:

driving the words above
[3] the returning clatter of stones
[2] with courage, labor and abandon
[1]   the word, the word, the word

The difference in the reading of the lines as a result of the rearrangement is largely a matter of emphasis; perhaps Williams thought the poem should end with the assertion of the "stones" against which the speaker hurls his voice—but that ending for the poem, ultimately, came to seem not forward-looking enough. In later typescripts this section was also preceded by a quotation from Whitman. (See also Sankey's discussion of this image in *A Companion to William Carlos Wiliams' "Paterson,"* pp. 201, 211.)

I suspect that part of Williams' reason for submerging this final image of Whitman into the image of the swimmer might be that the overt use of Whitman would seem to invite comparison with Crane's invocation of Whitman, in *The Bridge*. Compare the omitted lines from the Yale mss. with this image from Crane's poem (pp. 40–41):

> "—Recorders ages hence"—ah, syllables of faith!
> Walt, tell me, Walt Whitman, if infinity
> Be still the same as when you walked the beach
> Near Paumanok—your lone patrol—and heard the wraith
> Through surf, its bird note there a long time falling . . .
> For you, the panoramas and this breed of towers,
> Of you—the theme that's statured in the cliff.
> O Saunterer on free ways still ahead!
>
>   . . .
>
> Sea eyes and tidal, undenying, bright with myth!

14. For good discussions of the generative and regenerative effects in *Paterson,* see Koch, pp. 119–29, and Quinn, pp. 90ff.

15. Allen Ginsberg, *Notes After an Evening With William Carlos Willaims* ([New York?]: Samuel Charters [1969]), unpaginated.

16. Williams later claimed that the form of *Paterson* resulted from a suggestion by James Laughlin, who had mentioned the shape of Williams' *Life Along the Passaic River* as a possible analogy to the shape of a long poem. The stories of that book follow the track of the Passaic River, as does *Paterson;* 13 of the 18 protagonists in the prose book are doctors, usually making house-calls. (The observation is included, among other places, in the early notes to *Paterson* in the mss. at Buffalo; see also Joel Conarroe's discussion of the formal similarities between the poem and the short story collection in *"Paterson,"* p. 48.)

Of the several other critics who relate Williams' professional interests as a doctor to his professional interests as a writer, the most memorable is Dr. Robert Coles, whose book *William Carlos Williams: The Knack of Survival in America* (New Brunswick, N.J.: Rutgers University Press, 1975) sympathetically surveys Williams' prose, especially the three novels of the Stecher family. Of the other critics who write on Williams' medical and literary interests, some focus on the doctor-as-poet, others on the poet-as-doctor. Critics in the first group usually concentrate on the "scientific" technique of Williams' lyric poems, those in the second group on the tone of Williams' work (what Parker Tyler calls the "materialistic sadness" that is the result of Williams' compassion). For examples of criticism of the first group, see Linda Wagner's "William Carlos Williams: Poet-Physician of Rutherford," *Journal of the American Medical Association* (April 1, 1968), 204: 113–18; William B. Ober's "William Carlos Wiliams, 1883–1963: Physician as Poet," *New York State Journal of Medicine* (April 15, 1969), 69: 1085–86; and Nicholas Dewey's "Dr. William Carlos Williams: The Writer as Physician," *Academy of Medicine of New Jersey Bulletin* (December 1970), 14: 64–72. For examples of the second group, see Vivienne Koch, pp. 173ff; Richard Ellmann, "William Carlos Williams: The Doctor in Search of Himself," *Kenyon Review* (Summer 1952), 14: 310–12; and Ralph Nash, pp. 23ff.

17. Williams, *Autobiography,* p. 286. See Felix Stefanile, "Confessions of an Editor," *New York Times Magazine* (Feb. 17, 1980), p 23. Advising the young Stefanile in 1960 to "get a job," Williams claimed that the discipline of any regular work would help to keep a young poet from becoming "scattered." Aside from some inevitable conflicts in demands for his time, Williams seems personally to have integrated the two roles gracefully. The writing, he claimed, benefited from the organization the medical practice demanded, the medical practice offered him material for the stories especially (as well as contact with other people), and ultimately the medical practice gained personalism from his writing. When Williams delivered his one-thousandth baby, the staff of his hospital in Rutherford gave him an electric typewriter to commemorate the occasion.

18. Williams, *Autobiography,* pp. 288–89.

19. Williams, "Marianne Moore," pp. 123–24.

20. Williams, *Autobiography,* p. 289.

21. See Peterson, p. 161.

22. Williams, *American Grain,* p. 26.

23. William Shakespeare, *King Lear,* in *Complete Works,* ed. Alfred Harbage (Baltimore: Penguin, 1969), III.iv.96–103. Like Paterson, Lear speaks alternately in verse (for his lyrical or kingly self) and in prose (for his mad private self). See also Williams' comparison of Whitman and Lear, in his late essay on *Leaves of Grass,* "An Essay," p. 26. There Whitman, facing the Atlantic, is pictured receiving a "new language," a "great mystery" that ultimately escapes him because he lacks the power to "identify or control" it: Whitman lacks a formal self-awareness of the "private" self.

24. Carl Gustav Jung, "Psychology and Poetry," *transition* (June 1930), 19/20: 44. In his essay "The Poet," Emerson also pointed toward the same image of the poet as physician. "The sign and credential of the poet," Emerson writes, are that he announces that which no man foretold. "He is the true and only doctor; he knows and tells; he is the only teller of news, for he was present and privy to the apperance which he describes." The Jung essay ("Psychologie und Achtung" in German) has been retranslated for the English-language *Collected Works* of Jung as "Psychology and Literature." I cite here the translation Williams read.

25. Jung, p. 44.

26. Williams, "Caviar and Bread Again," *Essays,* pp. 102–3.

27. Jung, pp. 41, 45.

28. Williams, *Autobiography,* p. 358.

29. Williams, "Prose Essays, 1914–1929," *Embodiment,* p. 88. Interestingly, Williams points to his own "scientific" background and training as the most pertinent difference between himself and the young Pound. The "humility and caution" of the scientist, Williams writes in his *Autobiography,* oriented Williams toward the local place, toward an inconspicuous participation in the life around him, and toward a less ostentatious style. (*Autobiography,* p. 58.)

For his part, Pound was claiming a "scientific" orientation in his own work as early as 1913. In "The Serious Artist," published in *The Egoist,* Pound defines the distinguishing characteristic of the serious artist as a verbal precision paralleling the quantitative precision of the scientist:

The serious artist is scientific in that he presents the image of his desire, of his hate, of his indifference as precisely that, as precisely the image of his own desire, hate, or indifference. The more precise his record the more lasting, the more unassailable the work of art.

(*Literary Essays of Ezra Pound* [New York: New Directions, 1964], p. 46.)

30. See also Williams' "The Poem as a Field of Action," *Essays,* p. 286.

31. James E. Breslin also compares Williams' attitude toward democracy with Whitman's notions of the democratic individual considered *en masse,* concluding that Whitman's confidently democratic impulses became in Williams' estimation a potentially dangerous tendency to merge into formlessness:

For Williams, the sea is not our home; his sources are in the hard, definite earth, the limited compass of a small town. He is not advocating flight from the pull of these vast forces; he is simply urging movement into a defined area in which chaos can be contended with successfully. His scope is not as vast as Whitman's; but he seeks a similar organic extension of the self.

See Breslin's "Williams and the Whitman Tradition," p. 17.

32. William Empson, quoted in "Two More Cultures," *New Statesman and Nation* (January 24, 1964), 67:130. For an interesting counterargument, see Horace Gregory's "William Carlos Williams and the 'Common Reader,' " *Briarcliff Quarterly* (October 1946), 3: 186–89.

33. Williams, "Marianne Moore," pp. 126–27.

34. Bernard Duffey also observes this "dominance of a verb rather than a noun effect in Williams." See Duffey, pp. 61–73.

35. See also Breslin's "Williams and the Whitman Tradition":

The sharp, hard-edged quality of his work, its precise observation, is there to assure us that the emotion of the poem has been generated by *this* object—not brought to it by a rhapsodic poet. Williams' effacement before the object, like the leap into the sea or river, is his way of becoming emotionally identified with it; self-abdication is part of the process of re-creation (p. 172).

36. Yale mss. Once again, Williams' revisions seem to track a pattern of avoidance of Crane's *The Bridge.* Compare Williams' omitted description of America's ruined, paradisal "plenty" with these lines from Crane's poem (p. 60):

> This was the Promised Land, and still it is
> To the persuasive suburban land agent
> In bootleg roadhouses where the gin fizz
> Bubbles in time to Hollywood's new love-nest pageant.

37. Williams, "The Work of Gertrude Stein," *Essays,* p. 118.

38. Gertrude Stein, "The Gradual Making of 'The Making of Americans,' " *Writings and Lectures, 1909–1945,* ed. Patricia Meyerowitz (Baltimore: Penguin, 1967), p. 96.

39. Williams, "Stein," pp. 119–20.

40. Williams, "The Somnambulists," *transition* (1929), 18: 149. This insistence on the innate "opacity" of the American character, beneath which a brightness shines, may be Williams' oblique, delayed response to Pound's problematic praise of Williams' early poems. In 1917, while attacking Williams for affecting a native American-ness that in Pound's estimation he should not attempt, Pound had written in a letter to Williams: "the thing that saves your work is *opacity,* and don't you forget it. Opacity is NOT an American quality. Fizz, swish, gabble of verbiage, these are echt Amerikanisch." Pound, *Letters,* p. 124.

41. Williams, "Marianne Moore," p. 122.

42. Williams, *Autobiography,* p. 224. Often Williams' fascination with the simultaneously "ancient" and "vital" energies of the dance recalls his enthusiasm for the performances of Isadora Duncan, whose free-form, Greek-inspired choreography had thrilled Williams when he had seen her perform.

43. Conarroe, *"Paterson,"* p. 139.

44. Williams, dustjacket to *Paterson* III (New York: New Directions, 1949).

45. See the discussion of "male" and "female" principles in poems by Whitman and Williams, in the preceding section.

46. Williams described *Paterson* in this way in the early drafts to the poem (Yale mss.), and that sense of "Paradise" continues through the final version: in the plundered plenitude of the eels in Book I for instance (p. 36), in the pearl of great price that is ruined by greedy entrepreneurs (pp. 8–9), and in the image of the amplitude and fecundity of the undeveloped mountain. The working title of the poem was at one time "PATERSON ANY/ Every place," and one of the drafts asserts strongly the overarching social concern that made Williams choose this particular troubled paradise to illustrate through an objectified form the significance of America as a new place:

> [Paterson]
> a somewhat long episodic poem
> designed to be a counter-point to the shortsightedness, the
> blunders the illwill and all those defects born of indifference
> laziness, and unwillingness to accept the plain evidence of the
> senses that make the age in which we live something less
> than the Paradise it might be with Plenty staring us in
> the face to say nothing of other disadvantages

47. See N. M. Willard's "A Poetry of Things: Williams, Rilke, Ponge," *Comparative Literature* (1965), 17: 311–26; also Beth Archer's fine introduction to her translation of Ponge's *The Voice of Things* (New York: McGraw Hill, 1974).

48. William Wordsworth, "Preface to the Second Edition of 'Lyrical Ballads,' " *Poems and Prefaces,* ed. Jack Stillinger (Boston: Riverside, 1965), p. 453.

49. See Williams' admiration for Cézanne, especially for his attention to "design," "the relation of parts to themselves," in Walter Sutton's "A Visit," p. 322.

Bibliography

Adams, Richard P. "Whitman: A Brief Revaluation." *Tulane Studies in English* (1955), 5: 111–49.

Alegría, Robert A. *Walt Whitman en Hispanoamerica.* Mexico City: Studium, 1964.

Allen, Gay Wilson. "Walt Whitman: The Search for a 'Democratic Structure.'" *Walt Whitman,* ed. Francis Murphy. Baltimore: Penguin, 1970, pp. 407–24.

—— *The Solitary Singer.* New York: Macmillan, 1955.

—— *Walt Whitman Abroad.* Syracuse: Syracuse University Press, 1955.

Archer, Beth, trans. *The Voice of Things.* New York: McGraw Hill, 1974, Introduction.

Bachelard, Gaston. *The Poetics of Space.* New York: Orion, 1964.

Beauvoir, Simone de. *The Second Sex,* trans. H. M. Parshley. New York: Knopf, 1971 [rpt.].

Bennett, Joseph. "The Lyre and the Sledgehammer." *Hudson Review* VI, (Summer 1952), 6: 298–307.

Bergman, Herbert. "Ezra Pound and Walt Whitman." *American Literature* (March 27, 1955), pp. 55–61.

Black, Max. *Models and Metaphors.* Ithaca: Cornell University Press, 1962.

Blodgett, Harold. *Walt Whitman in England.* Ithaca: Cornell University Press, 1934.

Bloom, Harold, *The Anxiety of Influence.* New York: Oxford University Press, 1973.

Borges, Jorge Luis. *The Aleph and Other Stories.* New York: Dutton, 1976.

—— "Walt Whitman: Man and Myth." *Critical Inquiry* (June 1954), 1: 707–18.

Breslin, James. "Whitman and the Early Development of William Carlos Williams," *PMLA* (December 1967), 82: 613–21.

—— *William Carlos Williams: An American Artist,* New York: Oxford University Press, 1970.

—— "William Carlos Williams and the Whitman Tradition," *Literary Criticism and Historical Understanding: Selected Papers from the English Institute,* ed. Philip Damon. New York: Columbia University Press, 1967, pp. 151–80.

Brinnin, John Malcolm. *William Carlos Williams.* Minneapolis: University of Minnesota Pamphlets, 1963.

Burke, Kenneth. *Counter-statement.* New York: Harcourt, Brace, 1931.

—— *A Grammar of Motives.* New York: Prentice-Hall, 1945.

Chambers, Jessie ["E. T."]. *D. H. Lawrence: A Personal Record.* London: Cape, 1935.

Coles, Robert. *William Carlos Williams: The Knack of Survival in America.* New Brunswick, N.J.: Rutgers University Press, 1975.

Conarroe, Joel. "A Local Pride: The Poetry of 'Paterson.' " *PMLA* (May 1969), 84: 547–58.

—— *William Carlos Williams' 'Paterson': Language and Landscape.* Philadelphia: University of Pennsylvania Press, 1970.

Costello, Bonnie. *Marianne Moore: Imaginary Possessions.* Cambridge: Harvard University Press, 1981.

—— "William Carlos Williams in a World of Painters." *New Boston Review* (July 1979), 4: 11–14.

Crane, Hart. *The Bridge.* New York: Liveright, 1970 [rpt.].

—— *The Letters of Hart Crane,* ed. Brom Weber. Berkeley: University of California Press, 1965.

Darío, Rubén. *Azul.* Buenos Aires: Edicom, 1969 [rpt].

—— *Selected Poems,* trans. Lysander Kemp. Austin: University of Texas Press, 1973.

Davenport, Guy. "The Nuclear Venus." *Perspective* (Autumn 1953), 6: 182–90.

Dewey, John. *Art as Experience.* New York: Minton, Balch, 1934.

Dewey, Nicholas. "Dr. William Carlos Williams: The Writer as Physician." *Academy of Medicine of New Jersey Bulletin* (December 1970), 14: 64–72.

Dijkstra, Bram. *Hieroglyphics of a New Speech.* Princeton: Princeton University Press, 1969.

Donoghue, Denis. "For a Redeeming Language," *William Carlos Williams,* ed. E. H. Miller. Bloomington: University of Indiana Press, 1967, pp. 39–51.

Doolittle, Hilda [H.D.]. *Red Roses for Bronze.* Boston: Houghton Mifflin, 1931.

—— *Selected Poems.* New York: Grove, 1957.

Duffey, Bernard. "Williams' 'Paterson' and the Measure of Art." *Studies in "Paterson,"* ed. John Engels. Columbus, O.: Charles E. Merrill, 1971, pp. 61–73.

Eliot, T. S. *Four Quartets.* New York: Harcourt, Brace, 1968 [rpt.].

—— "Hamlet and His Problems." *Collected Essays.* New York: Harcourt, Brace, 1960, pp. 123–29.

Ellmann, Richard. "William Carlos Williams: The Doctor in Search of Himself." *Kenyon Review* (Summer 1952), 14: 310–12.

Emerson, Ralph Waldo. *Selections,* ed. Stephen Whicher. Boston: Riverside, 1960.

Empson, William. [In] "Two More Cultures." *New Statesman and Nation* (January 24, 1964), 67: 130.

Erkkila, Betsy. *Walt Whitman Among the French: Poet and Myth.* Princeton: Princeton University Press, 1981.

Fanon, Franz, *The Wretched of the Earth,* trans. C. Parrington. New York: Grove, 1968.

Fausset, Hugh. *Walt Whitman: Poet of Democracy.* New Haven: Yale University Press, 1942.

Fiedler, Leslie. "Images of Walt Whitman." *'Leaves of Grass' 100 Years After,* ed. Milton Hindus. Stanford: Stanford University Press, 1955, pp. 55–74.

Fussell, Paul. *Poetic Meter and Poetic Form.* New York: Random House, 1965.

Gerber, Philip. L. "So Much Depends: The Williams Foreground." *Profile of William Carlos Williams,* ed. Jerome Mazzaro. Columbus, O.: Chas. E. Merrill, 1971, pp. 5–25.

Gilbert, Sandra. *Acts of Attention: The Poems of D.H. Lawrence.* Ithaca: Cornell University Press, 1972.

Ginsberg, Allen. *"Howl" and Other Poems.* San Francisco: City Lights, 1956.

—— *Notes after an Evening with William Carlos Williams.* [N.Y.?]: Samuel Charters, [1969], unp.

Gregory, Horace. "William Carlos Williams and the 'Common Reader.' " *Briarcliff Quarterly* (October 1946), 3: 186–90.

Grigsby, Gordon K. "The Modern Long Poem: Studies in Thematic Form." Ph.D. dissertation, University of Wisconsin, 1960.

Guimond, James. *The Art of William Carlos Williams.* Urbana: University of Illinois Press, 1968.

Heyen, William. "The Poet's Leap into Reality." *Profile of William Carlos Williams,* ed. Jerome Mazzaro. Columbus, O.: Chas. E. Merrill, 1971, pp. 25–53.

Jarrell, Randall. "Three Books." *Poetry and the Age.* New York: Vintage, 1959, pp. 691–700.

Jaén, Didier Tisdall. *Homage to Walt Whitman.* University, Ala.: University of Alabama Press, 1969.

Jung, Carl Gustav. "Psychology and Poetry." *transition* (June 1930), 19/20: 23–44.

Kaplan, Justin. *Walt Whitman: A Life.* New York: Simon and Schuster, 1980.

Kenner, Hugh. *The Pound Era.* Berkeley: University of California Press, 1974.

Kermode, Frank. *Romantic Image.* New York: Macmillan, 1957.

Kinnaird, John. "Paradox of an American Identity." *Partisan Review* (1958), 25: 580–605.

Koch, Vivienne. *William Carlos Williams.* Norfolk, Conn.: New Directions, 1950.

Koehler, Stanley. "The Art of Poetry: William Carlos Williams." *The Paris Review* (Summer–Fall 1964), 32: 110–51.

Lawrence, D. H. *Collected Letters.* New York: Viking, 1962.

—— *Complete Poems.* London: Heinemann, 1967.

—— *Studies in Classic American Literature.* Baltimore: Penguin, 1971.

Levertov, Denise. *The Poet in the World.* New York: New Directions, 1975.

Lewis, R.W.B. *The American Adam.* Chicago: University of Chicago Press, 1975.

Lewis, R.W.B., ed. *The Presence of Walt Whitman.* New York: Columbia University Press, 1962.

Lieber, Todd. *Endless Experiments.* Columbus, O.: Ohio State University Press, 1973.

Lorca, Federico García. *Poet in New York,* trans. Ben Bellitt. New York: Grove, 1955.

—— *Poeta en Nueva York.* Buenos Aires: Losada, 1962 [7th ed.].

Loving, Jerome. *Emerson, Whitman, and the American Muse.* Chapel Hill: University of North Carolina Press, 1982.

Lowell, Robert. " 'Paterson II.' " *The Nation* (June 19, 1948), 166: 693.

—— "William Carlos Williams." *Hudson Review* (1961–1962), 14: 530–36.

Lukács, Georg, "Introduction to a Monograph on Aesthetics." *The New Hungarian Review* (Summer 1964), 5: 48–65.

MacDiarmid, Hugh. *Lucky Poet.* Berkeley: University of California Press, 1972.

Macksey, Richard. "A Certainty of Music: Williams' Changes." *William Carlos Williams,* ed. J. Hillis Miller. Englewood Cliffs, N.J.: Prentice Hall, 1966, pp. 132–48.

Mariani, Paul. *William Carlos Williams: A New World Naked.* New York: McGraw Hill, 1981.

Martí, José. "El Poeta Walt Whitman." *Obras completas.* 2 vols. Havana: Lux, 1946, 1: 1134–45.

—— [translation of above] "The Poet Walt Whitman." *Walt Whitman Abroad,* ed. Gay Wilson Allen. Syracuse: Syracuse University Press, 1950, pp. 201–13.

Martz, Louis. "The Unicorn in 'Paterson.' " *William Carlos Williams,* ed. J. Hillis Miller. Englewood Cliffs, N.J.: Prentice Hall, 1966, pp. 70–88.

Matthiessen, F. O. *American Renaissance.* New York: Oxford University Press, 1941.

Mayakovsky, Vladimir. *Polnoe Sobranie Sochinenii.* Moscow: Zydo. Lit., 1958.
—— *"The Bedbug" and Other Stories,* trans. Patricia Blake. New York: Meridian, 1960.
Mazzaro, Jerome. *William Carlos Williams: The Later Poems.* Ithaca: Cornell University Press, 1973.
McAleavey, David. "If To Know is Noble: The Poetry of George Oppen." Ph.D. dissertation, Cornell University, 1975.
Mencken, H. L. *The American Language.* New York: Knopf, 1949 [rpt. of 1919 ed.].
Mendelson, Maurice. *Life and Work of Walt Whitman: A Soviet View.* Moscow: Progress, 1976.
Middlebrook, Diane K. *Walt Whitman and Wallace Stevens.* Ithaca: Cornell University Press, 1976.
Miller, J. Hillis. "Introduction," in Miller, ed. *William Carlos Williams.* Englewood Cliffs, N.J.: Prentice Hall, 1966.
——. *Poets of Reality.* Cambridge, Mass.: Belknap, 1965.
Moore, Marianne. *A Marianne Moore Reader.* New York: Viking, 1965.
Morse, Samuel French. *Wallace Stevens: Life as Poetry.* New York: Pegasus, 1970.
Murry, J. Middleton. "Walt Whitman: The Prophet of Democracy." *"Leaves of Grass" 100 Years After,* ed. Milton Hindus. Stanford: Stanford University Press, 1955, pp. 120–48.
Nash, Ralph. "The Use of Prose in 'Paterson.' " *Studies in 'Paterson',* ed. John Engels. Columbus, O.: Chas. E. Merrill, 1971, pp. 20–29.
Neruda, Pablo. *Nuevas odas elementales.* Buenos Aires: Losada, 1963 [rpt.].
—— *Odas elementales.* Buenos Aires: Losada, 1980 [rpt.].
—— *Selected Poems,* ed. Nathaniel Tarn. London: J. Cape, 1970.
—— *Twenty Poems of Pablo Neruda,* trans. Robert Bly and James Wright. Madison, Wis.: Sixties Press, 1967.
Ober, William B. "William Carlos Williams, 1883–1962: Physician as Poet." *New York State Journal of Medicine* (April 15, 1969), 69: 1085–86.
Olson, Charles. *Call Me Ishmael.* London: J. Cape, 1960.
—— *The Maximus Poems.* New York: Jargon, 1960.
Pascal, Richard. "The Radiant Gist: Romantic Strains in 'Song of Myself' and 'Paterson.' " Ph.D. dissertation, Cornell University, 1971.
Pavese, Cesare. "Walt Whitman: The Poetry of Poetry Making." *Walt Whitman Abroad,* ed. Gay Wilson Allen. Syracuse: Syracuse University Press, 1955, pp. 188–200.
Paz, Octavio. *The Bow and the Lyre,* trans. R. E. S. Sims. New York: McGraw Hill, 1973.
Pearce, Roy Harvey. *The Continuity of American Poetry.* Princeton: Princeton University Press, 1961.
—— "Pound, Whitman, and the American Epic." *Ezra Pound,* ed. Walter Sutton. Englewood Cliffs, N.J.: Prentice Hall, 1963, pp. 163–78.
Perlman, Jim, et al., eds., *Walt Whitman: The Measure of His Song.* Minneapolis: Holy Cow! Press, 1982.
Peterson, Walter Scott. *An Approach to "Paterson."* New Haven, Conn.: Yale University Press, 1967.
Pocock, J. G. A. *Politics, Language, and Time.* New York: Atheneum, 1971.
Poe, Edgar Allan. *Poetic Works.* London: Ward, Lock, 1880.
Ponge, Francis. *The Voice of Things,* trans. Beth Archer. New York: McGraw Hill, 1974.
Pound, Ezra. *ABC of Reading.* London: Faber, 1961.
—— *Cantos.* New York: New Directions, 1971.
—— "Contemporania." *Poetry* (April 1913), 2: 8–10.

—— *Literary Essays*. New York: New Directions, 1964.

—— *Personae*. New York: New Directions, 1971 [rpt.].

—— *Selected Letters,* ed. D. D. Paige. New York: New Directions, 1950.

—— *The Spirit of Romance*. New York: New Directions, 1968.

—— "What I Feel About Walt Whitman," quoted in full in Herbert Bergman's "Ezra Pound and Walt Whitman," *American Literature* (March 1955), pp. 56–61.

Pritchett, V. S. *The Gentle Barbarian*. New York: Random House, 1977.

Quinn, [Sister] M. Bernetta. *The Metamorphic Tradition in Modern Poetry*. New Brunswick, N.J.: Rutgers University Press, 1955.

Racey, E. F. "Pound and Williams: The Poet as Redeemer." *Bucknell Review* (March 1963), 2: 21–31.

Sankey, Benjamin. *A Companion to William Carlos Williams' "Paterson."* Berkeley: University of California Press, 1971.

Santayana, George. "The Poetry of Barbarism." *A Century of Whitman Criticism,* ed. E. H. Miller. Bloomington, Ind.: Indiana University Press, 1967, pp. 127–35.

Schlesinger, Arthur. *The Age of Jackson*. Boston: Little, Brown, 1934.

Schapiro, Meyer. *Modern Art*. New York: Geo. Braziller, 1978.

Shakespeare, William. "King Lear." *Complete Works,* ed. Alfred Harbage. Baltimore: Penguin, 1967.

Simpson, Louis. *Selected Poems*. New York: Harcourt, Brace, and World, 1965.

—— *Three on the Tower*. New York: Norton, 1975.

Slate, Joseph E. "William Carlos Williams, Hart Crane, and 'The Virtue of History.' " *Texas Studies in Language and Literature* (1965), 6: 496–511.

Slatoff, Walter. *With Respect to Readers: Dimensions of Literary Response*. Ithaca: Cornell University Press, 1970.

Sontag, Susan. *Against Interpretation*. New York: Dell, 1969.

Sperry, Stuart, *Keats the Poet*. Princeton: Princeton University Press, 1973.

Stefanile, Felix. "Confessions of an Editor." *New York Times Magazine* (Feb. 17, 1980), pp. 10ff.

Stein, Gertrude. *How to Write*. Paris: Plain Edition, 1931.

—— *Writings and Lectures, 1909–1945,* ed. Patricia Meyerowitz. Baltimore: Penguin, 1967.

Stevens, Wallace. "Preface" to Williams' *Collected Poems, 1921–1931*. New York: Objectivist Press, 1934.

—— *Collected Poems*. New York: Knopf, 1967.

Sutton, Walter. "Dr. Williams' 'Paterson' and the Quest for Form." *Studies in "Paterson,"* ed. John Engels. Columbus, O.: Chas. E. Merrill, 1971, pp. 43–61.

—— "A Visit with William Carlos Williams." *Minnesota Review* (Spring, 1961), 1: 309–24.

Symonds, John Addington. *Studies of the Greek Poets*. London: A. and C. Black, 1920.

Thirlwall, John C., "William Carlos Williams' 'Paterson': The Search for a Personal Epic in Five Parts." *New Directions* (1961), 17: 252–310.

Thompson, Frank. "The Symbolic Structure of 'Paterson.' " *Western Review* (Summer 1955), 19: 285–93.

Tocqueville, Alexis de. *Democracy in America,* trans. Henry Reeve. New Rochelle, N.Y.: Arlington House, 1966, vol. 2.

Turner, Frederick Jackson. *The Significance of the Frontier in American History*. New York: Ungar, 1973 [rpt.].

Tyler, Parker. "The Poet of 'Paterson' One." *Briarcliff Quarterly* (October 1946), 3: 168–75.

Valéry, Paul. *Oeuvres,* ed. Jean Hytier. Paris: Gallimard, 1957, vol. 1.

Waggonner, Hyatt. *American Poets from the Puritans to the Present.* New York: Delta, 1968.

Wagner, Linda. "William Carlos Williams: Poet-Physician of Rutherford." *Journal of the American Medical Association* (April 1, 1968), 204: 112–18.

Wallace, Emily Mitchell. "Pound and Williams at the University of Pennsylvania." *Pennsylvania Review* (1967), 1: 41–52.

Weaver, Mike. *William Carlos Williams: The American Background.* Cambridge: The University Press, 1971.

Whitehead, Alfred North. *Science in the Modern World.* New York: Macmillan, 1925.

Whitman, Walt. *Complete Prose Works.* New York: Mitchell, Kennerley, 1914.

—— *Complete Poetry and Selected Prose and Letters,* ed. E. Holloway. London: Nonesuch, 1938.

—— *Complete Writings,* ed. R. M. Bucke et al. New York: Putnam's/Knickerbocker, 1902.

—— *"Leaves of Grass": Comprehensive Reader's Edition,* ed. Harold Blodgett and Sculley Bradley. New York: Norton, 1965.

Willard, Charles B. "Ezra Pound and the Whitman 'Message.' " *Revue de Litterature Comparée* (1957), 21: 94–98.

—— "Ezra Pound's Appraisal of Walt Whitman." *MLN* (1957), 82: 19–26.

—— "Ezra Pound's Debt to Walt Whitman." *Studies in Philology* (1957), 54: 572–80.

Willard, N. M. "A Poetry of Things: Williams, Rilke, and Ponge." *Comparative Literature* (1965), 17: 311–25.

Williams, William Carlos. *Adam and Eve and the City.* New York: Alcestis, 1934.

—— *Al Que Quiere!* Boston: Four Seas, 1917.

—— "America, Whitman, and the Art of Poetry," *The Poetry Journal* (November 1917), 8: 27–39.

—— "An Approach to the Poem." *English Institute Essays: 1947.* New York: AMS Press [rpt.], 1965, pp. 51–75.

—— *Autobiography.* New York: Random House, 1951.

—— *Collected Earlier Poems,* New York: New Directions, 1966.

—— *Collected Later Poems,* New York: New Directions, 1963.

—— *Collected Poems, 1921–1931.* New York: Objectivist Press, 1934.

—— *The Embodiment of Knowledge,* ed. Ron Loewinsohn. New York: New Directions, 1974.

—— "Essay on 'Leaves of Grass.' " *"Leaves of Grass" 100 Years After,* ed. Milton Hindus. Stanford: Stanford University Press, 1955, pp. 22–31.

—— "The Fatal Blunder." *Quarterly Review of Literature* (1944), 2: 125–26.

—— "Hart Crane (1899–1932)." *Contempo* (July 5, 1932), 2: 1–4.

—— "How to Write." *New Directions in Prose and Poetry,* ed. James Laughlin. New London, Conn.: New Directions, 1936, pp. 45–48.

—— "In Praise of Marriage." *Quarterly Review of Literature* (1944), 2: 145–49.

—— *I Wanted to Write a Poem,* ed. Edith Heal. Boston: Beacon, 1958.

—— *Imaginations.* New York: New Directions, 1970.

—— *In the American Grain.* Norfolk, Conn.: New Directions, 1925.

—— "Letter to an Australian Editor." *Briarcliff Quarterly* (October 1946), 1: 205–9.

—— *Make Light of It.* New York: Random House, 1950.

—— "Manifesto." *Pagany* (January 1930), 1: 1.

—— "Measure." *Spectrum* (Fall 1959), 3: 131–37.

—— *A Novelette and Other Prose.* Toulon: Cabasson, 1932.

—— "New from New Directions." News Release, May 31, 1951, unpaginated.

—— Notes, manuscripts, and drafts to *Paterson* in the Beinecke Collection (folders ZA 185–191 and uncatalogued papers and letters), Yale University, New Haven, Connecticut, and in the Poetry Collection, Lockwood Memorial Library, State University of New York at Buffalo.

—— *Paterson* [III]. New York: New Directions, 1949.

—— *Paterson* [I–VI]. New York: New Directions, 1963.

—— *Pictures from Brueghel.* New York: New Directions, 1962.

—— "Preface." *Quarterly Review of Literature* (1944), 2: 346–50.

—— "Reply to a Young Scientist." *Direction* (Autumn 1934), 1: 37–38.

—— *Selected Essays.* New York: New Directions, 1969.

—— *Selected Letters.* New York: Oblonsky, 1957.

—— "Some Hints Toward the Enjoyment of Modern Verse." *Quarterly Review of Literature* (1952), 8: 170–75.

—— "The Somnambulists." *transition* (1929), 18: 147–51.

—— "Sordid? Good God!" [1932], reprinted in *Twentieth Century Interpretations of "Miss Lonelihearts,"* ed. Thomas Jackson. Englewood Cliffs, N.J.: Prentice Hall, 1971, pp. 99–104.

—— "Work in Progress (Paterson V)." *Perspective* (Winter 1953), 6: 153.

Wilson, Edmund. *Axel's Castle.* New York: Charles Scribner's Sons, 1948.

Winters, Yvor. *Primitivism and Decadence: A Study of American Experimental Poetry.* New York: Arrow, 1937, pp. 41–48.

Wittgenstein, Ludwig. *Philosophical Investigations.* New York: Macmillan, 1958 [3d ed.], unpaginated.

Wordsworth, William. *Selected Poems and Prefaces,* ed. Jack Stillinger. Boston: Riverside, 1965.

Wright, James A. "The Delicacy of Walt Whitman," *The Presence of Walt Whitman: English Institute Essays,* ed. R. W. B. Lewis, New York: Columbia University Press, 1962, pp. 164–90.

Yeats, William Butler. *Collected Poems.* New York: Macmillan, 1969.

Zabriskie, George. "The Geography of 'Paterson.' " *Perspective* (Autumn 1953), 6: 201–16.

Index